AF479189

Impossible Domesticity

Impossible Domesticity

~ Travels in Mexico ~

Leila Gómez

Translated by Robert Weis

University of Pittsburgh Press

Published by the University of Pittsburgh Press, Pittsburgh, Pa., 15260
Copyright © 2021, University of Pittsburgh Press
All rights reserved
Manufactured in the United States of America
Printed on acid-free paper
10 9 8 7 6 5 4 3 2 1

Library of Congress Cataloging-in-Publication Data

Names: Gómez, Leila, author. | Weis, Robert, 1971- translator.
Title: Impossible domesticity : travels in Mexico / Leila Gómez ;
translated by Robert Weis.
Description: Pittsburgh : University of Pittsburgh Press, [2021] | Series:
Illuminations: cultural formations of the Americas | Includes
bibliographical references and index.
Identifiers: LCCN 2021032888 | ISBN 9780822946915 (cloth ; acid-free paper)
| ISBN 9780822988502 (ebook)
Subjects: LCSH: Travelers' writings--History and criticism. |
Mexico--Description and travel. | LCGFT: Literary criticism.
Classification: LCC PN56.T7 G65 2021 | DDC 809/.933272--dc23
LC record available at https://lccn.loc.gov/2021032888

Jacket art by Crissy Jarvis on Unsplash
Jacket design by Melissa Dias-Mandoly

To my children, Faustino and Gabriela

Contents

Acknowledgments

I am grateful to the Alexander von Humboldt Foundation in Germany for granting me a Humboldt Research Fellowship for Experienced Researchers, which allowed me to carry out research in Germany for this book project.

The Kayden Award contributed funds for the manuscript's translation, which was done by the historian Robert Weis.

Many thanks to the friends and colleagues who read parts of different drafts of the book and made observations and suggestions: Ángel Tuninetti, Annick Louis, Karen Genschow, Roland Spiller, Marcy Schwartz, Jenny Haase, Rob Buffington, and Emmanuel David.

I am grateful to the editors of the Illuminations Collection and the anonymous readers who evaluated the manuscript.

Thanks to my students who attended my seminars with enthusiasm and willingness to approach new readings. One of them, Javier Muñoz, helped format the bibliography and the index.

My friends and family, Roque Gómez, Enrique Bernales Albites, Mirta Reyes, Santiago Estrella, Sergio Macías, Eduardo Robino, Mariana Bolívar, Brais Outes, Dulce Aldama, and Alexander Fobes gave me constant company and emotional and intellectual support.

To my children, Faustino and Gabriela, thanks for your patience and generosity.

Impossible Domesticity

Introduction

Mexico has been perceived according to what Rob Shields calls a place-myth.[1] Since the colonial era, Mexico has been an imaginary geography, idealized and demonized in the accounts of conquistadors, a place upon which to project fears and desires, as well as religious, political, and economic anxieties. In different historical moments, for varied reasons, this place-myth continued to attract travelers from other European nations, from North and South America, who came to Mexico in search of utopias and dystopias. The presence of Mexico in Western scientific discourse and arts and humanities has played a fundamental role as a necessary and interdependent counterpart of the configuration of modernity.[2] As an object of study, Mexico constructed academic disciplines, university foundations, professional and artistic reputations, and a market replete with exotic and rare objects deemed by the experts to be worthy of capitalization and conservation.[3]

The travelers studied here reflect the representations of the Mexican place-myth. However, as a symbolic, contested space, Mexico also shaped these travelers and, along with them, their scientific disciplines and artistic practices. For all the authors studied here, the voyage to Mexico was their first trip, or at least the first trip for which they became known in their fields. Mexico made them famous. In this sense, their journey to Mexico represented a watershed moment in their lives. All of the travelers studied here were young; Mexico represented for them a journey of initiation, of radically new experiences that were, consequently, risky, incommensurate, and transformative. In his definition of the "badlands of modernity," Kevin Hetherington, following Latour, adds the notion of laboratory to the definition of a liminal place or place-myth: "Spaces like the laboratory are socially and technically constructed, contested, heterogenous, partial, contingent, and deferred. They act as important nodes, obligatory points of passage for the development of new modes of ordering."[4] This idea is easy to understand if we consider that experimentation in liminal places is substantiating, just as it is in laboratories. Narratives produced from laboratory experiments are not regulated only by the conventional language; they also open interstices of historical change and epistemological rupture. The narratives that arise from experimentation in liminal places can be, to greater or lesser extent, consensual in literary language, and yet they also enable transformations in the social order.

My intention is to highlight how journeys to Mexico challenged stereotypical or orientalist images. The experiences of these writers, artists, and scientists created a problematic and conflictive dialogue with metropolitan discourses and dismantled asymmetrical binaries between cultures. These experiences thus underscore Mexico's importance in the configuration of Western science and art. Complementing postcolonial reading of how the metropole represents "otherness" and following Aníbal Quijano's understanding of the intrinsic relationship between modernity and coloniality, this book argues that without Mexico there would be no modernity.[5] Mexico appears as a place of initiation, change, problem, and passage: a laboratory of modernity and modern subjectivity. The very definition of Mexico is at stake. Mexico appears in the flow of a discursive battle of modernity/coloniality, in which multiple types of knowledge and discovery compete. This book analyzes objects, instances, and characters that cross through these discursive struggles that overflow the stereotyped metropolitan images of Mexico.

Impossible Domesticity examines travelers' narratives that destabilize the fixed categories of nation, race, class, and gender in the experience of traveling. In his classic study *Travel as Metaphor*, Georges Van Den Abbeele notes that all travel requires an *oikos*—Greek for "home," "in relation to which any wandering can be comprehended (enclosed as well as understood)": "The positing of an oikos, or domus (the Latin translation of oikos), is what domesticates the voyage by ascribing certain limits to it. . . . That point then acts as a transcendental point of reference that organizes and domesticates a given area by defining all other points in relation to itself. Such an act of referral makes of all travel a circular voyage insofar as that privileged point of oikos is posited as the absolute origin and absolute end of any movement at all."[6] My reading of travel writing implies searching within the text's elements and signs that deauthorize the point of reference of the *oikos* and its circular economy.

Impossible Domesticity proposes to read this economy against the grain, thinking of the trajectory per se—the itinerary—as a place of encounter for multiple possible economies. Humboldt is paradigmatic in this regard. After five years in the Spanish colonies (from 1799 to 1804), Humboldt returned to Europe with dozens of boxes full of botanical, astronomical, and geological treasures. These crates contained the merchandise that guaranteed the success of his endeavor and the credibility of his scientific publications: six thousand equatorial plants, seeds, seashells, insects, and geological specimens never before brought to Europe from Chimborazo, New Granada, and the beaches of the Amazon.[7] Acutely aware of the importance of his treasures, Humboldt lugged them through the Andes and up the Orinoco River. There is, nonetheless, an agonistic aspect to this fruitless eagerness to capture, transport, and measure everything. The agency of the objects Humboldt collected was not easily domesticated.[8] Humboldt's archive is brimming with excess material, the difficulties of new scenarios, and his near-countless itineraries. These are objects that belong to a "messy archive," creating chaos and disorder where knowledge should be classified and organized. As Martin F. Manalansan IV argues in talking about the messiness of archives: "By refusing legibility and establishing an alternative (dis)order of things," such objects resist the orders of documentation.[9]

In my reading, all these authors evidence an impossible domesticity in their writings. Van Den Abbeele sustains that the beginning and end of every journey needs an *oikos*, the economy of which regulates the value of the trajectory. This is tantamount to saying that the point of departure determines the appraisal of every experience along the way. In contrast, like Humboldt, the travelers studied here are subjected to economies that oppose and resist the economy of home, stability, and security. In this way, they allow themselves to be modified by the travel experiences that destabilize their scientific disciplines, their professional formation, their political ideas, their national origin, and their class, race, and gender identity.

Through a reading of the flow of experience and the materiality of the travel, of the interaction of multiple and contradictory economies at stake, this book seeks to complement readings of the predominant postcolonial criticism of travel writing that follows Edward Said's *Orientalism* (1978).[10] The postcolonial critique highlighted the Western imperialist vision of travel narratives, arguing that such narratives revealed only the traveler's subjectivity, and the discourses and institutions of the metropolises the travelers came from—the *oikos*—thanks to the rhetorical machinery they used to describe the territories and cultures they visited. *Impossible Domesticity* proposes a new reading of these narratives by posing questions that incorporate but also transcend the traveler's imperial subjectivity. This book thus proposes a way of interpreting the agency exerted by territories and cultures. In this sense, *Impossible Do-

mesticity examines the types of knowledge that interact, critically and asymmetrically, in travel narratives. These other types of knowledge seep through the porousness, the hybrid elasticity, of travel narratives and enable decolonial readings.

Impossible Domesticity deals with travelers from a wide range of professions, scientific disciplines, and artistic practices. Studying them is a multifaceted task. More than examining each discipline, this book aims to understand the multiple constructions of Mexico as an object and the conflicts that their constitutive heterogeneity engenders between types of knowledge. In many cases, these narratives are paratextual to the disciplines; they reveal their seams, beginnings, ruptures, and epistemological transformations. The genre's heterogeneity itself defies categorization: travel books are part of literature, understood broadly, and also continue the tradition of *The Odyssey*, *Don Quixote*, *Robinson Crusoe*, and *Moby Dick*.[11] Scientific expeditions, imperial expansion, adventure, and colonialization of exotic lands made nonfiction travel narratives into bestsellers in the eighteenth and nineteenth centuries. Travel writing accompanied the birth of modern disciplines such as archeology, anthropology, and psychology.[12] In this book, the genre of travel writing is understood in a broad sense, including stories, fictional or not, written about Mexico by foreigners. The corpus of the book therefore includes treatises, letters, newspaper articles, chronicles, conferences, fiction, and poetry to the degree that these texts represent the Mexican experience and the knowledge derived from it.

The multiplicity of discourses running through travel narratives enables readings that locate the knots and fissures in the modernity/coloniality rhetoric. The main decolonial premise is that there can be no modernity without coloniality. The ore extracted from America was the base of the primitive accumulation of capital that initiated the global capitalist economy. America was not incorporated into a global capitalist economy; it brought it to life. Decolonial criticism further posits that the "New World" invented modernity because it emerged as a space of the new that questioned the tradition of authority of the ancient classics, founding the spirit of the modern as an orientation toward the future. The golden age migrates from the past to the future. In this tremendous global shift, the New World redefines Europe. Modernity/coloniality invented racism to legitimize the ideology of inequality and hierarchy between Europe and its others. Decolonial theory questions the postcolonial notion according to which, for the construction of the world-system, America is a peripheral—not central—material reality.[13] America is not the eccentric support for the construction of a center but rather the very font from which the center, modernity, emerges: "Coloniality names the underlying logic of the foundation and unfolding of Western civilization from the Renaissance to today of which historical colonialisms have been a constitutive, although downplayed, dimension. The concept as used herein, and by the collective modernity/coloniality, is not intended to be a totalitarian concept, but rather one that specifies a particular project: that of the idea of modernity and its constitutive and darker side, coloniality, that emerged with the history of European invasions of Abya Yala, Tawantinsuyu, and Anahuac, and the formation of the Americas and the Caribbean; and the massive trade of enslaved Africans."[14]

The texts studied in *Impossible Domesticity* were produced within the networks of a colonial matrix of power. In particular, given the travelers' different nationalities, social classes, professions, ethnic origins, and genders, the flexibility and porousness of travel narratives reveal the kaleidoscopic visions of modernity and its disciplines. In the following chapters, I study the images of Mexico that these travelers unexpectedly produced and reproduced within the coloniality of power. In constructing the planetary consciousness to which these travelers contributed, Mexico changed the understanding of art, the history of empires, the origin of humankind in America, and the value of the new continent in relation to Europe. Within the networks and tensions of the coloniality of power, new ways of conceiving popular revolutions and social utopias became possible; vanguards and radical artistic ideologies were born.[15]

Impossible Domesticity studies the travels of the German naturalist Alexander von Humboldt (1769–1859); the French photographer and archeologist Désiré Charnay (1828–1915); the Scottish wife of the first Spanish diplomat to independent Mexico, Fanny Calderón de la Barca (1804–1882); the US journalist and war correspondent John Reed (1887–1920); the Chilean educator and winner of the Nobel Prize in Literature, Gabriela Mistral (1889–1957); the French playwright Antonin Artaud (1896–1948); the Beat generation writers Jack Kerouac (1922–1969) and William Burroughs (1914–1997); and the Chilean writer Roberto Bolaño (1953–2003).

The chapters of this book are divided in three sections, each relating to a group of theoretical questions that explain different aspects of the problems discussed thus far. The first section includes three chapters on Humboldt, Charnay, and Calderón. The section focuses on the agency of objects found during the journey. It analyzes the role of things and objects as "quasi subjects" in constant production and the questioning of social relations and disciplines of knowledge as Bill Brown, Bruno Latour, Manalansan IV, and Jean Baudrillard have asserted.[16]

In his *Diary of a Trip to Mexico*, after bemoaning the loss of several trunks with books and treasures shipped from Guayaquil to Acapulco,

Alexander von Humboldt noticed the tidiness of the home of his Mexican hosts. He had never seen anyone more meticulous or any place so "remarkably clean." Humboldt then spoke of the surprising agency of things: "Unfortunately, upon opening our trunks, we infected the house with cockroaches, scorpions from Guayaquil, ants . . . ! The ships that bring cacao from that port resemble Noah's ark. Nowhere in the world are parasites and insects more abundant than in Guayaquil. The lizards of the gecko family train at night pursuing the new arrivals."[17]

This seemingly comical anecdote reveals the anxiety that the transported objects—in this case, trunks full of vermin—provoke. Agents of their own will, they resist scientific discipline and the imperial gaze. Describing the metropolitan scientific traveler's capacity to bring objects from the periphery, Bruno Latour in *Science in Action* analyzes the process of transportation and translation of objects into a language of reduced scale: maps, illustrations, samples, tables, images, diagrams, measurements, drawings, etchings, and photographs—all new codifications that enable their transportation, storage, and exhibition in centers of calculation, that is, the metropolises of knowledge.[18] The institutions of such places are laboratories, scientific associations, museums, and universities that develop theories about explored territories. The cycles of scientific accumulation are crucial to understanding the condition and logic of the mobility of objects in travel practices. But they also help trace the history of the accumulation of knowledge as distinction and asymmetry of power between the metropoles—where knowledge is accumulated—and their respective peripheries. Thinking about how these objects are translated and displaced forces us to think about the objecthood of things—that is, the condition of the objects per se before, during, and after being transported. This approach allows us to propose a decolonial reading of the objects as carriers of other epistemologies that are in constant friction with metropolitan accumulation. In the above example, the trunks that transport valuable objects for science also move animals that resist scientific pursuits.

Given their myriad itineraries, the travelers' objects studied in the first section resist fixation and problematize domesticity and the security of home. The travel narratives selected allow an examination of these objects in the constant disarrangement of the habitual, creating what Manalansan IV calls "the queer messiness of the archive."[19] Domesticity, habit, classification, and normativity are concepts problematized by the movement of travel—by their constant dislocation and permanent translation. In this context, Manalansan's proposal is especially relevant, in the sense that it conjoins movement and archive in capacities that are at once creative and destabilizing, that is, "queer":

> I would argue that mess is a word that can creatively illuminate the idea of queerness in general and queer archives in particular. My assertion of queer and queering as mess and messing up comes out of a critical reading of queer theory, popular culture, vernacular language, and everyday life. My use of queer and mess is not limited to bodies, objects, and desires but also relates to processes, behaviors, and situations. "Queering" and "messing up" are activities and actions as much as "queer" and "mess" can be about states/status, positions, identities, and orientations. . . . While people may balk at the idea of mess as "constituting" queer, it is precisely the discomfort elicited and provoked by the idea and realities of mess that is at the heart my formulation and provocation.[20]

Impossible Domesticity employs a queer reading of the travelers' archive.[21]

Chapter 1 holds that, conventional thinking notwithstanding, Humboldt was not the second discoverer of the New World. Rather, it was Mexico that situated Humboldt in the global center of the scientific and political scene. In his desire to see the world as a naturalist, Humboldt had planned two earlier trips—one to Egypt with Napoleon's navy (1798–1801) and another to India and the South Pacific with Captain Nicholas Baudin (1800–1803). Both plans were scrapped: the English blockage made expeditions to Egypt difficult, and Baudin fell ill and died before embarking. So, Humboldt finally headed to America. Since much of the continent was a Spanish colony, he had to request permission from the Bourbon monarch Charles IV. It was granted to him on the condition that he serve as the crown's "inspector of mines," though Humboldt still had to finance the entire trip using his personal inheritance. The trip to Mexico was a watershed moment for Humboldt, but also for the Spanish colonies and for the place of the New World in planetary consciousness.[22] Humboldt entered into the debate Clavijero and Jefferson carried on with Buffon and DePauw regarding the inferiority of humankind and nature in America to their European counterparts. Using the metaphor of Borges's "Aleph," chapter 1 studies Humboldt's works on Mexico from a kaleidoscopic perspective. The German traveler endeavored to offer knowledge about everything in Mexico. Humboldt examined the country from various angles, interests, and temporalities. Yet the object of study, "Mexico," could not be easily subjected to a single discipline or community of readers. What Humboldt's books show is precisely the impossibility of a closed and fixed archive. His story is excessive because the grandiosity of the archive and the agency of the collected objects must be translated according to the interests of multiple interlocutors across the world: European scientists and naturalists; the Spanish king; British investors interested in exploiting Mexican mines;

Jefferson, who harbored interests in expanding into Mexican territory; local creole and mestizo scientists who opened to him archives, museums, and libraries in Mexico; Latin American political leaders working toward independence; abolitionist philanthropists; and the general public. Humboldt became the most important scientist of his time, and the most famous man after Napoleon Bonaparte, thanks to his trip to Mexico and other parts of the New World during a crucial historical moment for the West.

Chapter 2 studies Désiré Charnay's trips to Mexico and the transfer of archaeological objects to the centers of calculation. In addition to his natal France, Charnay lived in England, Germany, and New Orleans in the United States, where he worked as a schoolteacher. In 1850, after reading John Stephen's *Incidents of Travel in Central America, Chiapas, and Yucatan*, he decided to secure funding from the French government to follow in the explorer's footsteps. Charnay's fame arose from his expedition to Mexico, during which he produced the narratives and photographs for his first book *Cités et ruines americaines: Mitla, Palenque, Izamal, Chichen-Itzá, Uxmal* (1862–1863). His photos, the first of these archeological sites, opened the door to his subsequent trips to Madagascar, Java, and Australia. As traveling explorers, Humboldt and Charnay shared persistence and dedication, characteristic traits of what I refer to as the "ideology of the hero of science." In the light of this ideology, their narratives enumerate the grand obstacles they overcame in the name of science, as they provided important documentation for the archeology of Mexico. Their relationships with scientific networks reveal how science drew on knowledge about Mexico (and other places in Latin America) throughout the nineteenth century and how European institutions legitimized the specific disciplines of Mesoamerican archeology. These obstacles tell us of objects that resist domestication and how they should be molded in the rhetoric of martyrdom or scientific heroism as a way of legitimizing the work. The explorers' narratives also sparked new discourses of political identity around what was called national archeological patrimony. Charnay's contemporary Auguste Le Plongeon presents an interesting example. President Porfirio Díaz prohibited Le Plongeon from taking away the statue of the Mesoamerican rain deity Chac Mool, which the explorer claimed to have "discovered." Le Plongeon engaged in a long, and unsuccessful, dispute with the Mexican government; his determination kept him and his wife, Alice Dixon, in Mexico for twelve years.[23] Charnay similarly discussed how the Mexican government controlled and supervised his excavations.[24]

Chapter 2 studies Charnay's photography as an object of circulation and production of knowledge about archaeological ruins. Of all the travelers in this book, Charnay is the one most closely linked to an imperial ideology and the European political and economic power over Mexico. In this regard, I study how Charnay's trip coincided with the political and economic interests of Maximilian von Habsburg and Napoleon III, who sponsored the Austrian nobleman in Mexico. The importance of guides in locating and excavating ruins is clear in Charnay's narratives. In addition to guiding the traveler through the countryside, they conserved the oral registry of travelers in the area, which helped establish a map and a chronology of the archaeologists' competition in the ruins and, therefore, of the process of artifact extraction and metropolitan scientific accumulation.

In Chapter 3, I study the letters that Fanny Calderón wrote to her relatives during her stay in Mexico. Like Charnay, Fanny Calderón, a descendent of Scottish nobility, had already emigrated before traveling to Mexico. As was the case for the Frenchman, the trip would make her name. Upon the death of her father, her mother and siblings settled in Boston in 1831. Fanny continued her education in a school for young ladies in New England. Fanny Erskine Inglis met William Prescott, who introduced her to her future husband, the Spaniard Ángel Calderón de Barca. In 1838, they were married. The following year, they moved to Mexico, where Ángel became Spain's first diplomat after the Mexican independence. The trip was an initiation for Fanny Calderón—a recently married woman on a diplomatic mission in a country she knew nothing about. She wrote *Life in Mexico* based on her letters to home and it became her most widely read book. *Life in Mexico* solidified her links with the Bostonian Hispanists, led by Prescott, Washington Irving, and George Ticknor. In the context of the Mexican-American War over Texas (1846–1848), the Hispanists played a crucial role in US–Latin American relations. As I assert in chapter 3, Mexico brought a deep change in Fanny Calderón's white, feminine, and imperial subjectivity. From overt racism in the first chapters—evident in the abject descriptions of Mexicans—she gradually moved to a playful and impassioned acceptation of local tastes and customs in the final chapters. Her progressive addiction to a nonhuman object—pulque—is proof of this transformation. The "disgust" for this beverage she describes in the first chapters is symptomatic of her rejection of what she considered threateningly alien to her socioeconomic and racial identity.[25] Nevertheless, the final chapters of *Life in Mexico* narrate a new construction of the object pulque, transformed now into part of her routine, a vital necessity. A redefinition of the limits between the familiar and the alien occur in the body-object-sign relationship. Although indicative of a pathological need, her addiction to pulque also suggests a new way of thinking about identity as the incorporation of what is initially perceived as alien. My reading of Fanny Calderón's Mexican transformation thus departs from more established critical visions of the Scottish-Bostonian-Spanish traveler.[26]

The second section, encompassing chapters 4 and 5 on Reed and Mistral, respectively, addresses the study of revolutionary and postrevolutionary Mexico as a utopian enclave. The politics and pedagogy of utopia and arcadia are studied here in light of postulates from Ernst Bloch, Fredric Jameson, and Roger Bartra.[27]

For both Reed and Mistral, the Mexican Revolution and the educational reforms that followed engendered utopian narratives that represented Mexico as a laboratory of change toward a more just society for peasants, women, and children. Both authors constituted themselves as witnesses of an enclave that was at once utopian and arcadian. We can see in their writings this temporal oscillation, between the present, on the one hand, in which change is being constructed for future generations (utopia), and, on the other, the rural and bucolic past, inhabited by the "noble savage" or the primitive man, uncontaminated by civilization (arcadia). Both authors thus projected one of the most forceful and persistent images of Mexico in the West, reproducing a key figure in the modernity/coloniality dialect that, as Bartra notes, has always accompanied the changes and the progress of European civilization: "The wild men of Europe zealously guard the secrets of Western identity. Their presence has faithfully accompanied the advances of civilization. Behind each landmark set in place by the march of European culture a savage is hidden, watching over the frontiers of civilized existence."[28]

For Reed, Pancho Villa is the centaur that Bartra analyzes in Piero di Cosimo's painting from the Italian Renaissance—tender, ferocious, and above all uncorrupted by modernity. For Mistral, utopia and arcadia become tangible in the rural school, where Indigenous children are led by the Christlike figure of modern Mexico, the teacher. Both Mistral and Reed were cast in the model of Romantic and primitive figures: for Reed, the revolutionary rebel; for Mistral, the saintly virgin mother. The analysis below shows the fissures and the contradictions within these images and their contextualization reveals a resistance to fixed classifications. For both authors, the trip to Mexico was the point of departure in a journey from which they would never return. The Mexico they visited distanced them definitively from their respective countries and made them critics of domesticity and nationality.

Chapter 4 studies John Reed's travels, describing a constant itinerary, not only because of the changing nature of the material his journalistic writing describes but also because of the impossible domestication of the traveler, as is evidenced by his death in Moscow, which forces us to rethink the question of the traveler's *oikos* or *domus*. Before going to Mexico, Reed wrote "War in Paterson" while covering the silk factory workers' strike in New Jersey.[29] Nonetheless, it was the trip to the Mexican Revolution that launched his career as a war correspondent and revolutionary journalist. Following Pancho Villa's army through northern Mexico, Reed wrote war chronicles for the *Metropolitan Magazine* and the *Masses*, which he later published in his 1914 book *Insurgent Mexico*. Danger, adventure, and a romantic vision of Villa and his men characterize these chronicles. Reed followed the journalistic style of Richard H. Davis, who had famously covered the American "Rough Riders," led by Theodore Roosevelt, who fought in the Spanish-American War. The "Romantic" war narrative—which forged the fame of war-heroes-cum-politicians—was the model for the chronicles of war, one of the most important arenas for the diatribes of presidential campaigns. The trip to Mexico established a path for Reed, professionally, politically, and ideologically: just a year later, he traveled to Moscow to write the epic narrative of the Russian Revolution, *Ten Days that Shook the World* (1918). Chapter 4 studies Reed as the war correspondent in labor strikes, World War I, and the Russian Revolution. It situates the narratives about Mexico and Pancho Villa in Reed's complete works. My interest here is to examine the deep connections between the news industry and the lucrative business that media companies made with war narratives. Reed, however, opposed the US interventionist policies in Mexico that sought to protect American economic interests. He was one of the few journalists of his time who went to the battle lines to witness and suffer violence. He describes barely dodging bullets, execution, and prison. His trip as a war correspondent, and the literary journalism he practiced, allowed him to dissent from the official discourses and explain the causes and circumstances of war through formal and informal interviews, always with firsthand knowledge of its main actors—which in Mexico were peasants, women soldiers, and bandits. Revolution, in his case, becomes a contested symbolic site in which everyday actors also participate. In terms of journalistic and literary genres, Reed's writings oscillate between the arcadian and utopian, epic and comedy, the rural past and the modern future.

Chapter 5 examines Gabriela Mistral's trip to Mexico to participate in the postrevolutionary educational reform. After the Mexican Revolution, the secretary of education and intellectual leader José Vasconcelos invited many academics, scientists, and educators to help construct a modern nation from the ruins of the revolution. As part of his plan to modernize the country, and specifically to professionalize women teachers, he also invited the Chilean Gabriela Mistral. Her residence from 1923 to 1925 inspired her to write poems and essays that described Mexico as an arcadian society and, at the same time, a "utopian enclave" that retained the innocence, purity, and uncontaminated authenticity of the New World while struggling to become a more just and independent future society.

The new peasant school was to be the foundation. Mistral created a Romantic image of primitive Mexico for the rest of Latin America. In her eyes, the woman teacher was a maternal figure for the modern nation. Although she had traveled extensively through Chile as a primary school educator and administrator, she had never gone abroad prior to receiving Vasconcelos's invitation. Her trip to Mexico was the beginning of a career that would bring fame to her work as lifelong consul for Chile; in 1945, she became the first Latin American to win the Nobel Prize in Literature. Thanks to this trip, her voice of provincial teacher could be heard throughout the Spanish-speaking world. In Mexico, Mistral became the icon of teaching as a woman's profession, of the traditional roles of mother-virgin. At the same time, she took up the cause of women working outside the home as teachers.

This chapter examines the tension between the image of the celibate woman and that of the mother during the intense professionalization of female teachers in the Mexican education reforms. I also explore the role Mistral played in women's historical shift from domesticity to the labor force, especially in rural schools over the course of Vasconcelos's education crusade. In addition, I address how the dreams of postrevolutionary modernity forged by Vasconcelos and Mistral fell apart in communities where agrarian reform had yet to be carried out and where labor laws regarding gender equality in schools were mere utopian aspirations. This abundance of plans for peasant schools amid the massive professionalization of women in education provoked an excess that called into question the official discourses of the Mexican nation. I interpret these dreams and this excess as part of the queer archive.

The third and final section includes chapters on Artaud, the Beatniks, and Roberto Bolaño. These chapters take on the spatial question of art and literature, investigating the definitions of art and poetics that these writers associate with Mexico, mostly in terms of the desert and the frontier. This section analyzes the relationship between these texts and space, following the theories of Rob Shields, Turner, and Bourdieu.[30] Moreover, Artaud, Burroughs, Kerouac, and Bolaño's experiences in Mexico are read according to Halberstam and Ahmed's critical framework of "queer" failures and "unhappy" subjects.[31]

In the case of the authors in this section, defiance of the bourgeois (hetero)normativity was capitalized in a literature that unsettled established models. Halberstam proposes a queer reading of how artistic production explores alternatives to "the usual traps and impasses of binary formulations":[32] "I argue that success in a heteronormative, capitalist society equates too easily to specific forms of reproductive maturity combined with wealth accumulation. . . . *The Queer Art of Failure* dismantles the logics of success and failure with which we currently live. Under certain circumstances failing, losing, forgetting, unmaking, undoing, unbecoming, not knowing may in fact offer more creative, more cooperative, more surprising ways."[33]

In this sense, failure is not restricted to queer as a nonbinary sexual orientation but rather as part of a subjectivity that separates from and challenges cultural binaries such as civilization and barbarism, order and chaos, West and non-West, capitalism and communism, and so forth. For Halberstam, "failure preserves some of the wondrous anarchy of childhood and disturbs the supposedly clean boundaries between adults and children, winners and losers."[34]

The space of home, its objects and bodies disciplined in sedentariness and routine, vanishes in the travel experience that jeopardizes fixed securities. As Sarah Ahmed notes, in capitalist societies happiness is associated with stable spaces and objects that reproduce the status quo. Artaud's trip to Tarahumara territory, his writings in psychiatric hospitals, the on-the-road trips of the Beatniks repudiated by the domesticity of Cold War US society, the vagabondage of the *realvisceralistas*, and the "savage" poets in Roberto Bolaño's work all produce writing that resists and questions "the foggy fantasy of the happiness" of the warmth of home, that is "domestic bliss."[35] At the same time, their writing proposes a new philosophy of failure, happiness, and adventure, one that yields literary, not economic or social, profits. This existential and artistic experimentation of rebels becomes symbolic capital that guarantees reproduction of the artistic field. These travelers are part of what Ahmed would call "the unhappy archive," which is not necessarily "unhappy" but rather evidence of an alternative history of happiness, formed by those who "enter this history only as troublemakers, dissenters, killers of joy."[36] My reading brings together travelers like Artaud, the Beatniks, and the real realvisceralistas, for whom travel signified a way to question conventions of happiness and their associated spaces and objects.

Chapter 6 studies Antonin Artaud's chaotic and exuberant journey. For Artaud, the voyage to the land of the Tarahumara was crucial to prove his theory on theater and its double. For Artaud, theater was a port that allowed hidden life to flow from its signs and beings. As he wrote in *Les Tarahumaras* (1937), this hidden life could be seen on the surface in Mexico. From the era's artistic point of view, Mexico was the terrain of magical dreams—the primitive and darker aspect of the repressed mentality of the West. Herein lies the interrelationship between surrealism and ethnology.[37] Artaud traveled to northwestern Mexico in 1936 to stay with the Tarahumara nation and experiment with peyote. Mexico, and the Mexican desert specifically, is often seen in Western eyes as an area of experimentation and liminality. An exoticist reading situates Artaud within the orientalist tradition. Yet, his travel narrative and his letters to psychiatrists and friends show a man torn, in search of something transcendent, which he thought he had discovered in the peyote ritual. In each of the successive versions of his narrative, Artaud gave free rein to his schizophrenia. Following his trip and return to France, he was interned in seven psychiatric hospitals. It was until the end of his life that he wrote about his trip to Mexico. He went over the experiences again and again, rewriting, clinging to them like a castaway, but at the same time revealing the impossibility of the focus of his trip.

Chapter 7 revisits William S. Burroughs's Latin American travel diaries and Kerouac's novels and poetry about Mexico in order to understand how visions of Mexico (involving sex, drugs, criminality, spirituality) predicated a critical questioning of the policies of the Cold War and North American conservatism. For the members of the Beat generation, and Jack Kerouac in particular, Mexico meant, as it also did for many contemporary tourists, a place of recreation, though they did not seek the safety of resorts for foreigners. For the Beats, a generation struck by the war policies of the United States and the censorship of the Cold War era, Mexico offered an escape, a reminder that another world was possible. Deeply American, Kerouac crossed the United States from east to west to learn its past and present and recognize its people, as he recounts in his famous book *On the Road* (1957). Nonetheless, the trip across the United States is a failure due to constant economic insecurity, police persecution, derision from abandoned wives, and paternal neglect. Consequently, following his heroes in cowboy stories, Kerouac went to Mexico to dodge the law and seek adventure. As an alternative literary movement in the postwar United States, the Beat generation—represented by Kerouac, Burroughs, Joan Vollmer, and Allen Ginsberg—saw counterculture in Mexico, a dystopian place where one could experiment with drugs, non-heteronormative sexualities, and criminality. They perceived the Mexican frontier as the ideal place for unregulated artistic creation, one in which normative points of reference would disappear.

Chapter 8 examines the work of Roberto Bolaño to show Mexico as the territorialization of poetry. For Bolaño, Mexico represents horror, damnation, and its antidote. The ideology of the accursed poet, which runs through all of Bolaño's writing, repeatedly comes to life in Mexico.

The vagabond poets in *The Savage Detectives* (1998) drift to the northern border, which also is the site of the massive femicides featured in his novel *2666* (2004). Bolaño began his literary career in Mexico, where his rejection of the status quo in literary circles earned him ostracism. In his work, Mexico is a dystopian place, excessive, and variegated, not only in literary and intellectual milieus, but also in terms of the atrocious murders of hundreds of women along the US border. In contrast to Mistral's utopian voyage to Mexico, Bolaño depicts the other face of the Mexican frontier: as the place where the neoliberal economy wreaks havoc, revealing an open colonial wound.[38] In contrast to the view of Mexico as a regenerator of humanity (held by Artaud and at times the Beats), Mexico becomes a site of human waste and gory capitalism.[39] For Bolaño, it is the symbolic and actual place of literature and horror. From different angles, Mexico continues to be narrated and lived as a laboratory of modernity/coloniality.[40]

All the travelers in *Impossible Domesticity* describe lived experiences that upend the certainties and happiness of the *oikos*. In the travel narratives of these writers, the object "Mexico" is defined in a variegated symbolic struggle that overturns Manichaean binaries and constantly recreates them in the logic of modernity/coloniality. Many, though not all, of the travelers here write from liminal situations marked by race, provincialism, homosexuality, insanity, foreignness, alcoholism, drug addiction, ideological persecution, war, scientific vilification, and/or illness. *Impossible Domesticity* explores this liminal, or chaotic, place as a possibility, a crack, from which to understand other visions and perspectives that fracture the homogeneity of imperial travel narratives.

Chapter 1

Humboldt in Mexico

The Aleph in Latin America

The voyage through Mexico and elsewhere in Latin America made Alexander von Humboldt the second most famous man of his time (after Napoleon Bonaparte), the second discoverer of the New World (after Christopher Columbus), and the second most important scientist of the nineteenth century (after Charles Darwin). From 1799 to 1804, Humboldt traveled through what would become Venezuela, Colombia, Ecuador, Peru, Cuba, and the United States. Some of his most outstanding feats include climbing Chimborazo (at the time considered to be the world's highest mountain), locating the confluence of the Orinoco and Amazon Rivers, and inventing the isotherms and isobars. His greatest accomplishment, however, was to make his journey at the prelude of Latin America's independence from Spain, a crucial moment in the history of the West. When the world focused on the political and economic affairs of America, Humboldt gave a detailed account of the continent's physical characteristics, politics, and economy. He was the perfect man, in the right place, at the right time.

In the context of the wars of independence, his trip to Mexico took on particular importance. His writings not only contributed to science but also legitimized Mexico's place on the political and economic map that sprang from the fall of the Spanish monopoly. His *Political Essay on the Kingdom of New Spain*, published in 1811, was a diplomatic letter that stressed to the great powers of the world that Mexico was, and would be, a privileged place: its geographic location between Europe and Asia favored world commerce; its mines and minerals contained vast wealth; its creole intellectuals were well learned; its cities were modern; its history was grand; and it boasted a variety of climates and natural regions. A compendium of facts that went from Mexico's physical characteristics to the distribution of its militias, touching along the way on demography, metallurgy, agriculture, manufacturing, commerce, and political administration, the *Political Essay*, and the section on Mexico in *Views of the Cordilleras and Monuments of the Indigenous Peoples of the Americas* (1810–1813), founded the vision of Mexico as a mythical place that would attract all subsequent travelers. In the first pages of his essay, Humboldt notes:

> Among the colonies subject to the king of Spain, Mexico currently occupies at present the first rank, both on account of its territorial wealth and on account of its favorable position for commerce with Europe and Asia. We speak here of the political value of the country, considering it in its actual state of civilization, which is very superior to that of the other Spanish possessions. . . . But on considering the greatness of the population of Mexico, the number of considerable cities in the proximity of one another, the enormous value of the metallic produce and its influence on the commerce of Europe and Asia; in short, in examining the imperfect state of cultivation observable in the rest of Spanish America, we are tempted to justify the preference which the court of Madrid has long manifested for Mexico above its other colonies.[1]

The narrative of Humboldt's discoveries was important not only for Spain but also for other nations and empires on the world map such as the United States, England, and the incipient Mexican nation itself. Humboldt deftly compiled knowledge about Mexico and other American territories with an eye to the political, economic, and scientific interests of several different reading publics. He understood how to present Latin America as merchandise in the market of symbolic goods.

Humboldt's sympathies toward the liberal, abolitionist pro-independence movements, as well as his friendships with leaders like Simón Bolívar and Thomas Jefferson, earned him a special place in Latin American national discourses during the nineteenth and twentieth centuries. But his writings on independence were more circumspect than his overt opposition to slavery. Humboldt arrived in the Spanish colonies with permission from Charles IV to work as an inspector of mines. The intersection of politics and science is crucial in Humboldt; it shaped not only his scientific career but also the pro-independence politics of the future American nations. Humboldt was acutely aware of the need to translate knowledge into the language of politics, which, in turn, would shape the object of his studies.

Scientists and sociologists have long debated the notion of science isolated from society. It is a fallacy to view the social dramas that surround the development of theories or scientific discoveries as divorced from laboratories and scholarly institutions, as if scientific endeavors were intrinsically impermeable to spheres of the real world and that society, politics, and the economy were separate from purely scientific pursuits. Following Bruno Latour's work on science and the interaction between humans and nonhumans, I propose that scientific endeavors rely for their very existence on political-social-economic relations. Latour uses the metaphor of the "blood flows of science" to refer to how scientific knowledge emerges from the feedback of multiple translations through which the objects of study (which he calls "nonhumans") gradually become part of the world of "humans." The process renders "nonhumans" accessible through the language of human interests, thus involving and convincing humans of the importance of specific scientific claims. Latour explains how Joliot's experiments with neutron bombs during World War II involved not just the scientists in his lab, but also the Belgian mining companies in Africa that discarded uranium, the anti-Nazi Norwegian producers of hard water (necessary for experiments with neutrons), anti-Nazi scientists in the United States and Europe who wanted to censure the publication of Joliot's findings in scientific journals such as *Nature*, and of course, the nationalist French government and public opinion. All these agents were constitutive parts of Joliot's research.[2]

Humboldt similarly "translated" Mexico and the continent into the general language of multiple and divergent interests and actors, creating links and alliances for a political-scientific project. These actors included the Spanish crown, British and German investors, North American republicanism, and scientific communities on both sides of the Atlantic. More than an alliance between separate spheres of society and science, the relationship shaped the study of nature and history in Mexico and America in Humboldt's writings. In this science-society relationship, the object "Mexico" is constructed in a discursive battle in which the objects—the nonhumans—are vehicles of knowledge that resist metropolitan disciplines. In this chapter, I explore the configuration of "Mexico" as a scientific object through three thematic axes: first, the mobilization of objects (the "nonhumans" in Latour's formulation) in the boxes, maps, and diaries that Humboldt carried from America to Europe; second, the debate over the inferiority of man and nature in America that Enlightenment-inspired European philosophers such as Buffon, DePauw, and Raynal sustained with Jefferson and Clavijero; and third, the role of mercury (another nonhuman) in Humboldt's research on gold and silver mines. Although I will consider several of Humboldt's texts in my analysis, many of the examples come from his writings—travel diaries but also essays and letters—about Mexico.

The Mobilization of Objects and the Agency of Nonhumans

For Bruno Latour, metropolitan science is characterized by the ability to bring "home" objects from the periphery. Latour analyzes the translation of objects into maps, illustrations, specimens, tables, photographs, diagrams, and other codifications of reduced scale that enable their transportation, indexing, and exhibition in the metropole. The "centers of calculation" (laboratories, scientific societies, museums, and universities) then construct theories about these objects and about the periphery itself.[3]

Travelers use a particular language to translate objects, transforming them from their personal collections into scientific objects. The successive translation of objects into scientific signs in the textuality of the journey means that travel writing is a privileged textual space in which to observe Latour's interaction between humans and nonhumans in scientific practices. Such a transformation relies on an abundant and sophisticated use of scientific and literary language that subjects/subjugates the nonhumans to a complex treatment of language while establishing alliances with politicians, fellow scientists, museums, laboratories, and the general public. Unlike increasingly specialized scientific discourse, travel narratives still did not separate humans and nonhumans. Latour calls these nonhumans "factische" (a portmanteau of fetish and fact).

Humboldt returned to Europe with many boxes full of botanical, astronomical, and geological treasures that had never been transported to Europe—six thousand equatorial plants, seeds, seashells, insects, and geological samples from Chimborazo, New Granada, and the shores of the Amazon.[4] Acutely aware of the importance of these nonhuman treasures, he lugged them through the most difficult circumstances. In a letter from Cumaná dated October 16, 1800, Humboldt emphasized the quantity and quality of his collection, as well as his meticulous methodology. Humboldt's narrative reveals the difficult interaction between humans and nonhumans—that is, between Humboldt as a scientist in the field and the nonhumans that he must force into submission before carrying them to centers of calculation. Humboldt painstakingly described his methodology, how he embalmed, sketched, and desiccated animals to observe their insides: "In the six months we have traversed the vast area situated between the coast, the Orinoco, the Río Negro, and the Amazon, citizen Bonpland has dried, easily, more than six thousand plants. Together with him on land, I have made descriptions of two hundred species, most of which appear to be of geneses not described by Aublet, Jacquin, Mutis, and Dombey. We have gathered insects, small seashells, woods for dye; we have desiccated crocodiles, *lamantins*, monkeys, *Gymnotus electricus* (the fluid of which is absolutely galvanic and not electric), and destroyed scores of serpents, lizards, fish."[5]

These objects followed him for the next five years through the Andes, New Spain, and up the Pacific Coast. Requiring more than twenty mules and Indigenous guides for the enormous caravan, the transportation of the boxes caused the expedition immense delays.[6] Humboldt was fully aware of his pioneering, and therefore perhaps precarious, methods of accumulating scientific knowledge. His travel diary is an exhaustive record of every measurement. In a letter to Baron de Zach, dated September 1, 1799, from Cumaná, he notes:

> I have also found that the daily functioning of my chronometer has changed
> somewhat in this warm country; it falls behind a second and a half each day.
> This is hardly strange, for the heat is such that one burns the fingers upon
> touching metal instruments exposed to the sun. Therefore, the longitudes
> measured on the trip may be too small; however, I believe not, for it was con-
> siderably cool on the high sea, 18 degrees Reaumur at 12 degrees latitude. I
> daily note the functioning of the chronometer and all other pertinent obser-
> vations; if I were to die and my papers saved, the results can be examined,
> reviewed, and corrected at will. Meanwhile, I have made, with patience and
> application, determinations, which I believe to be exact. In effect, a super-
> human patience is needed to make astronomical observations with precision
> and *con amore* in such heat. I have found the latitude of Cumaná by observ-
> ing the Sun with the aid of the two stars β and γ of Dragon, with the Bird
> quadrant and the Ramsden reflecting sextant.[7]

Humboldt had to construct a discourse that lent credence to his measurements, evident in his taking note of the how the tropical heat may have altered his instruments. The nonhumans thus reveal themselves to be objects with agency within scientific discourse. These rebellious nonhumans alter the precision of instruments and resist the subjugation of measurement and the corroboration of Humboldt's colleagues. The traveler thus reveals the seams of knowledge, predicated on an agonistic struggle with nonhumans. In his *Views of Nature*, Humboldt wrote:

> The Indians had left us in the middle of the cataract, proposing to take the
> canoe around a long narrow island below which we were to re-embark. We
> waited an hour and a half under a heavy tempestuous rain; night was com-
> ing on, and we sought in vain for shelter between the masses of granite. The
> little monkeys, which we had carried with us for months in wicker cages, by
> their mournful cries attracted crocodiles whose size and leaden-gray color
> showed their great age. I should not here notice an occurrence so usual in

the Orinoco, if the Indians had not assured us that no crocodiles were ever seen in the Cataracts; and in dependence on this assurance we had even ventured repeatedly to bathe in this part of the river. Meanwhile our anxiety lest we might be forced to pass the long tropical night in the middle of the Raudal, wet through and deafened by the thundering noise of the falling waters, increased every moment; until at last the Indians reappeared with our canoe.[8]

These "treasures" put Humboldt's life in danger. Monkeys interacted with the surroundings, attracting other, more dangerous animals. The role of the guides is ambiguous. The Indigenous were Humboldt's main informants, without whom the traveler would have not been able to explore the interior of the continent or collect the abundant information in situ. However, the presence of natives does not highlight Humboldt's dependence as much as the disagreements, mutual misunderstandings, and "erroneous" advice. In the same episode, Humboldt narrates his discovery of the tomb of the extinct Mapire tribe in the Ataruipe cavern. Taken to the cavern by the guides, Humboldt found approximately six hundred skeletons preserved in baskets made of woven palm fronds. He precisely describes the size of the baskets according to the age of the skeletons; he describes the preparation of the bones, the pigmentation, and the resin used. Then, he introduces the voice of the natives: "The Indians affirm that the flesh corpse is buried for some months in moist earth that gradually absorbs the muscle tissue; it is then exhumed, and any remaining tissue is scraped from the bones with sharp stones."[9]

Anticipating the reader's confusion over how contemporary Indigenous people knew so much about a remote, long-extinct tribe, Humboldt explains, "This is still a practice of some tribes in Guyana."[10] The practice, known by the natives, is not lost. The natives are an active, effective, and affective part of the collection of knowledge. They refused to help move the skeletons: "We left the cavern at nightfall, after collecting several skulls and the complete skeleton of an older man, much to the irritation of the Indian guides."[11] Humboldt adds that they left the cavern with a dark premonition. The skeleton, together with a large part of the entomological specimens, was lost in a shipwreck off the coast of Africa, the same site where Humboldt's earlier travel companion, the Franciscan missionary Juan González, had lost his life. The collection and transportation of objects enters the terrain of collaboration and dispute between metropolitan science and local epistemes. It hardly seems coincidental that the guides abandoned Humboldt and his fellow explorer, botanist Aimé Bonpland, to crocodiles and that his dependence on the guides seems ambiguous in his narrative.

The Debate on the Inferiority of Man and Nature in America

Humboldt's trip to the American continent took on new meaning in the context of the pro-independence revolutions. His writings were of interest to Latin Americans who sought to legitimize the new nations' place within new political and economic map that arose from the destruction of the Spanish monopoly. Humboldt's *Political Essay on the Kingdom of New Spain* was a diplomatic letter that affirmed to the world powers that Mexico's unique characteristics—its favorable geographic position between European and Asian markets, the enormous value of its mines and minerals, the erudition of creole intellectuals, the development of its cities, the grandiosity of its history, the variety of its climates and natural regions—meant that Mexico was a privileged place and would be even more so in the future. His *Veus des Cordillères et monumens des peuples indigènes de l'Amérique* similarly prefigured the view that the ancient American cultures were on equal footing with the classic cultures of antiquity and the Middle East.

In 1804, before returning to Europe, Humboldt shifted his itinerary toward Philadelphia and Washington where he met with Thomas Jefferson. As Sandra Rebok notes in *Humboldt and Jefferson*, the North American president was interested in the maps of Mexico, especially the maps of regions near Louisiana, which the United States had recently purchased from France. Humboldt and Jefferson agreed that nature and man in America were not inferior in size or development to those in Europe. The Mexican Jesuit Clavijero had already made similar claims in his dissertations and *The Ancient History of Mexico*. But Humboldt's account had added legitimacy, for, unlike Clavijero, he was European. Moreover, unlike Buffon, DePauw, and Raynal, Humboldt had traveled to the New World. With eloquent sarcasm, Clavijero had summarized what readers on the other side of the Atlantic could learn from DePauw: "To show the weakness of the American physical constitution, Paw offers evidence that we must face head on. First, Americans taken to Europe were irate during the voyage, and their rage lasted until death. Second, adult men in many countries of America have milk in their breasts. Third, American females give birth too easily, have extraordinary milk, and their periods are scarce and irregular. Forth, even the least vigorous European could defeat the strongest American in a fight. Firth, Americans cannot endure the lightest burden. And, sixth, they are subject to venereal and other endemic diseases."[12]

The controversy raged among enlightened philosophers and New World intellectuals during the first half of the nineteenth century. In his analysis of DePauw's treatise, Ottmar Ette argues that the discourse of American inferiority complemented the expansion of European slave traders, particularly from Germany and the Netherlands.[13] For Ette, this discourse sought to prevent colonial expansion in the Americas and to encourage the African slave trade. That is, by proclaiming the inferiority of the American man, it legitimized the transfer of Africans to the New World so as to "improve" the labor force in America. Humboldt, a staunch abolitionist, argued against African slavery in America. Speaking of men who labored in Mexican mines, he refutes DePauw:

> It is curious to observe how the Mestizoes and Indians employed in carrying minerals on their back, who go by the name of *Tenateros*, remain continually loaded for six hours with a weight of from 225 to 350 pounds and constantly exposed to a very high temperature, ascending eight or ten times, without intermission, stairs of 1,800 steps. The appearance of these robust and laborious men would have operated a change in the opinion of the Raynales, the Pauws, and a number of authors, however estimable in other respects, who have been pleased to declaim against the degeneracy of our species in the torrid zone.[14]

Humboldt adds that there were few Africans slaves in Mexico and the Indigenous people and mestizos who worked in the mines were free laborers.[15] For him, the equality of the American man applied to all classes and races, not only to Mexico but also in Havana, Lima, Quito, Popayán, and Caracas. He states that "everywhere a great thrust toward enlightenment is visible and the youth penetrate the principles of science with singular ease,"[16] and that "no city on the New Continent, including those of the United States, possesses scientific establishments as grand and solid as those in the capital of Mexico."[17] He praises Mexico's School of Mines, botanical gardens, and the academy of painting and sculpture. He celebrates the work of many local scientists—Clavijero, Alzate, Joaquín Velázquez, and Gama. On the latter, he wrote:

> He published several memoirs on eclipse of the moon, on the satellites of Jupiter, and on the almanac and chronology of the ancient Mexicans, and on the climate of New Spain; all of which announce a great precision of ideas and accuracy of observation. If I have allowed myself to enter into these details on the merit of three Mexican *savants*, it is merely for the sake of proving from their example that the ignorance which European pride has thought proper to attach to the creoles in neither the effect of the climate nor a want of moral energy; but that this ignorance, where it is still observable, is solely the effect of the insulation and the defects in the social institutions of the colonies.[18]

For the Mexican historian Juan Ortega y Medina, such statements contributed to the self-awareness and national consciousness of Mexican creolism that were necessary for independence and subsequent eras. The

Political Essay on the Kingdom of New Spain helped "solidify the national political, economic, and cultural aspirations of a now redeemed Mexico that awaited a glorious future."[19] In this sense, Humboldt was an ally of Latin American nations and their projects of modernity/coloniality. Nonetheless, what I hope to highlight here, complementing and diverging from Ortega y Medina's view, is that Mexico (and the rest of the Latin America), in its movement for political and economic independence from Spain, solidified Humboldt's fame and then drew on Humboldt for legitimacy as a modern nation. To speak of Humboldt as the new discoverer of the continent is to overlook the importance of the continent within the global political map, redefined by the movements of globalization and imperialism in the logic of modernity/coloniality. In his *History of Mexican Archaeology*, Ignacio Bernal acknowledges the importance of Humboldt's role as a diffusionist: "Humboldt was a diffusionist, like most Europeans. . . . He knew how to arouse the interest of European scholars; this was to be his great gift to Mexican archaeology. His books, skillfully edited in French, as well as his language of scholarship, all met with such success among the intelligentsia of the day that from them arose a renewed desire to become acquainted with things Mexican, and this desire arose not only in France but in England and Germany as well."[20]

The colonies' struggle for independence, including that of the United States in 1776, needed to place Americans on equal footing within the scientific and political map. In a letter dated April 14, 1811, six years after Humboldt's visit to the United States, Jefferson thanked Humboldt for sending him documents on his journey, which included a map of New Spain. Jefferson remarked on the political importance of the documents:

> It comes out to a moment when those countries are beginning to be interesting to the whole world. They are now becoming the scenes of political revolution, to take their stations as integral members, of the great family of nations. All are now in insurrection. In several the Independants are already triumphant, and they will undoubtedly be so in all. What kind of government will they establish? How much liberty can they bear without intoxication? Are their chiefs sufficiently enlightened to form a well-guarded government, and their people to watch their chiefs? Have they mind enough to place their domesticated Indians on a footing with the whites? . . . I imagine they will copy our outlines of confederation and elective government.[21]

During his stay in France, Jefferson argued with Enlightenment philosophers about the idea of the inferiority of man and nature in America, a point he also addressed in *Notes on the State of Virginia*. Refuting this supposed inferiority was vital to the ideological legitimacy of the independence project in America. Accordingly, the friendship between

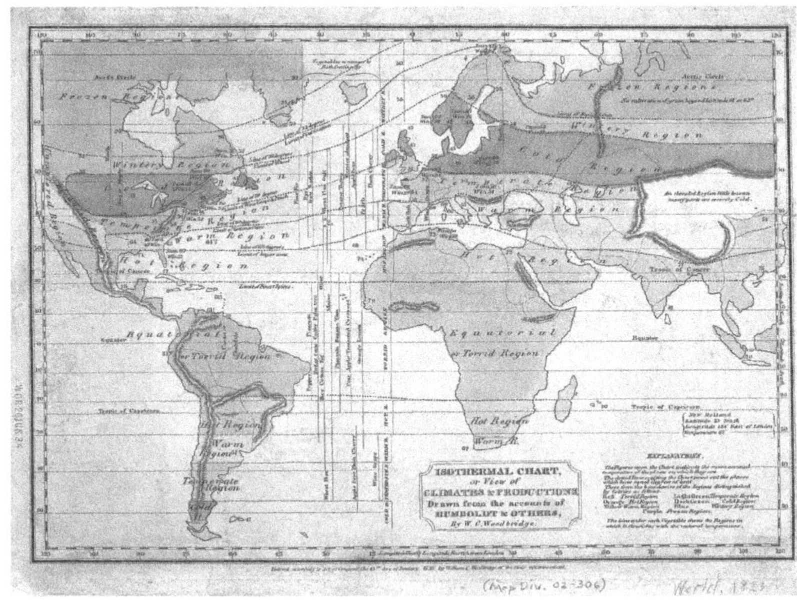

Isothermal chart, or, view of climates and productions drawn from the accounts of Humboldt and others, by W. C. Woodbridge, 1823.

Naturgemälde, Humboldt's diagram of the distribution of plants according to elevation on the volcanoes Chimborazo and Cotopaxi. The illustration first appeared in *Essai sur la géographie des plantes*, 1807.

Humboldt and Jefferson rested upon an alliance that was both scientific and political.[22]

Within this logic, as Ottmar Ette notes, the American continent is not perceived as Europe's "other," but rather as part of a global totality with interrelated parts.[23] The drafting of maps and illustrations of ecological regions joined by isotherms and isobars ratified the importance of including the American continent in a planetary consciousness (Pratt) or as part of world knowledge (Ette).

In the history of science, Humboldt's trip to Latin America placed him between Buffon and Darwin. As Rebok recalls, Enlightenment endeavors to measure and study nature followed Carl Linnaeus's famous system of classification of live organisms.[24] In *Systema Naturae* (1735), Linnaeus described species according to their physical appearance and their reproductive systems. He classified them by degrees of similarity. For example, he situated monkeys and man within the category of Anthropomorpha, arguing still for the invariability of species. In *Histoire naturelle, générale et particulière* (1749–1804), Buffon expanded the panorama by proposing that species could change when influenced by their environment. For Buffon, general laws, not theological doctrine, explained nature, a view that led to Charles Darwin's more expansive theory of natural selection and random mutation in *The Origin of Species* (1859). Humboldt sat between them. With his *Naturgemälde*—a scientific painting of Chimborazo—he insisted that the search for general laws of nature required more exact measurements in the field.[25] In his concept, nature was an organic whole, in which all components, species, and environments were interrelated. Nothing, therefore, could be studied in isolation.[26]

To understand the whole, it was necessary to understand how the parts were interrelated. Since his study of nature included societies, Humboldt's work is a compendium of natural and social sciences, a body of knowledge whose multiple disciplinary facets interacted in an organic whole. His knowledge of America, understood as a global totality on equal footing with Europe, opened avenues for the continent's political, social, and economic legitimacy. This expansive view allows us to study Humboldt in light of Latour's ideas on the blood flow of science, in which all knowledge is related to social and political institutions and has an agency that connects humans and nonhumans through reciprocal dialogue.

Views of the Cordilleras and Monuments of the Indigenous Peoples of the Americas (1813)

Humboldt argues most forcefully that American cultures were highly developed in *Veus des Cordillères et monumens des peuples indigènes de l'Amérique*. He wrote the book with a clear aesthetic goal of celebrating the beauty of the American vistas, especially the mountains, volcanoes, and other features of nature. But the book is also an argument in favor of the common origin of humanity, and he builds his case by adducing the advanced degree of civilization that pre-Columbian peoples had brought to America. By describing the majestic scenes of nature and ancient monuments, he refuted the supposed inferiority of America. His analysis of the Aztec calendar, the pyramids in Cholula, and the Nahuatl pictograms, and comparisons with the ancient cultures of Egypt, Tataria, China, and Mongolia, aimed to establish the common origin of the new and old worlds: "It was surprising to discover, toward the end of the fifteenth century, and in a world that we call new, the very kind of ancient institutions, religious ideas and shapes of buildings that in Asia seem to date back to the dawn of Civilization."[27] Here Humboldt extends his holistic hypothesis on the parts of a single whole by comparing societies to plants: "It would seem that the characteristics of peoples, not unlike the internal structure of plants, are disseminated across the surface of the Earth."[28] During his ascent of Chimborazo, this observation had been fundamental for his theory on the cosmos.

His argument draws on illustrations and descriptions of objects, ruins, and landscapes. As in Humboldt's other works, objects are transported through varied formats thanks to their reduction in size and to the graphic medium. The book is a mobile book-museum accessible to a broad public. It brings together objects and information that he gathered during his trip to America and also from his research in the Borgia Museum, the Vatican library, the Imperial Library in Paris, the Royal Library in Berlin, and other archives, where he collected information on Mexican codices. This allows Humboldt to compare and contrast how objects that would otherwise have remained separate now complement and shed light on each other. Yet, the archives were not enough for Humboldt. His holistic vision drove him to consider all possible perspectives. In addition to the sources offered by creole scholars such as Clavijero and Gama, he also consulted contemporary Indigenous peoples who lived near the ruins to see how they understood the pyramids and incorporated them into their everyday life. In his description of the pyramid in Cholula, for example, unlike descriptions made by other chroniclers of the veneration of Quetzalcoatl, Humboldt included the version of the Indigenous, for whom the origin of the construction had been gratitude to the mountain of Tlaloc, the caves of which had protected the seven giants (Tzocuillixequeme) from a raging storm. According to this legend, the bricks had been crafted in Tlalmanalco and carried to Cholula by a long column of men. Humboldt sought to corroborate this "remarkable legend" in the Vatican library. "After my return to Europe I examined the Mexica manuscripts in the Vatican Library in Rome and found record of this very legend in a manuscript by Pedro de Los Ríos, a Dominican monk, who, in 1566, had copied on site all the hieroglyphic paintings he could procure."[29] Humboldt thus presents a polyphonic book-museum that gathers complementary and contradictory visions to ensure the greatest objectivity. The resulting surfeit of information offers no conclusive theses. Rather, it offers a vision of American history as a palimpsest of a thousand fragments.

Humboldt complements the detailed description of the shape, interior, and legends of the pyramid in Cholula with a comparison with the pyramids in Egypt, Etruria, China, Tibet, and elsewhere. Yet, similarities aside, he points out that their purposes were very different. Unlike pyramids elsewhere, the Mexican ones were not only for burial. They were also temples (*teocalli*) and altars:

> At the dawn of civilization people chose high places for sacrifice to the gods. The first altars and temples were erected on mountains. If the mountains were isolated, they preferred to give them regular shapes by cutting terraces into them and making steps in order to climb to the summit more easily. Both continents offer numerous examples of hills that have been terraced and dressed in bricks or stone walls. The teocalli appear to me nothing more than artificial hills raised in the middle of a plain and designed to serve as a base for altars. Indeed, there is nothing more impressive than a sacrifice that can be seen by an entire people at the same time![30]

One of the longest entries relates to the description of the Aztec calendar (plate XXIII). Through a comparative linguistic analysis of the glyphs indicating days and epochs, Humboldt shows the surprising similarities with the Chinese calendar, as well as other parallels such as the ecclesiastical hierarchies, the number of the religious congregations, the austerity and penitence of their rituals, among many others. He thus engages with European philosophers in the debate on the inferiority of American civilizations:

> These people, who based their festival on the movements of the stars and who engraved their celebrations on a public monument, had likely reached a higher level of civilizations than that accorded to them by de Pauw, Raynal, and even Robertson, the most judicious of all historians of the Americas. These authors regard as barbarous any state of humanity that diverges from the notion of culture that they have established, based on their own systematic ideas. We simply cannot accept such sharp distinctions between barbarous and civilized peoples. In examining this work with a scrupulous

impartiality, everything that we ourselves have been able to discover about the former circumstances of the indigenous peoples of the new continent, we have tried to bring together the features that distinguish them individually, as well as those that appear to link them in various groups of Asian peoples. As it is with mere individuals, so it is with entire peoples; among the former, not all the soul's faculties manage to develop simultaneously, while among the latter, the advances of civilization do not manifest themselves all at once in the tempering of public and public morals, in a sense for the arts, and in the form of institutions. Before one can classify peoples, one must study them on the basis of their specific characteristics, for external circumstances produce infinite variations in the cultural nuances that distinguish tribes of different races, especially when, settled in regions separated by vast distances, they have lived for a long time under the influences of governments and religions more or less contrary to the advancement of the mind and the preservation of individual liberty.[31]

Here Humboldt summarizes the "scrupulous impartiality" of his method. He develops his opinion on the specific characteristics of each culture, as well as those shared by others, and is therefore able to "separate" the specific and individual characteristics of each culture from the "external circumstances," notably the influence of respective governments and religions, that account for differences between races and regions. For Humboldt, the Incan and Mexica cultures were "contrary to progress of the mind and the preservation of individual liberty."[32] Humboldt thus considers the peoples and their circumstances, applying, in order to understand them, his theory on the relationship between flora and the environment (altitude, climate, temperature) that he illustrated in his *Naturgemälde* of Chimborazo, according to which each species was distinct due to its relationship with its natural environment.

Humboldt established the need for a historical and natural explanation for the American tableau of ruins, mountains, statues, and glyphs. For him, they were produced in circumstances in which the elevation of the individual spirit had not yet reach the level of art. By means of comparison, he mentions the works of ancient Greece, whose exemplars do not require historical explanation in order to be regarded as works of art: "Although the theocratic government of the Peruvians favored the progress of industry, public works and everything indicative of mass civilization, so to speak, nevertheless hindered the development of individual faculties."[33] Development among the Greeks, by contrast, was "so free and rapid before the time of Pericles" that there was no parallel to the slow development of the massive civilizations of America.[34] For Humboldt, the evolution of the human spirit was more developed in Greco-Roman culture than in Asia Major or in America, precisely because of the political and natural circumstances. Nonetheless, the study of these American monuments allowed Humboldt to understand the "uniform and progressive spectacle of the human mind,"[35] revealing once again the logic of modernity/coloniality, according to which Europe was placing itself at the most evolved state of humankind in a linear trajectory of progress.

Humboldt thus struck a balance between the perspectives of inferiority and superiority, situating the American mountains as world sites of grandeur, Romanticism, and beauty. True art, for him, was in the cordillera of the Andes:

> The Andes are to the High Alps what the Alps are to the Pyrenees. Everything romantic or grand that I have seen on the banks of the Saverne in northern Germany, in the Euganean Hills, in the central mountain range of Europe, or on the steep slopes of the volcano of Tenerife—this is all combined in the Cordilleras of the new world. Several centuries would not be enough time to observe their beauties and to discover the wonders that nature has lavished upon an expanse of two thousand five hundred leagues, from the granite mountains of the Strait of Magellan to the coasts of the neighbor Asia. I will consider my goal fulfilled if the humble sketches in this book inspire *travelers with a passion for art* to visit the regions that I traversed in order to depict faithfully *these majestic sites*, which cannot be compared to those of the old continent.[36]

Certainly, Humboldt was an inspiration to scientists and artists. Among the latter, one of the most famous was Frederic E. Church, who traveled through Colombia and Ecuador in 1847 to paint the majestic scenes of volcanoes such as Cayambe, Chimborazo, and Cotopaxi. The Romantic and artistic veneration Humboldt felt for the mountains was inseparable from his fascination with the pyramids, which, like the mountains, elevated the spirit toward transcendence.

The Role of Mercury in Humboldt's Research on Gold and Silver Mines

In the era of great overseas expeditions, Humboldt arrived in the New World more by chance than meticulous planning. He had signed up for two earlier expeditions, one to Egypt with Napoleon's armada (1798–1801) and the other to India and the South Pacific with captain Nicholas Baudin (1800–1803). Fortunately for Humboldt, both plans failed. The English blockage ended the French journey to Egypt and Baudin fell ill and died.[37] Humboldt opted then for a third, and perhaps final, option: the trip to America.

Since much of the continent was held by Spain, Humboldt, a foreigner, had to request permission for his journey from Charles IV. The monarch authorized the trip under the condition that Humboldt work as a royal "inspector of mines," though he still had to fund the whole trip with his personal inheritance. The Spanish Empire only reluctantly allowed foreigners into its colonies (the Frenchman La Condamine led an expedition to Ecuador in 1735 and the Italian Alessandro Malaspina traveled from South America to Alaska and New Zealand from 1789 to 1794, both under restrictions and prohibitions). Consequently, knowledge about nature in the continent remained mostly a mystery outside of Spain. However, hoping to boost the economies and modernize the administration in the colonies, the enlightened Bourbon monarchs allowed Humboldt to travel to the New World as an inspector of mines. Since the silver and gold mines were the main reason for the conquest and colonialization of America, Humboldt's assignment underscores how valuable the trip was for Spain.

After shipping out of Ecuador, Humboldt disembarked in Acapulco in March 1803. Over a year, he traversed Mexico from west to east, visiting the Jorullo volcano, the Toluca lagoon, the mines of Taxco, Pachuca, and Guanajuato, and Mexico City, where he spent most of his stay. All the while, he collected information for his famous *Political Essay on the Kingdom of New Spain*. The book is an exhaustive compendium of the geography, the populations, agriculture, industry, and earnings of Mexico. Although he addressed the *Political Essay* to the king of Spain, the book inspired and justified the political and economic projects of multiple readers. Nonetheless, Humboldt explicitly dedicated the book to the king "for the favors that Your Majesty has inspired in me." Humboldt was entirely aware that the knowledge he offered the king—the "physiognomy of the country, grouping the mountains, extent of plains, elevation which determines its temperature; in short, whatever constitutes the structure of the globe"—had to relate to the progress and wellbeing of the population, agriculture, the ease of communication and internal commerce, military defense, and the colonies' protection from external enemies. Only in this way, he noted, "geological views can interest the statesman, when he calculates the force and territorial wealth of the nation."[38]

From the earliest pages, Humboldt addresses travel between the Atlantic and the Pacific, a topic of vital concern for the Spanish Empire. "The subject which we here summarily discuss is of the greatest interest for the balance of commerce and the political preponderancy of nations."[39] He then characterizes the nine points that facilitated interoceanic travel, from north to south, from Canada to Cape Horn. He discusses navigation in rivers that flow into both oceans, the mountain ranges that would make navigation and transportation of merchandise difficult; he corrects the errors in maps and chronicles drafted by previous explorers who miscalculated such features as the unevenness of the two oceans. As for the optimal spot for interoceanic transportation, he favored the isthmus of Panama, crossed first by Vasco Núñez de Balboa in 1513, although it needed to be measured and verified. He advises the king:

> I have sketched in one plate the nine points which appear to afford means of communication between the two oceans. . . . The long circumnavigation of South America would then be less frequent; and a communication would be opened for the goods which pass from the Atlantic Ocean to the South Sea. The time is past "when Spain, through jealous policy, refused to other nations a thoroughfare through the possessions of which she so long kept the world in ignorance." Those who are present at the head of the government are enlightened enough to give favourable reception to the liberal ideas proposed to them; and the presence of a stranger is no longer regarded as a danger of the country.[40]

Understanding that he was addressing an enlightened monarch, Humboldt articulated his liberal ideas on commercial openness and scientific developments in other countries. Such moments in *Political Essay* reveal Humboldt's underlying liberalism, as well as his ambiguous approach to the Spanish monarchy and its colonial administration. The study of Mexican mines occupies much of the *Political Essay*. Humboldt describes the mines with great precision, pointing out, for example, the advantageous altitude at which "nature has placed wealth of ore in New Spain."[41] Unlike the great heights in Peru, where vegetation cannot grow and water freezes, the richest mines in Mexico—Guanajuato, Zacatecas, Taxco, and Real Monte—were found between seventeen hundred and two thousand meters above sea level. The nearby fields, villages, and towns greatly facilitated the extraction of mineral wealth. Humboldt then provides a detailed description of the difficulties of transporting ore on rivers, making comparisons between different geographic regions. The colonial government and mine owners doubtlessly understood the value of this knowledge for commerce and the mining industry. Nonetheless, Humboldt's account goes beyond mere pragmatic descriptions and launched a criticism of the settlers who destroyed the ecosystems:

> The aridity of the central plain, the want of trees, occasioned, perhaps, in a good measure by the length of time the great vallies have remained covered with water, obstruct very much the working of the mines. These disadvan-

Table 1. La Valenciana's Profit

	Periods									Total of the nine years
	1794	1795	1796	1797	1798	1799	1800	1801	1802	
Produce of the sale of the minerals of Valenciana (in piastres)	1,282,042	1,696,640	1,315,424	2,128,439	1,724,437	1,584,393	1,4780,933	1,394,338	1,229,631	13,835,380
Expenses of working (in piastres)	799,328	815,817	832,347	878,789	890,735	915,438	977,314	991,981	944,309	8,046,063
Net profit divided among the shareholders (in piastres)	482,713	880,822	483,077	1,249,650	835,702	668,954	503,619	401,456	285,321	5,791,317

From Humboldt, *Political Essay on the Kingdom of New Spain*, book IV, p. 199.

tages have augmented since the arrival of Europeans without planting, but in draining great extents of ground have occasioned another more important evil. Muriate soda and lime, nitrate of potash, and other saline substances, cover the surface of the soil, and spread with a rapidity very difficult to be explained. Through this abundance of salt and these efflorescences, hostile to cultivation, the table-land of Mexico bears a great resemblance in many places to Tibet and the saline steppes of central Asia. In the valley of Tenochtitlan, particularly, the sterility and want of vigorous vegetation have been sensibly augmenting since the Spanish conquest; for this valley was adorned with beautiful verdure when the lake occupied more ground, and the clayey soil was washed by frequent inundations.[42]

But then he adds that, fortunately, this aridness does not characterize the plains and higher plateaus. On the contrary, "a great part of the vast kingdom of New Spain belongs to the most fertile regions of the earth."[43] Humboldt was convinced that Mexico, if properly cultivated, could produce all the world's fruits. The geographic placement of Mexico City presented inestimable advantages: "A king of Spain resident in the capital of Mexico might transmit his orders in five weeks to the Peninsula in Europe, and in six weeks to the Philippine Islands in Asia."[44]

Published first in French and later in English, the *Political Essay on the Kingdom of New Spain* fueled England's interest in Mexico's mines and, consequently, in Mexico's liberation from Spanish control. British investments in later decades failed, due to the neglect of mines during the wars of independence; however, at the time, European investors read Humboldt's detailed studies of the mines in Pachuca, Real de Monte, and Guanajuato with great interest. English companies even offered to hire Humboldt as a mining advisor. He rejected the offer, leaving the way open to his friend, the Mexican intellectual and mining expert Lucas Alamán.[45]

As part of his examination of mining in Mexico, Humboldt's account delves into the physical condition of miners. Refuting DePauw and Raynal's views on the American man, he notes that mine workers were strong, capable of enduring heavy burdens and high temperatures. They were neither slaves nor subjected to corvée labor regimes such as the Andean mita. Humboldt inserted comparative tabulations regarding Mexico's richest mines, including La Valenciana, that clearly display the advantages and the profits that investments in Mexican mining yielded.

Nonetheless, Humboldt stops short of presenting the continent and its natural resources as "merchandise," after the fashion of Columbus's diary, when he contemplates multiple aspects of mining with an eye to America's independence. Necessary to the amalgamation and extraction of minerals, mercury receives close attention in Humboldt's observations. He suggests that mercury could be the nonhuman agent that liberates the colonies from Spanish domination. To avoid importing mercury from Europe at elevated costs, Americans had to search throughout their territory for sources that were as large as those of Huancavelica in Peru and create routes to transport it. The agency of the nonhuman mercury would not only enable the colonies to free themselves from Spanish monopoly, but also to unify markets within the continent:

> America in its present state is the tributary of Europe with respect to mercury; but it is probable that this dependence will not be of long duration if the ties which united the colonies with the mother country remain long loosened, and if the civilization of the human species in its progressive motion from East to West is concentrated in America. The spirit of enterprise and research will increase with the population; the more the country shall be inhabited, the more they will learn to appreciate the natural wealth which is contained in the bowels of their mountains. If they discover no single mine equal in wealth to Huancavelica, they will work several at once, by which the united produce will render the importation from Spain and Germany unnecessary. These changes will be so much the more rapidly operated, as the Peruvian and Mexican miners shall feel themselves impeded by the want of the metal necessary for amalgamation. But we shall see what will happen to the predominance of America's silver mines if, amidst the wars that afflict Europe, they ceased to benefit from the mercury mines of Almaden and Idria.[46]

Seeing the continent as an alternative to Europe convulsed by Napoleonic wars, Humboldt contemplated the economic and political interests of America. Metaphorically, mercury's amalgamating properties could unite the American nations in the common pursuit of political and economic independence. Once again, "nonhumans" have palpable agency beyond their scientific significance.

The Aleph in Latin America

My analysis of Humboldt draws on three nodes or axes of what Latour calls "the circulatory system of scientific facts": 1) the mobilization of varied regions of the planet toward the metropole; 2) the dialogues and alliances between scientific communities and with politicians and economists (Clavijero, DePauw, Jefferson, British investors, etc.); and 3) the importance of knowledge for political movements. This sophisticated network of links and interconnections yields the unfinished textual representation of an object—in this case, Mexico and Latin America—that spills over unilineal and monologic narratives. Such writing must assume multiple perspectives to constitute the object of study. Humboldt's writings about Latin America, and Mexico in particular, in his *Political Essay on the Kingdom of New Spain*, thus resembles the Aleph as described by Borges:

> The Aleph's diameter was probably little more than an inch, but all space was there, actual and undiminished. Each thing (a mirror's face, let us say) was infinite things, since I distinctly saw it from every angle of the universe. I saw the teeming sea; I saw daybreak and nightfall; I saw the multitudes of America; I saw a silvery cobweb in the center of a black pyramid; I saw a splintered labyrinth (it was London); I saw, close up, unending eyes watching themselves in me as in a mirror; I saw all the mirrors on earth and none of them reflected me; I saw in a backyard of Soler Street the same tiles that thirty years before I'd seen in the entrance of a house in Fray Bentos; I saw bunches of grapes, snow, tobacco, lodes of metal, steam; I saw convex equatorial deserts and each one of their grains of sand; I saw a woman in Inverness whom I shall never forget; I saw her tangled hair, her tall figure, I saw the cancer in her breast; I saw a ring of baked mud in a sidewalk, where before there had been a tree; I saw a summer house in Adrogué and a copy of the first English translation of Pliny—Philemon Holland's—and all at the same time saw each letter on each page (as a boy, I used to marvel that the letters in a closed book did not get scrambled and lost overnight); I saw a sunset in Querétaro that seemed to reflect the color of a rose in Bengal; I saw my empty bedroom; I saw in a closet in Alkmaar a terrestrial globe between two mirrors that multiplied it endlessly; I saw horses with flowing manes on a shore of the Caspian Sea at dawn; I saw the delicate bone structure of a hand; I saw the survivors of a battle sending out picture postcards; I saw in a showcase in Mirzapur a pack of Spanish playing cards; I saw the slanting shadows of ferns on a greenhouse floor; I saw tigers, pistons, bison, tides, and armies; I saw all the ants on the planet; I saw a Persian astrolabe . . . *I saw the Aleph from every point and angle, and in the Aleph I saw the earth and in the earth the Aleph and in the Aleph the earth; I saw my own face and my own bowels; I saw your face; and I felt dizzy and wept,* for my eyes had seen that secret and conjectured object whose name is common to all men but which no man has looked upon—the unimaginable universe.[47]

Humboldt strove to describe every organic, inorganic, and cultural aspect of America and Mexico from "every angle of the universe": the scientific community in Europe, the Spanish Empire, British investors, pro-independence Latin Americans, Indigenous guides. This yields a written reflection of an agonistic subject struggling and desiring to chronicle "the unimaginable universe" that Borges mentions. Humboldt's fervor to capture an immeasurable object in the *Political Essay* provokes vertigos. The effect of writing that Borges describes in "The Aleph" is the same dizziness Humboldt experienced during his ascent of Chimborazo in Ecuador. This is why Humboldt cannot help but measure Chimborazo, despite the cold, the snow, the fog, the wind, the rarefied high-altitude air, the cliffs, the dizziness, the paths untrammeled by man, and the burden of his instruments weighing upon each step.

On June 22, 1802, Humboldt began to climb what was believed to be the highest peak on the planet. The claim was later proved to be inaccurate—Chimborazo is not even the tallest mountain in the Andes—unless its height is measured from the center of the earth. Upon reaching 4,700 meters, his porters refused to continue. Humboldt and Bonpland divided the measuring instruments among the two other members of the expedition, Carlos Montúfar and the *mestizo* José de la Cruz. The cold froze their hands and the metal of their instruments; the inhospitable soil made their feet bleed. Yet they continued to climb and made measurements with the barometer and the thermometer every hundred meters. Three hundred meters below the summit, continuing the ascent became impossible. Snow enveloped their bodies; the gorges were impassible. They relented, but as Andrea Wulf notes in her narrative of the Chimborazo ascent, "no one had climbed as high, not even the first astronauts in their balloons in Europe"—5,917 meters above sea level.[48] The Chimborazo ascent required, then and now, great physical strength, proper gear, adequate mountain clothing, and above all great spiritual integrity. Humboldt narrated the experience: "After an hour of cautious climbing, the ridge of rock became less steep; but alas! The mist remained as thick as ever. We now began gradually to suffer from great nausea. The tendency to vomit was combined with some giddiness; and much more troublesome than the difficulty of breathing. We have haemorrhage from the gums and lips. The conjunctiva of the eyes likewise was, in all, gorged with blood. These symptoms of extravasation in the eyes, and of oozing from the lips and gums, did not in the least disquiet us, as we had repeatedly experienced them before."[49]

In the narration, the experience of climbing Chimborazo was a via crucis. Yet instead of a saint, Humboldt was a modern man who risked everything for scientific progress. Humboldt's travel narratives are full of descriptions of martyrdom experienced during his trip; they are evidence of the difficult task of disciplining the object "America." The experiments are gestures of this rhetoric of martyrdom. Beyond the instruments, the travelers' very bodies measure extreme temperatures and altitudes and test the effects of poisonous plants. Humboldt thus sought to bear witness to the profound interaction between the human and the nonhuman in science:[50]

What joy, my dear friend, to live among the wealth of such majestic and imperious nature! My most ardent desires have been fulfilled; amid the thick forests of the Río Negro, surrounded by ferocious tigers and crocodiles, the body tortured by the bites of these formidable *mosquitos* and ants, having ingested no food for three months other than water, bananas, fish, and yucca; among the Otomac Indians who eat dirt, and on the banks of the Casquiare (below the equator), where no human soul can be seen for three leagues around; at the moments of greatest risk, I have never regretted my projects. The hardships have been great, but momentary.[51]

This rhetoric of danger aimed to establish the scientific traveler of modernity/coloniality as the new Romantic hero of scientific progress by cultivating and reaffirming the new global order in which science assumed the role once played by religion. In addition to validating the autonomy of the endeavor, the rhetoric of danger and martyrdom allows Humboldt, as Latour puts it, to establish his public image not so much for the scientific community but rather for the general public. This is how the trip to Latin America made Humboldt famous.

Chapter 2

Désiré Charnay in Mexico

Between Politics and Science

Napoleon III commissioned the French archeologist and photographer Désiré Charnay to travel to Mexico. His first journey lasted from 1857 to 1860. His second, from 1864 to 1867, coincided with the Mexican Empire of Maximilian von Habsburg. The third trip was from 1880 to 1882, and he returned for the last time in 1886. Characterizing each of these trips is a close relationship between politics and scientific expeditions. Charnay's journeys helped pioneer the mechanical reproduction of the Mayan ruins through photography, which made the ruins available to a vast audience. Further, Charnay crafted papier-mâché molds that rendered ruins' artifacts and glyphs mobile and accessible in the metropolis. Although his discoveries and theories never conferred him the prestige that later archeologists such as Alfred Percival Maudslay enjoyed in the scientific community, Charnay generated competition among important travelers who rushed to the archeological sites in the Maya territories, which prompted the Mexican government to defend its national patrimony.

The photographs of the Mayan ruins cemented Charnay's fame and introduced a crucial aspect into the modern travel enterprise. By vastly widening the circulation and diffusion of objects transported by travelers, mechanical reproduction created an "object Mexico" on a global scale. Codified according to Romantic and Gothic models associated with ruins, this object Mexico combined mythical images with an ideology of imperial decline. Nonetheless, Charnay's travel narratives reveal a more complex weaving, in which ruins, local guides, heavy photography plates, and equipment take on an agency that eludes the controlling intentions of scientific language.

On returning from his first trip, Charnay published *Cités et ruines américaines: Mitla, Palenque, Izamal, Chichen-Itzá, Uxmal* (1862–1863), a two-volume work consisting of a collection of seventy-one by fifty-four centimeter photographs and a smaller book of texts. The work gave Europe its first photographic vision of the mysterious Mayan ruins and monuments. Although the considerable size and price (five hundred francs) of the work limited access initially, the 1864 *Le Mexique et ses monuments anciens* contained twenty printed copies of the same photographs in a smaller format.[1] Furthermore, two of the photographs (*The Palace of Mitla, in Oaxaca* and *The Governor's Palace, in Uxmal*) were included in an exhibit in the Palace of Industry that ran from May 1 to August 31, 1863. Also, several of Charnay's impressions were exhibited in the 1862 International Exposition in London, which earned Charnay an honorable mention. Although his first album was only available to academics and wealthy patrons, these exhibitions brought samples of his work to a broader public.[2] This first group of photographs from Mexico was the most significant accomplishment of Charnay's career as a photographer.

This chapter studies the temporal meaning of the objects from Charnay's journey—the Maya archaeological pieces and their reproductions, including photographs—from the perspective of Jean Baudrillard's proposal regarding "antique objects": "The antique object no longer has any practical application, its role being merely to *signify*. It is astructural, it refuses structure, it is the extreme case of disavowal of the primary functions. Yet it is not afunctional, nor purely 'decorative,' for it has a very specific function within the system, namely the signifying of time."[3] For the traveler, and the metropolitan collector of antiques (or their photographic representation), the "antique" object signifies the always frustrated possibility of controlling the cyclic temporal flow of life and death represented in the ruins. The traveling collector can never stop it, but does try to capture it. My analysis considers this postulate in light of how imperial policies and nostalgic Romanticism relate to modes of archaeological legitimization in the figure of the pathfinder as an integral aspect of the expeditionary enterprise.

In addition to trophies of Charnay's adventure, the objects collected were a valuable symbolic sample of France's imperial designs in Mexico. *Le Mexique* clearly expresses this imperialist vision. Charnay discusses not only the advantages of the French liberal government in Mexico, but also the dispute between France and the United States over Mexico. One of France's objectives was to stop US expansion into the continent and thus preserve Latin culture in America. France invaded Mexico during the American Civil War, when the United States had to address pressing internal political affairs. Charnay's first expedition to Mexico brought together the scientific objectives with France's political and economic interests. France appears as the civilizing force: "It was reserved for France to shake Mexico from its numbness."[4] Moreover, France was also the creditor in charge of collecting Mexico's debt through the imposition of the French monarchy:

> But it took extraordinary circumstances: the cataclysm of a great people, and the genius of a great prince, to snatch it from the fatal slope that carried it to America.
>
> The split of the United States for a long time rejects Mexico under the influence of Europe, and the current expedition assures France a preponderance undoubtedly over this richest country in the world.
>
> At its origin, the Allied expedition, directed for the simple purpose of a claim for debt, engaged in an impracticable enterprise, and could only run up against the impotence of an insolvent debtor. Mexico, in the state in which the civil war had been reduced, deprived of resources, and in spite of the best will in the world, could not have made up for the slightest delay, and the seizure of its customs could only precipitate it in new ones orders. But it seems that Providence opens to this country a new perspective.[5]

The 1857 trip was not overtly political, but it did provide useful information for the French government. The publicity around the ruins that the trip generated in France made Mexico a more desirable place, at once close and distant. It was an enterprise of appropriation on multiple levels: political, economic, military, and symbolic. Mexico's ruins fascinated France as much as its mines. Charnay supported the ill-fated regime of Maximilian in Mexico. After the emperor's execution in 1867, Charnay had to leave Mexico. No documents or photographs remain from this trip, which lends credence to the hypothesis that Charnay was secretly working for Maximilian's government. In any case, after Maximilian's execution, to be a French explorer in Mexico became a dangerous task.

Amid the debts and crises of Benito Juárez's government, the idea of reestablishing a monarchic government in Mexico gained strength among conservatives and the clergy there. They turned to Napoleon III, who nominated his cousin Maximilian von Habsburg as emperor of Mexico. Maximilian wanted to establish a liberal government, and even get close to some Mexican republicans, which is why José Fernando Ramírez was among his collaborators. Nonetheless, the Mexican Empire's profligacy and poor administration, and the constant need to finance French troops in the fight against the republican soldiers, led to Maximilian's defeat and execution" in Querétaro. In that moment, Charnay was headed to the United States and, from there, to Java and Australia. Between his first two trips to Mexico, Charnay also traveled to Madagascar on a French political mission. These voyages helped consolidate his position as an imperial traveler between politics and science.

Although his first expedition to Mexico focused almost entirely on photography and his second left few traces, the third trip, from 1880 to 1882, helped pioneer techniques of excavation and documentation. Once the Civil War ended, the United States turned to Mexico and gave economic support to the French scientific mission. Because this was now a Franco-American joint effort, Charnay sent material not only to France but also to the Smithsonian Museum in Washington, DC. This trip was the most scientific: it was a journey of excavations, site measurements, artifact collection, and molds.

Although photographs did not feature as prominently in the third expedition, Charnay proposed new areas of expansion in archeological knowledge of the Mayan ruins. For two and a half years, he traveled to Mitla, Palenque, Izamal, Chichén Itzá, and Uxmal. The resulting book, *Les anciennes villes du Nouveau Monde* (1885), was meaningful because of its thesis on the age of man in America, the discoveries in excavations, and the maps of the main archeological sites like the temples of Comalcalco. During this excavation, Charnay carried out several transformational operations of the Mayan ruins that, together with the photographs, rendered them more accessible to a metropolitan audience. Part of what he translated was the knowledge of his local guides. Charnay conducted excavations of ancient cities and tombs, he collected ceramics and bones, he drew maps and makes papier-mâché molds of adornments, glyphs, and bas-reliefs. As they translated and transported valuable archeological pieces to metropolitan museums, these molds replaced photographs.

Despite the innovations in excavations that the book presented and its successful sales, *Les anciennes villes du Nouveau Monde* was not well received. The scientific community remained skeptical of Charnay's claims that the Toltec culture originated American cultures from a common trunk from which sprang all the groups that constructed the temples and pyramids in the Yucatán. Furthermore, the discovery of toys with wheels gave rise to a series of conjectures that many scientists doubted, although they were later proven to be true. The ancient Maya had the wheel, which implied an advanced degree of civilization.[6]

Compared to Humboldt, Charnay set out on a scientific journey of more modern scale and proportions. Humboldt collected, catalogued, and transferred specimens with a sense of holistic unity. Each collected specimen conserved an aura of the original. Even the drawings that Humboldt made of these specimens retained an artistic aura of the original.[7] Charnay's collecting and transporting methods and tools, in contrast, were revolutionary, in the sense of Walter Benjamin discussion of aura in the era of mechanical reproduction. [8] The technological reproduction of the photograph and the paper-mache molds enabled the transportation and diffusion of samples and specimens without a trace of originality. At the same time, these reproductions appear at least as real as the originals and drawings, thanks to the documentary illusion of photography and the precision of details reproduced in the molds.[9] And, they were at everyone's reach.

Mechanical Reproduction of the Ruins

Mayan ruins had already been captured in illustrations and daguerreotypes. John Lloyd Stephens and Frederick Catherwood made daguerreotypes of the Uxmal ruins during their 1841 trip to Yucatán. Daguerreotypes' popularity began to rise in the early 1840s. Daguerreotypes of Greece, Niagara Falls, and the Kremlin (through often anonymous photographers) appear in the series *Excursions Daguerriennes* (1840–1844).[10] Images of Egypt by Frederic Goupil-Fesquet and his uncle, the painter Horace Vernet, also became famous. Other pioneering photographers in the era of daguerreotypes were Baron Jean Baptiste Louis Gros, who made prints of Bogota (1842) and Athens (1850), and Joseph Philibert Girault de Prangey, who made more than a thousand daguerreotypes of Arabic architecture in the Middle East between 1842 and 1844.[11]

Yet daguerreotypes did not lend themselves to reproduction and wide distribution. They were single, unique images on silver-coated copper plates; reproduction, by hand or by photomechanics, was difficult. In contrast, the invention of paper negatives facilitated the distribution of originals in books and brochures. As a result, it allowed for expeditionary photography. Invented by William Henry Fox Talbot, the technique made use of a light-sensitive sheet of paper that was developed chemically; when pressed onto another light-sensitive sheet of paper, it yielded the positive image. The application of the calotype, or negative, process to travel photography resulted in many important publications of journeys. *Egypte, Nubie, Palestine et Syrie* (1849–1851) by Gustave Flaubert and Maxime DuCamp featured 125 copies of photographs. In 1856, the archeologist and photographer Auguste Salzmann published 174 images of Jerusalem and Palestine. In France, Edouard Baldus, Henri LeSecq, Gustave LeGray, and Charles Negre used the negative paper process in the 1850s to document famous monuments and cathedrals.[12]

This process dominated photography from the 1850s to the 1880s. It required the use of a light-sensitive glass plate coated in liquid emulsion. The liquid, collodion, dried quickly, so each negative had to be prepared moments before exposure; the photograph had to be developed in situ immediately. It was a cumbersome process involving different chemicals that the photographer had to carry to the archeological sites. Charnay relied on liquid negative photography to create his images of the Mayan ruins during his first trip. In 1862, forty-nine large photographs, developed mostly with the collodion process, were published in Paris in *Cités et ruines américaines*. They soon became famous throughout Europe and America.[13] Photography was also a vital tool for later researchers, including Charnay's competitors in Mayan archeology exploration, Augustus LePlongeon and Teobert Maler.

Expeditionary photography was an arduous task that involved considerable obstacles—inclement weather, thick vegetation, and mosquitos that got stuck in the negatives. Heavy equipment—cameras, tripods, dozens of fourteen-by-eighteen-inch glass plates, hundreds of gallons of developing chemicals, a tent that served as a darkroom—needed to be transported to inhospitable places. R. Tripp Evans notes that the equipment Charnay brought to the port of Veracruz in 1858 weighed more than four thousand pounds.[14]

The difficulties of the photographic endeavor enhanced the image of the expeditionary traveler as "hero" or "martyr." The images contributed to a vision of the non-Western as mysterious depositories of secrets into humanity's past. Charnay's most "scientific" work from the 1880s, *Les anciennes villes du Nouveau Monde*, dedicates considerable space to the antiquity of the Maya who constructed the cities.[15] His first book, *Cités et ruines américaines*, included a dissertation by Viollet-Le-Duc in which the French historicist used Charnay's photographs and the *Popol Vuh* to compare the ancient peoples of America to those of Asia and Africa.[16] Viollet-Le-Duc and Charnay sustained that the Toltecs were the descendants of Asians and Vikings with Arian features who had migrated from the east and the west to America. Charnay believed that the Toltecs had migrated from North America before founding the city of Tula. Searching for Toltec features elsewhere, he posited that Teotihuacan and Palenque were constructed after Tula, a hypothesis that was later disproved.

Charnay's disquisitions on a common Toltec origin not only of the Maya but of American man in general were fundamental to efforts by the United States to appropriate the region culturally and economically. Stephens had already been planning to buy Copán in order to "remove the monuments of a by-gone people from the desolate region in which they were buried, set them up in the great commercial emporium (New York City), and found an institution to be the nucleus of a great national museum of American antiquities."[17] These travelers often criticized the total neglect in which local governments had left the sites. In keeping with the civilizing mission, appropriation by the United States was thought to be a way to recover and oversee the continent's patrimony. The idea of American man's common origin strengthened the ideology of property and patrimony within the Monroe Doctrine's framework of America for Americans. Since Humboldt's trip to the United States, Jefferson had stressed the importance of the monuments of pre-Columbian civilizations to counterbalance the accusations of American inferiority. As evidence of the advanced degree of civilization and archeology, the ruins legitimized the discourse of American equality in the global panorama.

In Charnay's case, this became more complicated since both France and the United States commissioned his trip and both countries had imperial designs. Charnay's photographs from his first trip brought the ruins closer to an imperial French public. On the third trip, his theories on the origin of American man bolstered the United States's claim over the region. In both cases, the mission consisted of transporting ruins—be they excavated archeological pieces, photographic reproductions, or paper-mache molds—to the metropolitan museums of the Trocadero and the Smithsonian. Charnay pioneered the use of paper-mache molds, a predecessor to plaster casting. His technique consisted of placing several layers of newspaper on bas-reliefs or decorations, wetting them with water and flour, removing the excess liquid, and leaving them to slowly harden. Still damp, they were removed and dried by fire. This technique had several virtues. Molds could be easily transported and quickly reproduced. Charnay also boasted that by creating molds instead of reproductions, local authorities could not accuse him of transporting original archeological pieces.[18] From these molds, Charnay later made plaster reproductions. Beyond carrying pieces from the ruins to the Smithsonian, he wanted to reproduce the experience of travel inside the museum: "It is true that the quiet student at Washington will, of necessity, remain cold to . . . the feelings which have moved enthusiastic travelers. But, though the future investigator may have no share in the genial enthusiasm of the explorer . . . he will, in effect, have before his eyes Copán, with all its mysteries, its columns scored with hieroglyphs, its rows of death's heads on sculptured walls, its nameless kings and gods."[19]

This transfer is essential to understanding the role of travelers in the production of knowledge and subject within modernity/coloniality. For Bruno Latour, the capacity to render objects "mobile and stable" in order to bring them "home" is a principal characteristic of Western science. The notion of a "center of calculation" is key to understanding the economy that structures the production, distribution, and consumption of imperial travel narratives. In what Latour describes as the "circles of accumulation of science," imperial travelers select, edit, and prioritize the cultural goods they find on their trips and take them "home" as mobile objects of a reduced scale.[20] Nonetheless, Charnay often complains about cumbersomeness of the enterprise, the weight of his camera, and the climate of constant rains that made it difficult to work with paper-mache and forced him to dry his models by campfires that could spread out of control. All these instances reveal the true materiality of objects that refuse to flow into social life and professional activities, that resist domestication and the economy that rules the subject-object relationship from the metropole. Bill Brown notes that the materiality of objects is revealed when "they stop working for us," when the subject-object relationship—in which the former dominates the latter, that is, when the subject colonizes the object—shifts. For Brown, the power of things lies in this latent materiality.[21]

Ruins and Romanticism in Modernity/Coloniality

The images of explored territories, forged by modern travelers for metropolitan audiences, involved more than the production of scientific knowledge. The Romanticism and exoticism of otherness, which strengthened imperial dreams, is among the prevalent imperial discourses during the period examined by Edward Said and others. Viollet-Le-Duc, whose essay appeared with the photographs in *Cités et ruines américaines*, adhered to a Romanticism with "remnants of obscurantism" and an eagerness to recover the spirit of the past. This Romanticism was common in the literary salons of the Arsenal and among French thinkers such as Luis Bertrand, Victor Hugo, and Charles Nodier, who rejected the academicism and the scientific rationality of the Enlightenment's faith in progress. As an architect, Viollet-Le-Duc had participated in the restoration of the Cathedral of Notre Dame in Paris in 1844, in the works at Saint-Denis in 1848, and in 1852 he proposed a plan for the medieval city of Carcassonne, which continued until his death in 1879. Viollet-Le-Duc was also a student of geology, archeology, and the author of several books and dozens of studies during Napoleon III's era of splendor.[22] Viollet-Le-Duc combined scientific study with the Romantic spirit and the photographs that Charnay brought from the Mayan ruins.

On the one hand, photography provided travelers with documented evidence of ancient cultures, and available texts such as the *Popol Vuh* aided their search for explanations. On the other hand, the ruins possessed the phantasmagoric and Gothic aura that characterized Romanticism. Charnay's photographs highlighted the decay of constructions amid exuberant nature. The active role of the thick jungle in the photographic plane underscored the Romantic interest in the cyclical battle between man and nature. The ruins pointed to what was no longer

Désiré Charnay, Chichén Itzá

there but remained as a memory of perishing life. They were a memento mori, a ghost that emerged in the fissure between life and death.[23] In this sense, the images of the ruins capture that which, in Baudrillard's words, generates demand for such objects—the completeness of being: "'The antique is always, in the strongest sense of the term, a 'family portrait': the immemorialization, in the concrete form of an object, of a former being—a procedure equivalent, in the register of the imaginary, to a suppression of time."[24]

The shots of the pyramids against the background of the sky, as well as the details of the glyphs, created a mysterious and transcendental image of the ruins. The secret messages of the glyphs and the height of the pyramids that communicated with the Mayan gods were signs of an unresolved mystery, an ancient pagan religiosity that awoke the Romantic imagination.

Charnay's trip to the Mayan ruins continued the tradition of French travelers that began with Napoleon's 1798–1801 invasion of Egypt. The expedition aimed to secure the political and economic power of France in Egypt and block England in India and the East Indies. Four hundred ships carried 167 scientists, including the mathematicians Gaspard Monge (one of the founding members of the École Polytechnique) and Jean-Baptiste Joseph Fourier, the physicist Étienne-Louis Malus, the chemist Claude Louis Berthollet (inventor of bleach), the geologist Déodat de Dolomieu, and Baron Dominique Vivant Denon, who later became director of the Louvre. The main goal was to explore the possibility of constructing a canal between the Mediterranean and the Red Sea from Suez, which was effectively accomplished during the empire of Napoleon III. These scientists traversed Egypt exploring archeological sites, drafting illustrations of buildings, copying ancient texts, making measurements and maps, and carrying out geological, botanical, and zoological studies. Their efforts produced the twenty volumes of the *Description de l'Égipte* (published between 1809 and 1822), which gave rise to the discipline of Egyptology.

Two aspects of this journey are fundamental to understanding the role of science in politics and the economy. First, it is the way that science legitimizes power, both in triumph and defeat. Napoleon brought scientists to legitimate the triumph of France in territories that were strategical in the dispute with England. The discovery of the Rosetta Stone, the key to deciphering Egyptian hieroglyphics through its blocks translated from Egyptian to Demotic and Greek, was one of the most important breakthroughs in the history of linguistics and archeology. England's defeat of Napoleon in the famous battle of the Nile brought on the two-year land siege. To leave Egypt, the French had to turn over the Rosetta Stone to the English. Second, although Napoleon's invasion of Egypt was a political and economic failure, it generated an exacerbated orientalism in the decorative, archeological fever apparent in French furnishings and artistic style. The military reverse, the loss of the Rosetta Stone, and the defeat of Napoleon's imperial ambitions gave rise to the nostalgia characteristic of Romanticism.

There was a clear alliance between imperialism and Romanticism, then. The latter included a marked interest in ruins, imperial decline, and orientalism. The Romantic taste for lost empires is also a product of an imperial fantasy that is conscious and fearful of its own possible decline, its cyclic existence, like the crumbling buildings slowly being invaded by vegetation. The journeys to the Mayan ruins, just like the expeditions to the Orient, revealed such sentiments in which different empires fought for possession.

Competition between Archeologists

In *Science in Action*, Latour discusses how Capitan Lapérouse's shipwrecked expedition to the Pacific in 1787 was successful. For the metropole, it was a success. Lapérouse managed to send maps, letters, and native testimonies that ended the controversy over whether the Strait of Segalien was part of a peninsula or an island. The information was vital for the commercial relations between Versailles and China. Lapérouse carried out a series of actions that favored the accumulation of scientific knowledge: he translated "local knowledge" into scientific knowledge and contributed a substantial discovery to the project of metropolitan geography, navigation, and commerce. The next ship, the *Neptune*, successfully arrived at the coast of Segalien, confident with the information supplied by its sunken predecessor. While the Lapérouse expedition's lack of native knowledge put it at a disadvantage, the voyage of the *Neptune* was able to accumulate a great corpus of information. Thanks to the map drawn by natives and translated by Lapérouse into more abstract and portable information, the *Neptune* employed more sophisticated communication and navigation technology. The Lapérouse expedition was a success because he "brought home" mobile and stable pieces that facilitated the accumulation of scientific knowledge.

In this sense, Charnay's first book, *Cités et ruines américaines*, completed and even rectified earlier travelers' works that initiated studies of the Maya region. The first expedition, led by Antonio del Río, was in 1787; delayed by the systematic opposition of the Mexican clergy, his documentation was not published until 1822. Dupaix led explorations in 1805 and 1808; his narrative was published in 1836, together with drawings by Castañeda. Later appeared *Antiquities of Mexico* (1830) by Lord Kingsborough, Waldeck's *Voyage pittoresque et archéologique dans la province d'Yucatan pendant les années 1834 et 1836* (1838), and *Incidents of Travel in Central America, Chiapas and Yucatán* and *Incidents of Travel in Yucatán* (1841, 1843) by Stephens and Catherwood. These travelers brought attention to the ruins, opening the way for Charnay and his contemporaries, among them Augustus and Alice Le Plongeon who traveled through the Yucatán in the 1880s, when Charnay was on his third expedition, and published *Ancient Cities of the New World*.

The Englishman Alfred Percival Maudslay (1850–1931) was the most important archeologist to explore the Maya area in the nineteenth century. He was also an excellent photographer. Maudslay made seven trips to Central America between 1881 and 1894 and his methodical research was published in *Biologia Centrali-Americana* (1889–1902). The volumes contain reproductions of the Maudslay's photographs, most of which were taken with a dry-negative technique that improved upon Charnay's. In his desire to document the ruins accurately and give them a uniform tone, Maudslay scrubbed the stucco with wood ash and white scales. At the same time, scaffolding allowed him to photograph the highest sections of the facades. Maudslay's documentation of the Copán is particularly impressive and exhaustive.[25]

In his narrative, Charnay discusses the feverous looting of archeological pieces and the competition between travelers to be the first to discover, excavate, and photograph the ruins. A newly documented site meant fame for the traveler who revealed it to the ruin-thirsty public. This fame, in turn, yielded commissions from museums for new expeditions and payment for the archeological pieces. The accumulation of scientific knowledge that Latour discusses reflects the logic of commerce. In this case it includes transactions in legal and illegal markets of knowledge. As Charnay notes:

> It is a curious circumstance, that Mexicans, even the best informed among them, as well as foreigners, should so often be victimized by vulgar forgers of antiquities, who trade on the passions of the collector and the gullibility of the public; and that such things cannot be done in Europe without immediate detection, can only arise from the superior knowledge of our savants, and the greater facility afforded them of observing, classifying, and comparing the productions of all the civilized nations of the world, in the numerous collections with which our museums, both public, and private, abound. In my own case, after my excavations, I never could have been so grossly imposed upon by pottery modern in shape, over which ancient bas-reliefs had been incongruously reproduced, forming a monstrous medley of things old and new, without any originality whatever.[26]

Charnay thus warned of the illegal fraud market while erecting himself as the "savant," who, after conducting his excavations can no longer be fooled like other less-informed adventurers. In a competitive field where many vied for the symbolic capital of the travel experience and the archeological scoop, this was his claim to legitimacy.

Guides and pathfinders

What role do guides play in this construction and legitimation of knowledge? In the situation described above, their labor was indispensable. It is impossible to think about the figure of the guide without evoking famous examples from literature and history. Recall legendary fictional characters such as the wise Virgil in Dante Alighieri's *Divina Comedia*, the story of betrayal in the figure of Hernán Cortés's Malinche, Fenimore Cooper's Pathfinder, and others. In the region of the Río de la Plata, the writer, teacher, and national politician Domingo F. Sarmiento dedicated one of the most emblematic pages of his famous text *Facundo: Civilización o Barbarie* (1845) to a specific type of gaucho guide known as the *baqueano*.[27] One of the most admired human figures of the Argentine pampas, the baqueano possessed the virtues of a precise and sophisticated map in a war zone. In a geographical area as featureless as the pampas, the baqueano remembered where to find trails, creeks, and other signs in the landscape. The baqueano's services were indispensable for guiding soldiers to victory. According to some orientalist critiques of *Facundo*, contemporary linguistic studies suggest that baqueano is an archaic term borrowed from Arabic. The archaic nature of the term suggests that the original baqueano was a marginal and fugitive figure from the conquest into the early colonial period (the sixteenth and seventeenth centuries).[28] In most of the travel narratives discussed above, the baqueano is portrayed as a dark and solemn figure whose position is ambiguous due to his association with a socially subordinated group; at the same time, his geographical and cultural knowledge confers him status as an authority. Nonetheless, the figure of the guide or baqueano is obliterated from the importance of the narrative.

The local guide is often seen in opposition to maps, as if each belonged to two different cognitive worlds. In fact, the cartographer and the baqueano use similar rational systems. In this sense, I diverge from the vernacular conception of the pathfinder and integrate it into the scientific aspects of travel narratives. The main difference between the cartographer and the baqueano lays in the scale of representation and in the capacity to transport knowledge and make it useable for the traveler and broader audiences. In Charnay's narrative, the appearance of guides varies from the first and the second book, depending on the mission of each trip. In the first trip, dedicated to photography, Charnay paid attention to the guides whenever they saw a monument, a temple, or a palace that the foreigner's eye, unaccustomed to the landscape, could not have found:

> The ruins are at least twelve kilometers from the village; it's a pretty long race. The sound of knocking on tree trunks warned me that we were approaching; yet we did not perceive the slightest trace of the monuments, the virgin forest enveloped us in the depths of its shadows, and we advanced with difficulty. I soon arrived in the clearing that had just been made by the ax of the workers, and I did not see the palace at all times.

—Oh that! but my friend, I say to the guide, where is the palace hiding?
"There it is, señor," he replied, pointing to a blackish mass, covered with vegetation as vigorous as that of the soil, and whose facade was half hidden beneath a clutter of creepers. In truth, one could go to ten meters and not see it. I understood at once the difficulties which awaited me in the reproduction of these monuments; everything was black, vermiculated, ruined, lost; I could not, however, put myself to work soon, because the work of the Indians did not go as fast as I thought at first, they needed two more days to allow me to take a perspective of the facade. It was necessary, moreover, to cut down at least the most troublesome trees which covered the roofs of the building and to clear the front of climbing plants which obstructed the view.[29]

Thanks to the baqueanos, the monuments that Charnay, unfamiliar with the terrain, could not have noticed are seen, cleaned, and photographed for cosmopolitan audiences. The camera completes the translation from the local vision of the guide to the gaze of the public. Still, Charnay had earlier complained of having to pay his guides with his own money even though the Mexican government had assigned them as guardians of the nation's patrimony. As in Humboldt's case, we can see here the traveler's ambivalent relationship with the guides, upon whom the success of the whole trip largely depended:

> For the last two days, Don Agustin had sent twelve Indians for me to the ruins to cut the woods and clear the palaces; the work was to advance, and I left to join them. I was accompanied by my servant and a guide whom the State of Chiapas imposes today on every traveler, for a pay of five francs a day. This one should serve me for two purposes: to guide my explorations in the monuments and to supervise my conduct with regard to the palaces, its instruction being to prevent me from committing any degradation; four Indians also followed us, loaded with my luggage, a table, various kitchen utensils, and food.[30]

Charnay's description of the guide changes in the narrative of his second, more scientific and less aesthetic trip. He occasionally mentions his "Indian" scouts, pathfinders, excavators, servants, and cooks. These sporadic references reveal and question the general silence on the local guides, giving them a phantasmagoric appearance. Nonetheless, the guides become more visible when Charnay needs to show his readers the arduousness of his endeavor. His guides explained the active and intense archeological projects in the country. In an episode from *Les anciennes villes du Nouveau Monde*, Charnay mentions an old guide who traveled with him. This time, there was more at stake than the baqueano's knowledge of the terrain, powerful memory, and ability to recognize sites and routes; even more important was the guide's role in the transfer of archeological artifacts to the centers of calculations.

> My impatience to find the cemetery was so great, that I could not stop long to contemplate the fine view to be seen here; we immediately began our search. But though I seemed to recognize the plateau, it looked somewhat different—strewn with flat stones I had not observed before—consequently I climbed higher, followed by an old Indian who had been with me in my first expedition, and who opened the ground in several places. It was very hard, compact, gravelly, without any appearance of ever having been disturbed; so, after many fruitless attempts, I returned to the first place, when the old Indian, who had not breathed a word hitherto, said:
>
> "Señor, this is the place where you found some vases the last time you were here."
>
> "But how do these flags get here?"
>
> "Oh, from subsequent excavations."
>
> "Then I am sold, robbed, done out of my find," I cried in my disappointment, as though the cemetery were my property.
>
> "But," objected the old *volcanero*[31] softly, "only a few loads of detritus were taken away; there must be more to come out."
>
> Acting on advice, which seemed so reasonable, I soon discovered numerous *tepalcates*, fragments of vases, cups, and various potteries; we had lost so much time, however, in looking about, that we were soon obliged to abandon the mountain, trusting in what the morrow would bring forth.[32]

In this passage, the guide's extraordinary memory contrasts with Charnay's inability to remember all the archeological sites he had visited. Moreover, the guide's information reveals the competition among scientists and archeologists over who could make rightful claims on the ruins, who arrived first, and who could handle the booty of vases and pottery. On the one hand, the value of the archaeological pieces, their exchange value, is thus in part delimited by social and professional factors, in the dispute over which traveler arrived first and how to situate the discovery in relation to previous and future trips. On the other hand, the value of the ruins' absolute singularity, Baudrillard argues, "arises from the fact of being possessed by me—and this allows me, in turn, to recognize myself in the object as an absolutely singular being. This is a grandiose tautology, but one that gives the relationship to objects all its density— its absurd facility, and the illusory but intense gratification it supplies."[33]

The cited passage from Charnay also clarifies the guide's role in the process, establishing him as the authority who grants travelers permission to carry off the artifacts. The pathfinder is therefore represented as an accomplice to the circulation and the transport of archeological pieces, as well as to the gratification of the traveler's narcissistic possession. Furthermore, following the trope of the spiritual guide in hagiographies and classic literature, the guide's sage advice calms Charnay: "Only a few loads of detritus were taken away; there must be more to come out." In the narrative, the local elder, whose name the reader never learns, grants legitimacy to the whole enterprise.

We can take this reading further still if we consider Charnay's nostalgic description of the archeological excavations, which, for him, had been a primitive, archaic landscape full of mysteries for the modern traveler. Charnay contrasts the condition of the ancient ruins during his third trip with those he photographed during the first a couple of decades earlier. Much had happened in the meantime to alter the landscape: several scientific expeditions of metropolitan archeologists, individual adventures who collected valuable pieces to sell to museums or on the black market, the Mexican government's recent regulations on the traffic of such pieces, now considered to be part of the nation's patrimony. The old volcanero acts as a witness and an active participant throughout the processes. For Charnay, the local guide is the living memory of the transformation of the landscape and the competition among agents for treasures: "I notice many changes since I was here before; portions of walls, the whole front of the Temple of the Cross has given way, and in the Lion's Temple the fine bas-relief over the altar has disappeared. It is sad to calculate how much more havoc another fifty years will make; there will be nothing, probably, but a mass of smoldering ruins, such as are met with in the woods, on the low hills, and the plain around."[34]

On the one hand, Charnay feels nostalgia for this type of "lost pristine paradise." On the other, he is thrilled to have been the first to discover archeological pieces and propose a new theory of the history of the New World. In this situation, Charnay faced the predicament of modernity and modern scientists between the fascination of the rural past and the scientific future. In this future, it becomes fundamental to remember the role that the baqueanos and local guides played in the creation of maps and the validation of the travelers' knowledge. As Charnay's case makes clear, the guides' authority legitimizes the traveling archeologists. As Jacob mentions in his detailed study of maps, "Between mapmakers and map viewers, there are mediators, such as the individual agents or the institutions who have the power to prescribe, to render authoritative, to bestow legitimacy."[35] Here, to a large measure, guides fulfilled the role of such mediators.

A Journey to the "Embryo or Mother Cell"

Charnay's narrative adheres to the Romantic rhetoric of adventure and imperial decline by emphasizing an imaginary of Mexico as a "place-myth."[36] In this story, the object of the Mayan ruin is refashioned for transfer, circulation, and global diffusion, as Latour, Brown, and Baudrillard note. Yet, along the way, objects and figures appear that cannot be easily submitted to the Romantic or scientific models, for in travel narratives disciplinary lines—in this case, Romantic literature and archeology—are not taxonomic or exclusive. Rather, they are open to porousness that enables the agency of the object. Charnay narrates a paradigmatic passage regarding insects that attack during a rainy night in the Palace of the Nuns in Uxmal. Exhausted, Charnay decided to sleep inside the palace, despite warnings from his guides: "I slept alone in the palace; the Indians constantly refused to spend the night in the ruins; the idea alone inspired them with a mortal fear."[37] The scene is Gothic: the insects literally eat and suck Charnay's blood, the natural otherness is abject, and the subject is at risk of disintegrating and becoming the object that threatens him.[38] He describes the encounter as mortal combat:

Night came, I rolled on my hammock, where I soon fell asleep the sleep of the just. But unfortunately! just I was not, for I suddenly awoke in excruciating pain. A sound of wings filled the room, and, carrying my hands at random, I felt a multitude of cold, flat insects the size of large cockroaches. Horror! A multitude of them passed over my face; I rushed to light a candle, and my eyes were struck by the most distressing sight that could be seen. In my hammock, more than two hundred of these frightful creatures remained as if caught in the net; at least thirty of these animals, which I hurried to shake off, remained on me; I had in my face, my hands, my body, swelling which caused me unbearable pain. A large number of those in the hammock were fat, bouncy, and swollen with the blood they had shot at me; the walls were covered with companions of the same kind, who seemed to be waiting for their friends, satiated, to give way to them. How to get rid of so many enemies? I armed myself with a small board and began the massacre. It was an atrocious and disgusting task to lift the heart; the fight lasted two hours, without pity, without mercy: I crushed everything. When I saw the cleaned place, that there were only corpses, I closed the door hermetically and tried to go back to sleep, two hours later it was necessary to start again. . . . For eight days, I endured this torture, which was one of the most atrocious of my life of travel. Fifteen days later, I was still wearing the marks of my opponents' stings.[39]

In this Gothic narrative, the threat is the otherness that resists colonization. Charnay emerges victorious from battle but not without wounds inflicted by the other in combat. From his white, masculine, and European subjectivity, the traveler disdained the natives' knowledge of the inside of the temple while nonetheless including it, thus revealing, however implicitly, its effective usefulness.

Something similar happens with the baqueanos and volcaneros who, in Charnay's narrative, oscillate between the characteristic Romantic type and the authority that legitimizes the traveler's enterprise. The baqueanos possessed the knowledge, the mental maps of an antagonistic territory. As a foreigner without modern maps, Charnay relied on their abilities to see what he cannot discern due to his lack of familiarity with the density of nature. The story constructs the baqueanos as the legitimizers of the excavation and the extraction of archeological pieces in a terrain where their knowledge is authoritative. The competition between the expeditionary photographers, and the success of the entire project, hinged on the baqueanos' trustworthiness. Read carefully, the baqueanos left their mark on the narrative of the excavations as much as the insects in the Temple of the Nuns of Uxman left their mark on Charnay's body.

The antique objects Charnay transported acquire their meaning in a temporal and symbolic journey toward what is original, primary, and in a certain sense, anachronistic. They are not mere cultural accessories or scientific objects. For Baudrillard, these objects recall a journey to the "embryo or mother cell," a fantasy with secular mythic functions, of the temporal completeness of being, the past, present, and future of humanity: "In a civilization where synchronism and diachronism strive to establish systematic and exclusive control over reality, a third dimension, that of anachronism, nevertheless emerges (and this as much at the level of objects as at the level of behaviors and social structures). This regressive dimension, though it attests to a relative setback for the system, nevertheless finds a place within that system and even, paradoxically, enables the system to function."[40] Charnay's journey reveals that nonhumans are integral to human completeness.

Chapter 3

Fanny Calderón in Mexico

Objects and Identity

Few female travel writers have suffered criticism as harsh as what Frances Calderón de la Barca has faced. She was the first foreign woman to chronicle her experiences traveling through Mexico during her stay from 1839 to 1842 as the wife of the first Spanish diplomatic in independent Mexico. Due to the patronage of William Prescott, the letters she wrote to relatives back in Boston were published as *Life in Mexico, during a Residence of Two Years in that Country.* Perhaps because Calderón was a pioneer, because she had received support from important figures, or simply because of how her writings documented nineteenth-century Mexican society, *Life in Mexico* is required reading for specialists in travel narratives in Latin America and Mexico. However, at the time of its publication, the book was not well received. Felipe Texidor, who translated the letters into Spanish, notes in the prologue how *Life in Mexico* and its author were remembered in Mexico:

> If people who only knew her through her book mention her by accident, it is with a terseness tinged with resentment, without the slightest testament to her figure and the challenges she faced in Mexico. The book had been published a year when the ill-fated writer Martínez de Castro cited Calderón de la Barca's name apropos of Loewenstern's "Memories of Mexico": 'There are other [travelers], more than a few, who like house painters, only know how to paint with white what is black and, more often, vice-versa. They are of a new lineage of gossips, who profess to bring news that is often outdated and false. . . . But, returning to the analogy, it will always seem to me a profanation to confuse Madame Stäel, or Lady Montagu, with Madame Calderón de la Barca.[1]

Manuel Payno, author of the *Bandits of Río Frío*, said of Fanny Calderón: "Every traveler since Humboldt has slandered us, from

Löwenstern and Mrs. Calderón de la Barca to the court writers of Maximilian, who profit off the public's curiosity, selling their Menippean satires against us."[2] Mathieu de Fossey similarly wrote, "Madame Calderón de la Barca, English by birth and *basbleu* by habit, is only concerned with frivolities: *elle n'entend rien a la synthése*."[3] Views of Fanny were no more favorable on the other side of the Atlantic. Early reviews of the book in England were hardly flattering. In an 1845 issue of *Quarterly Review* dedicated to women travelers, Elizabeth Eastlake wrote:

> Though the book engages the attention to a high degree, and exhibits great and various ability, it fails to interest us in the writer. Something of this, however, may be owing to a reason, which is perhaps meritorious, and certainly fortunate in her as the wife of a foreigner; and to the very un-English nature of her writing. Madame Calderón was a Scotch woman and a Presbyterian, we have reason to suppose; she is now a Spaniard and a Roman Catholic, as we have more than reason to suppose. And, accordingly [*in Life in Mexico*], we have a Spanish indifference to bloodshed, a Spanish enthusiasm for bullfights, a Murillo glow of colour, a Cervantes touch of humour, a gentle defense of the cigarito, and a hard hit at John Knox, which can leave no doubt of our quondam countrywoman being perfectly at home in her adopted land.[4]

Fanny was born Frances Erskine Inglis (1806–1882) in Edinburgh, Scotland; her position as a foreign woman in constant cultural transit in part accounts for the negative reception. On the death of her father, her mother brought her and her sisters to Boston, where they founded a school for girls. The Hispanist writers George Ticknor and William Prescott introduced her to her future husband, Ángel Calderón de la Barca, who was bound to Mexico as a Spanish diplomat. Fanny converted to Catholicism and followed her husband to all his political posts— Mexico, Washington, and Boston. Finally, she lived for many years in Madrid, where she acquired the noble title of marquise and died as a widow.

Critics such as Jean Franco emphasize Calderón's imperial, condescending gaze charged with racial stereotypes.[5] Others situate Calderón within the crossroads of identity, studying her multicultural belongings as a Scot married to a Spaniard and a resident of the United States and Mexico.[6] In this view, the epistolary nature of her writing makes her texts fluid receptors of her identitary shifts.

My reading of Calderón's letters published as *Life in Mexico* focuses on the role played by objects—mainly pulque, as an object of consumption, and the remains of Hernán Cortés, as an object of "collection" disputed by Prescott, the Calderóns, and Lucas Alamán in the correspondence between the Calderóns and Prescott. The china poblana dress that Fanny Calderón yearned to wear has already been studied by critics, so I shall refer to it only briefly here. Pulque, in contrast, has not been studied as an object with agency that produces and reveals identitary shifts in Calderón. What happens when an object enters and transforms the subject? The object becomes body, literally. The inability to distinguish between the subject and the object, once consumed, effaces not only the distinctions between human and nonhuman; it also broadens our understanding of the agency of objects. Our corporal and sensorial relationship to the objects organizes our affection with other bodies in space. As Sara Ahmed notes, "The word 'disgust' is then transferred from the event [or object] to the bodies of those others who are held responsible for the event [or object]. But how are those others ingested and expelled? What does this do to the bodies of those who narrate their disgust?"[7] Objects define social and affective relationships. For Calderón, pulque defined a national and class identity. Associating it with the Mexican lower classes, she initially reacted with rejection or disgust. Her later attachment to it speaks to her identitary modification and her relationship with Mexico and its inhabitants.

The final section of this chapter returns to the circulation of scientific objects and the collectorship studied in earlier chapters to show how the secret possession and the concealment of objects—such as the remains of Cortés—were ways to prevent or motivate revolutions and, at the same time, revealed the rival imperial ambitions of Spain and the United States. Amid this tension, Mexico's refusal to surrender objects to travelers underscores the intrinsic compenetration between objects and social relations, in which disputes over power occur through the possession and retention of objects. Therefore, as Latour notes, any study of social relations should not exclude nonhumans. Consciously or not, our practices spring from the nonhuman "delegates" that configure them and, consequently, our social life: "The bizarre idea that society might be made up of human relations is a mirror image of the other no less bizarre idea that techniques might be made up of nonhuman relations. We deal with characters, delegates, representatives, lieutenants . . . —some figurative, others non-figurative; some human, others nonhuman; some competent, others incompetent."[8]

Humans and Nonhumans in Life in Mexico

Analyzing *Life in Mexico*, Lindsay notes how Fanny Calderón fetishized the china poblana dress that she wanted to wear to a high society ball in Mexico City. Partly because she was prohibited by social conventions from wearing it, Fanny's letters repeatedly mention the dress. For Lindsay, the fixation on the china poblana dress is a sign of Calderón's hybrid identity in transition. Admiration for the dress is clear in an early description:

> The dress of the Poblana peasants is pretty, especially on fete-days. A white muslin chemise, trimmed with lace round the skirt, neck, and sleeves, which are plaited neatly; a petticoat shorter than the chemise, and divided into two colours, the lower part made generally of a scarlet and black stuff, a manufacture of the country, and the upper part of yellow satin, with a satin vest of some bright colour, and covered with gold or silver, open in the front, and turned back. This vest may be worn or omitted, as suits the taste of the wearer. It is without sleeves, but has straps; the hair plaited in two behind, and the plaits turned up and fastened together by a diamond ring; long ear-rings, and all sorts of chains and medals and tinkling things worn round the neck. A long, broad, coloured sash, something like an officer's belt, tied after going twice or thrice round the waist, into which is stuck a silver cigar-case. A small coloured handkerchief like abroad ribbon, crossing over the neck, and going through the broach, the ends trimmed with silver, and going through the sash. Over all is thrown a reboso [*sic*], not over the head, but thrown on like a scarf; and they wear silk stockings, or more commonly no stockings, and white satin shoes trimmed with silver. This is on holidays. On more common occasions, the dress is the same, but the materials are more common, at least the vest with silver is never worn; but the chemise is still trimmed with lace, and the shoes are satin.[9]

Following Ruth Olivera and Liliane Crete, Lindsay notes that the china poblana is associated with mythic and legendary stories. The dress was allegedly inspired by the outfit of a princess of India from the seventeenth century who was kidnapped and sold as a slave to a merchant in Puebla, where she lived out her days married to a Chinese immigrant.[10] The dress is a sign of the hybridization of a foreign woman who underwent several cultural transitions that register her constant movement. The china poblana dress expresses Fanny Calderón's own condition as a foreigner in transatlantic movement from Scotland to Boston to Mexico and to Spain. Her letter's recurrent mentions of the prohibition of her wearing the dress reveal a veiled rebellion against censorship. The outfit was associated with women with less-than-conservative, even common, tastes. As the wife of the Spanish ambassador, she had to follow a protocol that limited and redefined her identity and forced her to neglect her own desires.

Something similar happened with publication. Her first book was originally published with only her initials. In a letter to Charles Dickens, Prescott explained why: "The name of the beautiful author is hidden under her initials. In the opinion of her 'dear husband,' it would counter the rules of diplomatic etiquette, etc. for the name of the Ambassador's wife to be displayed on the cover of a work that exhibits the official world and the country in which they were residents. He believes it would not be seen well in Spain."[11] For her second book, *Attaché in Madrid*, published in New York in 1856, on the lives of the monarchs Ferdinando and Isabel, Fanny Calderón used the pseudonym of a young German diplomat in Spain. The object of the china poblana dress carries her desire and her repression.

The diplomatic mission of Ángel Calderón de la Barca was certainly delicate. He was the first Spanish diplomat in Mexico after independence. Mexico was the first former colony that the crown recognized as an independent nation. As historian Antonia Pi-Suñer Llorens notes, Mexico needed Spain to recognize its independence before it could reestablish commercial ties. To this end, the republican government of Mexico had assumed debt left by both the colonial government and by the leaders of the wars of independence. The reestablishment of overseas trade would promote the circulation of capital necessary to pay creditors. At the same time, Mexico took on the debt instead of paying the reparations that Spain demanded of its former colonies as the condition of reestablishing commercial ties. Because of the long negotiations, Ángel Calderón's mission in Mexico was highly difficult.[12]

The patient contemporary reader who endures the racial stereotypes in *Life in Mexico* and makes it to the end of the book will see Fanny Calderón's aesthetic and ideological shifts. The change in conscience happened gradually, during a stint in the countryside after her first stay in Mexico City, where she and her husband witnessed the first of two uprisings, or *pronunciamientos*. The trip to the countryside was a catalyst for change. The letters manifest the fluctuations of her identity. As an intimate genre, letters are open to discursive hybridity, flows of consciousness, and experiential flexibility. A progressive evolution in Fanny's relationship to objects and perils, as well as the constant movement and fluctuation even within her established role as the wife of a diplomat, explains her fixation with the hybrid quality of the china poblana dress. Her relationship with pulque exemplifies this fluctuation. She goes from feeling repulsion to the popular fermented drink to becoming addicted to it. To paraphrase Sara Ahmed, the shift reveals the incorporation of an alien object through the elimination of barriers that delimit certainties of identity. Consumption and disgust are instances of intercorporeal encounters that show the relationships between the body, objects, and the other.[13]

It is therefore important to be mindful of the chronotopes that Fanny Calderón shapes in her letters. The countryside appears as a subsidiary of her experience in the capital, insofar that it becomes a reference to a return to the primitive, where travelers may find a superior truth or a more transcendental understanding of life. The countryside is a phase of distance necessary for rites of passage and transformation. Here again is the idea of Mexico as a "place-myth." It is in the countryside where the traveler develops her addition to pulque.

Calderón's first stay in Mexico City coincided with the federalist uprising against Anastasio Bustamante in July 1840. At the time, Fanny expressed that she was unable to interpret political events; she only saw spectacular scandals. Her ignorance about the habits and codes in the city is clear, as well as her acute fear of its agents, revolutionaries, servants, and the poor. Mexico City seemed about to burst. The idealized vision that she had developed from her reading about Hernán Cortés's conquest of Tenochtitlan crumbles amid the everyday life of the city. There, differences in wealth are abysmal; rural immigrants and idle masses fill the streets with threats of crime. Independent Mexico was characterized by the military recruitment of hordes of young men from the countryside who failed to find work in the city. The 1813 abolition of guilds and royal corporations affected vast numbers of the workers, especially artisans whose trades now had to compete with imported manufactured goods.

Critics have emphasized Fanny Calderón's impressions of the eclectic dress and the illiteracy of elite Mexican women; however, the phantasmagoric figures of the poor—known as leperos—on the street and the suspicious shadows of criminals occupy an equally predominant place in her writings. Appearing in the most unexpected places, these figures destabilize the secure sense of demarcation about the self. Images of abject leperos, threatening criminals, and indifferent Indigenous people, mestizos, and poor white men and women in the pulquerias stand out in her early descriptions.

> Whilst I am writing a horrible lépero, with great leering eyes, is looking [at] me through the windows, and performing the most extraordinary series of groans, displaying at the same time a hand with two long fingers, probably the other three tied in, "Señorita! Señorita! For the love of most Holy Virgin! For the sake of the most pure blood Christ! By the miraculous Conception!" The wretch! I dare not look up, but I feel that his eyes are fixed upon a gold watch and seals lying on the table. That is the worst of a house on the ground floor. . . . There come more of them! . . . What groans! what rags! What a chorus of whining! . . . I try to take no notice and write as if I were deaf. I must walk out the room, without looking behind me and send the porter to disperse them. I come back again to write, hardly recovered from the start

that I have just got . . . when I heard a footstep near me, and looking up! Oh, there was my friend again standing within a yard of me, his hand stretched out for alms! I was so frightened, that for a moment I thought of giving him my watch to get rid of him.[14]

The city council of the capital concurred with Calderón's impressions. In 1828, it created the Tribunal de Vagos (Tribunal for Vagrants) in order to control the masses in Mexico City by fining them, throwing them in jail, or sending them to the army where they could be of use to the nation. These vagrants were considered criminals morally, even if they had not committed any specific crimes beyond failing to offer their labor to industry and the progress of the nation. After independence and the abolition of colonial castes, the multitude became a legally indecipherable body, a problem for the Tribunal de Vagos to address. In keeping with modern ideals, the independent nation put more emphasis on the morality of production and the control of free time than the colony had.[15] For authorities, vagrants were a threat to the social order, especially during periods of political crisis such as the pronunciamientos, the outbreak of the Mexican-American War, and the US invasion, which happened four years after the Calderóns' stay in Mexico.

The Tribunal de Vagos was in charge of regulating a new moral code for bodies in alignment with the "decency" of work and the "indecency" of idleness. Pulquerias were considered hidden spaces of everyday resistance where every vice and unbridled passion mixed. Since servants of wealthy families frequented pulquerias while running their errands, the city council proposed the panoptical measure of limiting the taverns to the city center and markets where supervision was possible.[16] Precisely because customers were not only vagrants and beggars but also servants, pulquerias were seen as sites of sociability that connected the worlds of Mexican rich and poor. Servants acted as mediating agents between the homes of the wealthy and the autonomy of lower classes. Servants were some of Fanny Calderón's chief sources of information.

After the first pronunciamiento of 1841, the Calderóns traveled to the countryside. They visited the mines of the Real del Monte, the city of Cuernavaca, the caverns of Cacahuamilpa, and Michoacán, where they rode horseback for five weeks. Nigel Leask argues that the predominant aesthetic in Fanny's descriptions is feminine picturesque.[17] Through this visual aesthetic, Calderón could express her contradictory experiences in Mexico and her cultural ambivalence in a zone of contact. The Romantic picturesque offers an alibi for imperialist utilitarianism. The picturesque generally empties a landscape of people, stripping it of its history. However, Leask points out that people are not totally absent in Calderón's picturesque accounts. Ruins and ghosts (such as the ghost of La Malinche in the ruins of Chapultepec), as well as Indigenous people in rural areas whom Calderón presents as descendants of a grand, archaic race, occupy much of her descriptions. Leask calls this presence-absence in the history of descriptions of nature the "trembling historical narrative."[18]

As for the letters' chronotope, the picturesque aesthetic that Leask studies is clearer in the countryside than in the city. The image of the rural Indigenous person as a figure of solitude and resistance is juxtaposed with the unexpected and abject presence of the Indigenous and non-Indigenous urban leperos. Still, the picturesque aesthetic allows Fanny Calderón to make peace with Mexico since the countryside is the catalyst for the change in her conscience. In the countryside, Fanny had nostalgic visions of her childhood in Scotland. In the countryside, she was victim to what critics call "reverse colonization"[19] due to the presence of all kinds of vermin such as scorpions and snakes, which, unlike the urban leperos, could be perfectly seen and classified.

It is mainly in the countryside where Fanny Calderón turns to the trope I call "the naked traveler." In a fundamental scene in letter 25, right in the middle of the book, her luggage falls apart due to the rattling of the stagecoach along the rustic road. Her dresses, combs, and jewelry fall over a cliff. For a traveler so eager to uphold her identity through the superiority of her European clothing and merchandise, the moment can only be read as key to the narrative structure of the trip, a hinge in the cultural passage. In her discussion of Mungo Park in Africa, Mary Louise Pratt points out that the supremacy of the white man emerges from the hardships of the traveling "naked white man."[20] The naked Álvar Núñez Cabeza de Vaca derives virtue and innocence from the tribulations that followed his shipwreck.

It should come as no surprise, then, that Fanny Calderón eventually confesses her love for pulque: "The Indians come in the morning to drink pulque (which, by the way I now think excellent, and shall find it very difficult to live without!)."[21] Like Álvar Núñez, Mungo Park, and other travelers who lose their possessions, Fanny Calderón underwent a process of adaptations to the customs of otherness. The pulque (and the pulqueria) that she viewed as abject in the city becomes a transcultural test in the countryside. In the following quote from an early section of the book, Fanny shows her total dislike of the drink. Her disgust at the smell and flavor of pulque set up, with patronizing sarcasm, a comparison with the beverage enjoyed by the gods on Olympus:

> [At La Ventilla] we were obliged to eat and praise—though, except the
> chirimoyas, all seemed bad to me. They also made us taste pulque; and on

a first impression it appears to me that as nectar was the drink in Olympus, we may fairly conjecture that Pluto cultivated the maguey in his dominions. I should regret to attempt describing the smell—the reverse of roses we may say. The taste and smell combined took me so completely by surprise that I am afraid my look of horror must have given mortal offense to the worthy alcalde, who considers it the most delicious beverage in the world; and in fact, it is said that when one gets over the first shock it is very agreeable. The difficulty must consist in getting over it![22]

Elsewhere, the irony turns to outright fear for she associated pulque with the lower classes, the Indigenous race, and urban bandits. The passage recalls Ahmed's proposal on (dis)taste and the social and cultural associations related to food and everything else that is ingested in the cultural encounter: "Disgust does something, certainly: through disgust, bodies 'recoil' from their proximity, as a proximity that is felt as nakedness or as an exposure on the skin surface." Ahmed notes that "disgust" is more than a "gut feeling" because our relationship with "gut feelings" is indirect, mediated by our ideas and impressions of other bodies.[23] In the case of pulque, the drink is associated with a fear of the lepero and the thief whose bodies provoke the same type of "disgust" as pulque:

> When we arrived at the lower part of the Alameda all was still, and as we walked outside under the long shadows of the trees I expected every moment be attacked, and wished we were anywhere, even on the silvery top of Popocatepetl! We passed several crowded *pulquerias*, where some were drinking and others drunk. Arrived at the arches, we saw from time to time a suspicious blanketed figure half hid by the shadow of the wall. A few doors from our own domicile was a pulque shop filled with léperos, of whom some were standing at the door shrouded in their blankets. It seemed to me we should never pass them, but we walked past and reached our door in safety.[24]

However, the change of scenery in the countryside alters her perceptions of people, and pulque takes on new associations: "Another bullfight last evening! It is like pulque; one makes wry faces at it at first, and then begins to like it."[25] The picturesque and bucolic space of the countryside modifies her perceptions of pulque. Certainly, pulque is now removed from the leperos and bandits in the city, but the adaption of taste here is apparent in the broader changes that Mexico exerted on her through a cultural passage: "It has a small garden adjoining, amongst whose tangled bushes a pretty little deer was playing, with its half-startled look and full wild eye. I found an excellent breakfast prepared, and here for the first time, I conceived the possibility of not disliking pulque. We visited the last buildings where it is kept, and found it rather refreshing with a sweet taste and a creamy froth upon it, and with a much less decided odor than that which is sold in Mexico."[26]

After the couple returned to Mexico City for their second stay, the radical federalist Santa Anna overthrew Anastasio Bustamante in a second uprising in September 1841. Gunshots and the fear of death no longer raised the traveler's adrenaline so much. Now she confesses to fearing not for herself but for her Mexican friends of wealthy families who will suffer the consequences of the political events. Calderón quotes the Count de la Cortina who does not understand why foreigners were so alarmed by Mexican thieves who are no more numerous than their counterparts in London and treat their victims with greater consideration. During this second stay in the capital, she develops more picturesque descriptions of common characters in the city.

A scene in one of Calderón's final letters, written in the coach en route to the port of Veracruz from where they would embark to Europe, catches the reader off guard. The fearsome thieves who had been a constant concern for her finally appear. However, they find a different Fanny Calderón, one who accepts her fate without perturbation or doubt:

> Their approach was first discerned by a Spanish lady who was with us, and who was travelling with strings of pearl and valuable diamonds concealed about her person, which made her peculiarly sharp-sighted on the occasion. Ladrones! said she, and everyone repeated Ladrones! in different intonations. They rode across the fields, came up pretty close to the diligence, and reconnoitered us. I was too sleepy to be frightened, and reconnoitered them in return with only one eye open. The coachman whipped up the horse, the escort came in sight, and the gentlemen struck into the fields again. The whole passed in a minute or two.[27]

The fictions of travelers who undergo a cultural transition reveal the barbarism, described in orientalist terms as the violence of precolonial chaos, which traps the travelers, and makes them "deserters," entities indistinguishable from the otherness. Casting aside concerns about her own destruction, Fanny Calderón refutes the images that distinguish and reinforce the civilization-barbarism binary in this episode; she seems even playful. This the acceptance of fate that Borges discusses in "The Story of the Warrior and the Captive."[28] As Fanny Calderón's relationship with pulque makes clear, in the dichotomy of civilization and barbarism, the civilized subject needs to separate itself from the barbarous object in order to safeguard its identity and the superiority of its rationality, laws, and institutions. In my reading, the end of Calderón's journey reveals the absence of the fear of losing her objects and, therefore, her identity. The end of the journey reveals an embrace of the abject, defined by Kristeva as the critical moment in which the "I" and the "other" collapse and the subject ceases to struggle with its lack of difference with otherness: "[The Abject is] neither the subject nor the object . . . it represents the crisis of the subject . . . insofar as it would not yet be, or would no longer be separated from the object. Its limits are no longer established. It would be constantly menaced by its possible collapse into the object. It would lose definition. It is a question, then, of a precarious state in which the subject is menaced by the possibility of collapsing into a chaos of indifference."[29]

Fanny Calderón and Hispanism in Correspondence with William Prescott

The Boston Hispanists introduced Fanny to her future husband. The couple married, and soon after the Spanish crown assigned Ángel the diplomatic post in Mexico. For Fanny, the trip was a ritual, a kind of honeymoon, and a difficult "conversion" to married life, the Catholic faith (during her trip she was still a Protestant), and Hispanic culture. It was doubtlessly helpful to have a circle of Bostonian friends who valued the literature and the history of the Spanish Empire. It is important to note the Calderóns' strong connection to William H. Prescott's *History of the Conquest of Mexico*, published in 1843, a year after their departure to Mexico.

The Bostonian Hispanists had great expectations for the Calderóns' trip. After the independence of Mexico and other Spanish colonies in 1821, the United States began to pay more attention to diplomacy and commerce in the new American republics. Interest in Latin American cultures also grew and universities like Harvard began to teach courses in Spanish. As Iván Jaksić notes, this cultural interest, paradoxically, turned more attention to Spain than to Latin America for, as an exemplum of imperial decline, Spain offered important lessons to the building empire of the United States.[30]

Fanny Calderón was the ideal intermediary between the Boston Hispanists and the object of study. Protestant, Scottish, brought to live in Boston at an early age, married to a Spanish diplomat destined for Mexico, she was the perfect translator. She was competent in linguistic and cultural diversity, and her husband's position gave her privileged access to sources in Mexican archives. These different perspectives, identitary shifts, and cultural affectivities are visible in Fanny Calderón's narrative. On asking Charles Dickens to recommend *Life in Mexico* to a publishing house, Prescott emphasized the author's privileged position:

> He (Ángel) was sent two years since to Mexico to arrange a treaty, etc., with
> that country, and as he was the first minister sent by the mother country to

the rebel child since the latter had set up for herself, his journey through the land was a sort of triumphal progress, and during his stay there he had everything of interest thrown open for inspection. The consequence was that he and his wife saw society in a way in which no foreigner has seen it. . . . The English and Americans who visit these countries are so little assimilated to the Spaniards that they have had few opportunities of getting into the interior of their social life. Madame Calderón has improved her opportunities well and her letters are those of a Spaniard writing in English.[31]

Prescott was nearly blind and lived with his parent. He was never an adventurous explorer like his Hispanist friends George Ticknor, Washington Irving, and Frances Calderón de la Barca. Nonetheless, his biographers, both detractors and defenders, highlight the powerful tentacles of his networks in Europe and the United States that afforded him access to information, objects, archives, and faraway collections. With his personal wealth, he deployed secretaries and connections to constantly search for useful cultural artifacts. He was able to call on personalities such as the American ambassador to Spain, Obadiah Rich; Henri Tirnaux in Paris; Lucas Alamán in Mexico City; Pascual de Gayangos in Madrid and London; and, of course, his intimate friends the Calderóns. Fanny and Ángel were instrumental in shipping documentary materials that became the foundation of *History of the Conquest of Mexico* to Prescott. The size of Prescott's archive was monumental, but it was also focused. As John Eipper points out, the *History of the Conquest of Mexico* established the canon of Hispanic-American colonial literature in the United States, thanks to the inclusion of (mostly Spanish) chroniclers such as Sahagún, Las Casas, Oviedo, Gómara, and Bernal Díaz.[32] This canon was cut, classified, and read from the hermeneutics of the conquest and colonization as an enterprise of heroes of the Christian empire who were, at once, medieval and modern.[33]

The correspondence between Fanny Calderón and Prescott while both were working on their respective books is documented in *The Correspondence of W. H. Prescott 1833–1847*, which also features letters exchanged with Ángel Calderón. With the first-hand information from the Calderóns, Prescott was able to write the *History of the Conquest of Mexico*. The main difference between Prescott's book and *Life in Mexico* is that, in line with the tradition of female travel writing,[34] the history of Mexico that Fanny Calderón tells does not seem to have been conceived for publication. She wrote letters to relatives that were later compiled in a book. From the fragmentation of letters, without encyclopedic ambitions, Calderón viewed independent Mexico from the perspective of an aristocratic woman, married to a Spanish diplomat, and from the perspective of at least three nationalities, English, American, and Spanish.[35]

Like the adaptation of her taste for pulque, her letters show an evolving transculturation. In her last letter to Prescott, written from Havana on her way back to the United States, Fanny Calderón writes, "With all its sinful doings [pulque and pronunciamientos] I must say, that Mexico's a pleasant place to me."[36] Both *Life in Mexico* and her letters to Prescott published in *Correspondence* are full of descriptions that mix everyday affairs with history and archeology, largely because Prescott encouraged her to adorn the information with such "color" as the names of Mexican trees and birds.

The letter cited above shows the strong bonds between the Calderóns and Prescott that facilitated the shipping of materials that Prescott requested. Mexican intermediaries such as Lucas Alamán and Count Cortina were able to acquire engravings of Moctezuma and Malinche and a daguerreotype of Cortés's cenotaph, and to discover the site of Cortés's remains. The controversies that surrounded all these objects (which were more than mere objects) reveal the objects' almost superhuman capacity to inspire passion, lies, and hidden interests. The Calderóns found contradictory accounts about the engravings of Moctezuma and Malinche. Alamán believed that they did not exist, for natives did not make portraits. Nonetheless, an indignant Cortina insisted to Fanny that a famous Mexican painter in the time of Cortés had made the portraits and that the artist's descendants still kept them. Certain that the portraits were authentic, Cortina assured her that he would send them along.[37]

As for Cortés's remains, Lucas Alamán, in a hand-written letter transmitted to Prescott through the Calderóns, wrote that Count Fernando Luchesi and Duke Terranova had opened the tomb and moved the bones to a safe place to protect them during the wars of independence: "Their present whereabouts must be kept secret to avoid further insults and it is therefore best to say that they were sent to Italy."[38] In another letter to Prescott, Fanny writes that:

> The body of Cortés is in Alamán's house—concealed. Before leaving Mexico, Alamán promised Calderón to send him a detailed account of all these circumstances; it was not ready when we came away, but as Alamán may be depended upon, no doubt we shall receive it. But at all events, Calderón will write now to Alamán, not only to remind him of this but requesting his permission to disclose to you how the body of Cortés came into his possession, or rather begging him to write down where the body is. Some suppose it to be in one place and some in another. It is generally thought to be hid in a Convent. I dare say Alamán will have no objection now to its being known.

At all events he will write a clear account of the whole affair and say what may and what may not be published.[39]

In earlier letters to Ángel Calderón, Alamán had been evasive on the topic, turning him instead to the cenotaph in the Church of Jesus and inscriptions regarding the tomb, which he was able to acquire. Nonetheless, Alamán clearly had no intention of revealing to the Calderóns or Prescott the exact location of Cortés's remains or the circumstances under which they were removed.[40] In fact, there was no further mention of the "clear account" that Fanny told Prescott he could expect from Alamán.

The correspondence between Ángel Calderón and Prescott focuses on the shipping and transfer of materials, manuscripts, engravings, first editions, letters, and unpublished chronicles. Here we see once again in Prescott the eagerness of a collector. The complex network between Prescott's envoys and the Mexican personages and institutions that held power over local merchandise is also clear. The business of collectors and archeological treasure hunters provoked diatribes. Ángel Calderón wrote to Prescott about the obstacles that Mexican intermediaries raised:

> During all this time I have not forgotten your errands or your kindly friendship for a single day. I have talked several times with the Count de La Cortina, who has assured me that he has already sent you various papers; he keeps promising me to seek others and keeps repeating to me the eternal refrain of the Mexicans, *mañana, mañana,* a kind of Mexican *yes* which means—*in the next century, if I find the thing to my hand without search—or never.* But in the course of my inquiries I have been fortunate enough to find Dr. Lucas Alamán. I enclose a pamphlet of his in which there are some good *hints.* He has placed at my disposal all the existing documents of the house of Hernan Cortes which are in the Hospital of Jesus. He has shown me the autograph signature of that great man, from which he will allow me to take a facsimile if you want it; he has shown me and will allow me to take a copy of his portrait, painted as we think after his prosecution in Spain, and in short has promised to point out to me the way to get other data. As everything here is disorder and procrastination, it is necessary to seek these papers where they are, and keep the day and the season, because so-and-so is in the field or in the council, and the clerk who is to do the copying is ill or busy and will come tomorrow; and tomorrow never comes. So, I am occupied and shall be occupied without losing sight of it, with what you want and with whatever relates to your work; and whenever I may find a printed book that I think bears on your object or that you ask me to send to you. I only ask the indulgence that I must myself grant in the highest degree—patience and

more patience. Alamán has said to me, and I agree with it, that you would do well to come here for a short time, where you would find things that would compensate for the fatigues of the journey.[41]

Prescott and Ángel Calderón looked for things that existed but they did not know where those things were or if they could obtain them. If we stop to think about the things they were hunting, it seems that they were more valuable as collectable items than as elements of an archive. Possession itself—fetishism without any explanatory or scientific end—satisfies the ego, which, for Baudrillard signifies the fruitless desire to detain the decline of the subject while, at the same time, seeking its completeness.[42] Although Ángel Calderón complained of all the work involved, the hunt for cultural objects was gratifying for him, as well. By shipping off sources conserved in Mexico to a prominent metropolis of knowledge, he was fulfilling the two-fold objective of representing his country, and its former empire, while protecting the interests of the Spanish history and its heroes. Embraced by such an author as Prescott and featured in his book on the Spanish Empire in Mexico, the lost objects that the independent Mexican nation had perhaps failed to appreciate would recover their epic glow as they entered into the lofty new discipline of Hispanism in the United States.

Nonetheless, Prescott's book sang the glories of the decline of the Spanish Empire in order to open the way for another imperial power. The *History of the Conquest of Mexico* was published shortly before the Mexican-American War (1846–1848). The war and the Treaty of Guadalupe-Hidalgo established the independence of Texas and led to the sale of California and New Mexico to the United States. American soldiers read about the conquest of Tenochtitlan in Prescott's book. Seeing the Spanish conquest as analogous to their own, they associated victories in battle with the civilizing mission of manifest destiny. In his letters, Prescott noted that his book headed to Mexico aboard US Navy vessels. "Combatants in Winfield Scott's expeditionary force came to view their exploits in central Mexico as the re-enactment of the Cortes conquest. The U.S. army followed the original Spanish invasion route into Mexico City / Tenochtitlan almost exactly, a coincidence which served as a starting point for an analogy of sweeping socio-cultural proportions: the Mexicans became the swarming, superstitious 'Aztec' hordes, and Cortes, the emblem of civilization and progress, was symbolically inducted in to the U.S. Army as 'our great predecessor.'"[43]

This doubtlessly bellicose reading of US Hispanism was not what Prescott seems to have intended with his book. He frequently expressed his opposition to the war.[44] Still, as his biographers note, he was eager to take advantage of the American invasion, asking his correspondent from Massachusetts, General Caleb Cushing, to search archives and libraries in Mexico City for valuable manuscripts for his collection, revealing, once again, his voracious appetite for things that would enlarge his collection despite his opinion of the invasion.[45]

José Fernando Ramírez offered a response to Prescott in his *Notas y esclarecimientos a la* Historia de la Conquista de México *del Señor W. Prescott*. Born in Chihuahua and educated in Durango, Ramírez became a state representative, lawyer, historian, politician, writer, journalist, military strategist, and drafter of legal codes and constitutional principles. During the empire of Maximilian I in Mexico, he was the director and curator of the National Museum and director of the National Library, where he read and copied everything for the Mexican archive.[46] Like Prescott, he was a collector and bibliophile: his personal library featured more than seven thousand volumes. During the Mexican-American War, one of his chief concerns was safeguarding the historical documents from the museum and the National Archive, the same documents that Prescott was eager to attain. Written between 1844 and 1845, *Notas y esclarecimientos a la* Historia de la Conquista de México *del Señor W. Prescott* includes an introduction and ten notes on different chapters from Prescott's book. Drawing on extensive sources from his collections and manuscripts, Ramírez's approach differs sharply from Prescott's philosophy of history, and Ramírez proposes an alternative canon to colonial literature. With different collections and archives, both historians vied for the canon of Hispanism and Mexicanism.

At the outset, Ramírez points out "three weaknesses that spring from the author's pen that, in their nature and origin, would be difficult to classify and censure: the often immoderate use of the rule of criticism; the instinctive detachment from the race that, fighting against its noble and conscientious efforts, tends to reach at times its victories, and finally, the exaltation of his [immoderate] enthusiasm for Hernán Cortés."[47] On the pre-Hispanic peoples, Ramírez sarcastically notes that "Mr. Prescott wields his pen to write the history of the barbarians, a word which, together with savages, runs throughout the history. Being an army of *barbarians* who fought against invaders, their war cries could not have the same designation as those of a cultured people; the Mexicans *howled*. Their armies did not fall back or retreat orderly, rather they *fled*. An ear accustomed to such harmonies as *Yankee Doodle* could hardly be a competent judge."[48]

In Prescott's account, Cortés effectively stands as a model conquistador, faithful to the Spanish crown but with a clear entrepreneurial spirit—qualities that the Calderóns, and especially Ángel, would appreciate.

Prescott also valued the principles of patriotism and private initiative in the heroes of the United States. In keeping with the New England historiographic model of scholars such as George Bancroft, Francis Parkman, and John Lothrop Motley, whose historical studies resemble the novels of Sir Walter Scott,[49] Prescott's Cortés is a Romantic hero: handsome, driven, cunning, an adroit strategist. Burning the ships to force seditious Spaniards to fight with him for the conquest of Tenochtitlan instead of returning to his enemy Velázquez in Cuba, Cortés is the leader willing to pursue his objectives to the final consequences.[50]

In a letter to Ángel Calderón, Prescott declared his Hispanist goals to shed positive light on Cortés instead of othering a more "Mexican" version, as Ramírez would say. The letter also articulates the circle of affections and preferences that surrounds the selection of the material for his study (what Benjamin calls the "magic circle"[51]):

> I shall now talk to you about my own little affairs. I am getting on ancient Aztecs—a confoundedly hard and bothering subject. This half civilization breed makes a sort of mystification like twilight, in which things appear as big again as they are, and all distorted from the truth. I have now nearly disposed of them and shall soon be on my march with the great *Conquistador*. I am persuaded you will not be able to pick up anything of value for me in Mexico. I do not want anything relating to the ancient history, and I am most generously supplied from Spain with ammunition for the Spanish invasion; *5000* pages of fair manuscript, of letters, state papers, chronicles . . . all contemporary and on which the public breath has never blown; the united collections of Munoz, Vargas Ponce, and Navarrete—rare luck, the greatest that ever befell a man, and for which I may well thank your kind offices. I have received one case of these, which completes the collection, since I wrote you, and I am now satisfied that it will not be worthwhile to lay out a good deal of money in order to get a little additional matter, of not much importance, from Mexico. If any *contemporary* document relating to the Conquest should come under your notice, I will thank you to have it copied for me. Humboldt mentions two manuscripts, one of Cortes on the road, and another Libro del Cabildo, begun three years after the siege, giving an account of the city, soon after the capture. It was in the convent of San Felipe Neri. These may perhaps contain some things useful to me. . . . I should be very glad to learn any tidings of the personal history of Cortes, his family and descendants, and estates in Mexico. His remains lie there, I believe. But I leave the whole to your better judgment, who know my views and are on the spot, knowing that whatever you advise will be right. If you meet with a good engraving of him I should like it much, also a facsimile of his handwriting. Manning and Marshall have sent me one of Moctezuma, quite curious . . . [52]

This quotation from Prescott is significant for several reasons. First, it reintroduces the concern with acquiring "things," not only sources: the portrait, a sample of Cortés's penmanship, testimonies that the conquistadors' descendants made to Prescott. His eagerness to collect things is an attempt to recreate the events and characters of his story. What interests me here are the connotations of the word "recreate" in light of what Benjamin calls the "rebirth of old books" in the acquisitions of collectors, "their renewal of existence."[53] Objects in a personal collection seem to guarantee the veracity of the account and validate Prescott's figure as "father" of modern Hispanic history. Secondly, Prescott here unwittingly confirms Ramírez's argument about his overzealous Hispanism and admiration for the conquistador. The circuits through which pieces were transferred to his collection, mostly from Spain and not from Mexico, is clear in the manifest geopolitics in the *History of the Conquest of Mexico*: things, measurements, and channels all reveal hierarchies and ideological preferences. "Nothing of value" about the conquest remained in Mexico. Prescott had no interest in collections about the Aztecs or other ancient Mexican cultures. He turned away from the important tradition in Mexico of collecting and preserving pre-Columbian objects and archeology that runs from Sigüenza y Góngora and Javier Clavijero in the colonial era to Ramírez after independence.[54]

Richard Kagan argues that the Bostonian and his Harvard colleagues (Ticknor, Irving, Henry W. Longfellow) helped delegitimize Hispanic history and historiography by describing the policies of the Spanish monarchy as despotic and orientalist.[55] Kagan focuses on Prescott's 1837 book *History of the Reign of Ferdinand and Isabel*, and does not include *History of the Conquest of Mexico*, or the work of Ramírez. In the expression of Romantic paradigm that Kagan identifies, Spain is the other. As an empire, it is the antithesis of the US empire animated by the ideals of republican liberalism. This view contrasts with Ramírez's vision in *Notas y esclarecimientos*. For Ramírez, the invading US empire identified with Cortés, the faithful vassal and modern conquistador that Prescott portrayed as the protagonist of his story. In this view, Prescott associates Cortés with the ideology of a modern empire. For Iván Jaksić, Spain was a historical case study of "national character"; it exemplified how despotism and Catholicism "most decidedly represented by counter-reformation Charles V, had managed to corrupt a once-promising nation."[56] The United States could learn valuable lessons about its own history and future in imperial politics. Moreover, the United States could also distance itself from the advent of slavery in the New World by blaming Spain and Portugal: "By critiquing the Spanish (and Portuguese) origins of slavery, Americans could remove themselves from full responsibility for the persistence of the institution at home."[57]

Exotic and Familiar Fanny Calderón

In the circuit of Bostonian Hispanists, Fanny Calderón knew what was expected of her. She was an excellent mediator between English and Spanish, between both sides of the Atlantic, between north and south, and between knowledge and politics. Her attempted "Mexicanization" was legitimized by the fact that, unlike Ángel Calderón, Prescott, and Ramírez, she had no political interests at stake. Although she was married to a Spanish diplomat, her Scottish origin distanced her from imperial interests. Like the original wearer of the china poblana, she was a relocated woman, an icon of the uncanny. She was sufficiently exotic and familiar at the same time. The everyday relationship with pulque and other objects described in her letters reveals the construction of affection toward Mexico and the agency that objects take on as they condition social relations. Toward the end of her voyage, the loss of her travel objects no longer mattered to Fanny Calderón. She had already interacted with them, and now she could let them go (or let them be stolen). This would have been unthinkable for Prescott or Ramírez.

Fanny Calderón does not apparently need to possess objects to (re)create history. In the case of Ramírez, possession refers to the preservation of national heritage. Prescott, in contrast, needs for the collection to confer him authority as the principal holder of objects related to the imperial history in Mexico. In this accumulation, there is a desire for completeness similar to that of Humboldt. Prescott's "eschatological" interest in Cortés's remains is linked to the cycle of life and death—according to which the possession of the remains would give new life (or "rebirth" in Benjamin's words)—or perhaps to the eternity of the Spanish conquistador now in a new iteration of empire, the United States.

Chapter 4

John Reed in Mexico

Between Comedy and Epic

"Utopia is always political," writes Fredric Jameson in *Archaeologies of the Future*, his study of narrative forms of utopia, which he explains as a meditation on the radical otherness.[1] With the understanding that narrations on utopia are a formal meditation on otherness and its radical difference,[2] here I study the chronicles of John Reed in the Mexican Revolution. Reed traveled to narrate the chronicle of the deep social and political changes being forged in northern Mexico under Pancho Villa. Any interpretation of Reed's trip and his chronicle of utopia in Mexico between 1913 and 1914 would be incomplete without a consideration of his later trip to Russia in 1917. There, the Bolshevik Revolution was creating another utopia, one that, in Reed's mind, could perhaps be more perfect than the Mexican.[3] My aim in this chapter is to think about John Reed's trip to the Mexican Revolution from the perspective of utopia, insurgency, and revolution, paying special attention to his role as a war correspondent. I am interested in reading the journalistic chronicle as a movable and stable object, in Latour's sense. The war chronicle is an object that moves quickly; it transfers information about war, but also the images and symbols that influence national and international politics and public opinion. The correspondent's chronicle shows war and "utopia" in movement. However, it is an *in-situ* narrative of the vicissitudes of extreme danger. In the "business" of war, so exploited by the press, correspondents take on a predominant role. This was especially true for *Metropolitan Magazine*, the early twentieth-century publication for which Reed was the star reporter. Therefore, I will focus special attention to the Mexican chronicles Reed published in the *Metropolitan* in 1913 and 1914. Although some of these chronicles later appeared in *Insurgent Mexico* (1915), they lost some of their urgency once rendered into book form.

More than Mexico per se, Reed was interested in seeking out what Jameson calls "utopic enclaves." Following Ernst Bloch's *The Principle of Hope*, Jameson discusses these "utopic enclaves" as new spatial and social totalities distinct from the fragmented "utopic impulses" found in every individual gesture and action that aims to change the future state of things. Reed's war chronicles feature both enclave and impulse.[4] Mexico was the utopic place he could not find in the United States because an entirely new society could be (or would be) created in Mexico.

I want to highlight two characteristics that Jameson associates with utopic enclaves. The first has to do with the temporality of utopia. All these enclaves interrogate and project into the future an illusion of eternity; however, at the same time they allude to the memory of infancy as a lost paradise—the past as an existential experience. In Reed, paradisiacal infancy with arcadian tones appears in the symbolization of Pancho Villa and his men as primitive or manifestations of "wild man." Villa is the original man, uncorrupted by "civilization" and partisan revolutionary ambitions. As Bartra writes, following Michel de Certau, the "homo sylvaticus" confronts the "homo economicus."[5] As the next chapter will discuss, Gabriela Mistral saw schools as the utopic enclaves of postrevolutionary Mexico and children as the protagonists. Both cases reveal an infantilization of the revolution. More than a narrative of utopia, they show a return to arcadia. But Reed and Mistral also reveal much more. Their infantilization of the revolution is inextricable from the political and philosophical worldview that emerges as a social model of "being" as opposed to the "becoming" in Western modernity.[6] It is not that this society (revolutionary Mexico) will become more just; rather, its nature possesses the necessary conditions to be just. There is thus a tension between, on the one hand, utopia as a program or projection into the future and, on the other, the arcadian past prior to the modern city in which the "wild man" is essentially the "noble savage."

The second characteristic of the Mexican utopic enclave I would like to highlight here is the "negativity inherent to every utopia." Evil is no longer present, although how it has disappeared is rarely mentioned. In Thomas More's canonic *Utopia* (1517), money, the source of evil, does not exist; however, More never says how money, and the relationships it generates, disappeared. The most interesting aspect in Reed and Mistral is that both travelers witness the process of evil's "eradication." Their narration of the process shows a "utopia in the making." The narrations of both travelers thus diverge from the classic utopic forms that tend to showcase already established and functioning enclaves. Without abandoning their faith in utopia as a finished form, self-conscious and autonomous (Jameson), Reed and Mistral show the seams of the revolution.

Reed explores two different forms of textualizing utopia. In Mexico, the form is comedic; in Russia, epic. I draw this distinction following Mikhail Bakhtin's theory on serious and comic genres. For Bakhtin, the epic hero is distant from the reader (or the audience). There is a total absence of perspectivism from which to consider his acts. Comedy, in contrast, involves the hero's closeness to the audience; proximity humanizes the hero, rendering him vulnerable to the spectator's criticism and laughter.[7] Reed's narration makes the Mexican soldiers into actors in an enjoyable story, close to the American reading public, in part by reproducing stereotypes around codes of peasant masculinity and infantilism. In Reed's *Ten Days that Shook the World* (1919), in contrast, Russian soldiers are exemplary—models to revolutionary workers, peasants, and soldiers the world over—since they are conscientious revolutionaries engaged in class struggle.

The "wild man" that Reed sees in Villa and the peasants in the Mexican Revolution is a readaptation of the longstanding Western myth.[8] Reed rearticulates the humanist Renaissance version of the myth, according to which the "wild man" is the incarnation of the primary goodness inherent to all men, to oppose the demonizing versions of Villa and the revolution used to justify a US invasion of Mexico. From his writings in the *Metropolitan*, Reed defended the noninterventionist principle.

John Reed, the Union of Workers, and Anti-War Ideology

"When there is war, John Reed is the writer to describe it." Born in Portland and educated in Harvard, Reed became famous for his reporting on armed conflicts and worker uprisings such as the steelworkers' strike in Paterson, New Jersey (1913), and the massacre of mining families in Ludlow, Colorado (1914). According to his biographers, the events in Paterson established Reed as the militant voice of American workers in the press. His coverage of the strike launched his political career. From that moment on, his journalism was inseparable from his role as a chronicler. Reed was thrown in jail together with veteran labor leaders like Haywood and Carlos Tresca and fifty striking workers. The detention in Paterson of the "Harvard Poet" caused more flurry in the press than the strike itself, but it did bring widespread attention of the workers' plight. After a friend from Harvard, Edward Hunt, paid his bail, Reed returned to New York to write about the euphoria of the moment in the *Masses*. He titled the article "The Paterson War."

> There is war in Paterson! But it's a curious kind of war. All the violence is the work of one side—the Mill Owners. Their servants, the police, club unresisting men and women and ride down law-abiding crowds on horseback.

Their paid mercenaries, the armed detectives, shoot and kill innocent people. Their newspapers, the *Paterson Press* and the *Paterson Call*, publish incendiary and crime-inciting appeals to mob-violence against the strike-leaders. Their tool, Recorder Carroll, deals out heavy sentences to peaceful pickets that the police-net gathers up. They control absolutely the Police, the Press, the Courts. Opposing them are about twenty-five thousand striking silk workers, of whom perhaps ten thousand are active. Let me tell you what I saw in Paterson and then you will say which side of this struggle is "anarchistic" and "contrary to American ideals."[9]

The need to connect the workers' struggle to a profound sense of Americanism is clear in Reed's earliest reporting. For him, the industrialists were powerful agents opposed to the nation's ideals and values. He substituted the discourse of labor struggle for the discourse of war as a forger of patriotic fervor. Although the unions and the workers' struggle were largely formed by immigrants, they were patriotic. In contrast, war, especially World War I, was a pretext to increase the wealth of the powerful—herein lay its anti-Americanism. Reed's opposition to war rose not from pacifism, but from an anti-capitalist critique of war. He did not oppose the wars of peasants in Mexico, workers in the United States, or Bolsheviks in Russia.

Reed's war chronicles made him famous, despite (or perhaps due to) his anti-war positions. "When there is war, John Reed is the writer to describe it," reads the opening of the June 1914 article "The Colorado War" that Reed wrote for *Metropolitan* magazine on returning from Mexico. "That is why the *Metropolitan* sent him straight from Mexico to Colorado."[10] Reed traveled to Trinidad, Colorado, to cover the clash between the Colorado National Guard and workers at Colorado Fuel & Iron, the largest coal company in the area, owned by John D. Rockefeller Jr. Workers were demanding eight-hour shifts, safer conditions in the mines, a reduction of the company's control over their lives, and the right to organize. Some of the demands were later met, but only after workers paid with their lives. When the union called the strike, the miners evacuated their houses and were forced to live in a camp. Rent for the grounds and the tents was provided by the United Mine Workers of America (UMWA), founded in 1890. Reed's article in the *Metropolitan* mentions that more than twelve hundred people lived in two hundred tents in Ludlow during the strike without running water, electricity, or any other comforts.[11] The strike lasted from September 1913 to December 1914. The massacre of April 20, 1914, a day after Orthodox Easter, was the most intense moment. The strikers' camp was burned down. During armed confrontations with the police, workers' families hid in the "death pits." Two women and eleven children died of smoke inhalation. The war continued through April until President Woodrow Wilson sent federal troops to put down the clash. After the 1914 Colorado strike, the union led and supported important protests and strikes in places like Matawan, West Virginia, in 1920.

Reed wrote about the international community of workers—a culturally diverse group of local Hispanics and European immigrants who spoke twenty-four different languages—that maintained solidarity during the strike.

> The largest of these colonies was at Ludlow, lying at the crossing of the two roads leading to Berwin and Hastings and Delagua on the other. There were more than twelve hundred people there, divided into twenty-one nationalities, undergoing the marvelous experience of learning that all men are alike. When they had been living together for two weeks, the petty race prejudices and misunderstandings that had been fostered between them by the coal companies for so many years began to break down. Americans began to find out that Slavs and Italians and Poles were as kind-hearted, as cheerful, as loving and as brave as they were.[12]

"The Colorado War" builds on characteristics evident in Reed's earlier writings on Paterson and the peasants of the Mexican Revolution. Protests arose from conditions of extreme desperation among genuine, well-intentioned people—poor, humble, good-hearted victims. The image of the immigrant further reinforced the idea of the American dream: the honest search for opportunities. The "Boss" (with capital b) was the contrast to the promise inscribed upon the Statue of Liberty. The supreme symbol of capitalist exploitation, the Boss revealed the contradiction between American ideology and actual economic practices. The workers were not politicized, Reed argued; their demands were purely human. For him, the right to organize was part of the human condition.

At this point, Reed was not discussing, as he would years later, class consciousness, the abolition of capitalism, and class struggle. Nonetheless, this can be read as a narrative strategy to ensure the reader's sympathy for striking workers. The article notes that businessmen, small-property owners, and common people from Trinidad and nearby towns all supported the strike. These immigrant workers were real Americans because they believed in the American values represented by the Statue of Liberty. The anti-Americans were the rich and powerful such as John D. Rockefeller Jr., "The Boss":

> There is nothing revolutionary about this strike. The strikers are neither Socialists, Anarchists nor Syndicalists. They do not want to confiscate the

mines nor destroy the wage system; industrial democracy means nothing to them. They consider the Boss almost a god. Humble, patient and easily handled, they had reached a desperation of misery in which they did not know what to do. They had come to America eager for the things that the Statue of Liberty in New York harbor seemed to promise them. They came from countries where law is almost divine, and here, they thought, was a better law. They wanted to obey the laws. But the first thing they discovered was that the Boss, in whom they trusted, insolently broke the laws. To them the union was the first promise of happiness and of freedom to live their own lives. It told them that if they would combine and stand together, they could force the Boss to pay them enough to live on, and make it safe for them to work.[13]

Like the *Brief History of the Destruction of the Indies*, in which Bartolomé de Las Casas draws on allegories of conquistador wolves and native lambs, Reed's writings on Paterson, Ludlow, and Mexico depicted peasants and workers as innocent victims, forced by circumstances to rise up in arms. Nonetheless, unlike Las Casas, Reed adhered to the noninterventionist principle in both politics and culture. For Las Casas, the goodness of the Indigenous revealed their humanity and, therefore, their possible conversion to Christianity. For Reed, in contrast, striking workers and revolutionaries did not need to be subjected to any indoctrination. In Ludlow, for example, the workers were mostly desperate immigrants—homeless, poor, unarmed. They did not seek out violent confrontations. The constant harassment by mine guards and local police of workers' families forced them to organize and strike. Something similar happened in Mexico. Neither Marxist rhetoric of politics and class struggle nor adhesion to capitalist values of a society like the United States occupied prominent places in these chronicles. In Reed's eyes, these ideologies were foreign for both the Mexican revolutionaries and the Ludlow workers.

Journalism and war are tightly intertwined in Reed. Before his trip to the Soviet Revolution, *Metropolitan Magazine* sent him as a correspondent to France and then to Eastern Europe during World War I. He also wrote for *Liberator* and the *Masses*, independent leftist magazines that frequently came under fire for their anti-war editorials. Because of his combative reporting and opposition to the war, Reed was put on trial several times in New York and thrown in jail in Finland upon trying to return from Russia. He suffered ideological persecution. Even before his trip to Russia, his ideas were considered "anti-patriotic" and unpopular. In April 1917, he writes in the *Masses*:

I know what war means. I have been with the armies of all the belligerents except one, and I have seen men die, and go mad, and lie in hospitals suffering hell; but there is a worse thing than that. War means an ugly mobmadness, crucifying the truth-tellers, choking the artists, side-tracking reforms, revolutions, and the working of social forces. Already in America those citizens who oppose the entrance of their country into the European melee are called "traitors," and those who protest against the curtailing of our meagre rights of free speech are spoken of as "dangerous lunatics." We have had a forecast of the censorship—when the naval authorities in charge of the Sayville wireless cut off American news from Germany, and only the wildest fictions reached Berlin via London, creating a perilous situation. . . . The press is howling for war. The church is howling for war. Lawyers, politicians, stock-brokers, social leaders are all howling for war. Roosevelt is again recruiting his thrice-thwarted family regiment.[14]

For Reed, the world war was a war of bankers, investors, speculators, plutocrats, not the "peaceful strikers, and their wives and children . . . shot to death, burned to death, by private detectives and militiamen."[15] *Ten Days that Shook the World* dedicates several pages to the cease-fire between Russian and Germany, which the Bolsheviks achieved after the revolution in order to open avenues to socialist internationalism.[16]

Reed in Mexico is not the same as Reed in Russia. During the Soviet Revolution, Reed's political commitment becomes radical and brings him into active engagement with the Communist International as a delegate to the Baku Congress of the Peoples of the East. There, he contracts typhus and dies in Russia. His tomb in the Kremlin Wall Necropolis reads, "John Reed: Delegate of the Communist International." In the 1987 "John Reed Centenary," organized by companions at Harvard for the hundredth anniversary of his birth, Reed's niece noted that during her trip to Russia she saw that even kindergarten children knew who John Reed was, "a true hero of the revolution." Speeches at the Harvard homage highlighted that John Reed was better known in Russia than in the United States and that John Reed can be interpreted as a bridge of reciprocal understanding between both countries at the end of the Cold War. Corliss Lamont, chairman at the encounter in the Harvard Club, declared in the opening speech: "We do believe that this 100th anniversary of Reed's birth comes at an opportune time when tension between the United States and the Soviet Union has much decreased. And we hope that our meetings, centered around a man dear to both countries, will further American-Soviet understanding."[17] For his part, the Soviet ambassador to the United States, Victor Zvezdin, remarked that: "In my country, John Reed is now a legend. But his legend lives together with us. We use the example of his life to bring up our children in the spirit of internationalism. We come to his grave at the Kremlin Wall not only to pay respect to this great American but to learn once again how peoples must try to understand each other and live in friendship for the benefit of all."[18]

It was no accident that Reed's centenary was celebrated in the context of the ending of the Cold War. *Reds*, the Oscar-winning 1982 movie by the director and actor Warren Beatty that popularized the figure of Reed, is another testament to the international political environment. Reed thus became a Romantic character. Admiration in both countries makes him a unifying, not separating, figure. From then on, Reed shed a different kind of light on Russia-US relations.

War Correspondent in Mexico

Speeches at the John Reed centenary noted that Mexico's influence on Reed's life and work tends to be overlooked. The commemoration therefore explicitly emphasized the significance of *Insurgent Mexico* for future work. Reed's writings on Mexico prefigured his itinerary and consciousness as a war correspondent. Before Petrograd and his assignment as a WWI correspondent, Reed traveled to northern Mexico to report on the advance of the Pancho Villa's revolutionary troops. He sent dispatches on the 1914 battles in Gómez Palacio and Torreón, where Villa managed to come back from defeat to drive federal troops from northern Mexico. At the time, Villa and Venustiano Carranza were allies; unlike Villa, Carranza aspired to become president of Mexico.

In the United States, coverage of the revolution focused on the US's billion-dollar investments in Mexico and the forty thousand Americans residents in Mexico who called for intervention. With the extension of railroads in northern Mexico, much of the territory was dominated by American capital linked to haciendas. Demands for military intervention reflected the financial interests of investors such as William Randolph Hearst, whose investments in Mexican properties were threatened by the instability of the government: the fall of Porfirio Díaz's dictatorship, the assassination of Francisco Madero by Victoriano Huerta in 1913, and the revolution.[19]

President Woodrow Wilson initially declared a policy of neutrali ty until Huertistas and Constitutionalists or Maderistas began to clash. The United States later refused to recognize Huerta as the legitimate president of Mexico and imposed an arms embargo. This led Huerta to seek alliances with Germany and Japan, rivals of American interests. Huerta's anti-democratic administration, the threat of civil war, and the pressures of the American press persuaded Wilson of the need to intervene in Mexico. In March 1915, Theodore Roosevelt wrote in the *Metropolitan:*

> Here are American private citizens, men, women and children, and American soldiers, all on American soil, scores of whom have been killed or wounded by bullets shot across the line. Some of the killing has been done through sheer carelessness and contemptuous indifference for our rights; some has been done maliciously and of purpose; and yet President Wilson's Administration has failed to take any action. The record of the preceding Administration as regards Mexico was not a pleasant object of contemplation for Americans brought up to honor the flag; but the present Administration has made Americans in or near Mexico feel that they have no flag to honor.[20]

The occupation of Veracruz by American troops in 1914 marked the beginning of the military intervention. Reed expressed his opposition in his writings and even in a personal meeting with Wilson.[21] Reed writes an editorial from Mexico in June 1914 in the *Metropolitan* against American intervention. He argues that most Americans knew little about the peasant revolution in a country where 80 percent of the population was subjugated and exploited by the wealthiest 10 percent of Mexicans and foreigners. The objectives of the revolution concerning land, Reed insisted, were just:

> We Americans, if we enter Mexico, are going to check all this. The first American soldier across the Rio Grande means the end of the Mexican Revolution. We are taking upon ourselves the responsibility of establishing a government in Mexico City suitable to the foreign powers. The government of the United States has already expressed itself as opposed to the confiscation of private property; and the land question in Mexico cannot be settled in any other way. The new government will be bankrupt. If it is forced to buy back the lands and redistribute them among the peons, it must sell more concessions to foreign speculators or borrow money from them, which will simply create more pressure upon the peons. We have said that we will recognize a government elected by popular vote; but the peons would probably elect someone who represents them—perhaps even a peon like Francisco Villa. And the governments of the civilized world could not accept Francisco Villa—in the first place, because he was once a bandit, and therefore disreputable; in the second place, because he would probably restore some of the illegal foreign concessions to the people in whose blood and sweat they are bathed, and the land to those who were robbed of it. And that is confiscation—a crime under the law.[22]

The *Metropolitan* included Reed's essay as an editorial in June, although he had sent it in April, the same issue that included a semblance of Pancho Villa. "We have given the editorial page of this issue to an important statement by John Reed, our correspondent for several months with the Constitutionalist Army in Northern Mexico." The magazine granted the piece a privileged place emphasizing that, "The attention which Mr. Reed's comments and observations have aroused in all quarters, including the highest official circles, is a striking proof of their value."[23] Once Reed left for Europe to cover WWI, *Metropolitan Magazine* shifted its posture on Mexico, as seen in Roosevelt's article a year later, as I will analyze in more detail below.

As long as Reed was the correspondent in Mexico, the magazine was highly critical of Carranza and the American intervention, in contrast to its glowing coverage of Villa. Indeed, Reed's writings in the *Metropolitan* pointed to Villa as a candidate for the presidency of Mexico and advocated for American support of Villa over Carranza. Contrary to the official press that demonized Villa as a "savage bandit," Reed attempted to strengthen the international image of Villa as just and popular, a born leader.

On December 13, 1914, the *New York Times* published the headline "Villa, Bandit and Brute, May Be Mexican President" with the subtitle "The Conqueror of Chihuahua and Taker of Juarez Has a Lifelong Record of Murder—Compared to This Presidential Possibility, Huerta Is Mild and Innocent."[24] In addition to demonizing Villa, blaming him for hundreds of deaths and executions, the article ridiculed him by portraying him as fearful of North American generals. Villa was naturalized by his supposed criminality and by his race. "When the Madero revolution started, Villa was a hunted man in the vastness of the Chihuahua Mountains. He was the most-hated man in that part of Mexico. 'Half Indian and half beast' is how an El Pasoan once described Villa."[25] Once establishing Huerta's constitutional ineligibility for the presidency and Villa's acts of "bestiality," the American press paved the way for the approval of Carranza as the future president of Mexico following American intervention. Reed, however, expressed his opposition in the *Metropolitan*. Between Villa and Carranza, he favored Villa:

Chihuahua, December 26, 1913. This is more wonderful than Italy. It is the last word in charm. Chihuahua is an exquisite place. There is absolutely no danger here. Villa rules with a rod of iron, and the town, to all appearances, is just as it was in times of peace. Villa runs the electric light plant, the telephone, the street-cars, the brewery, and almost every public utility. Every night the band plays in the plaza, and the soldiers and señoritas parade around in groups of four. The constitutionalist currency, of which I send you a sample, is flooding the town—but it is accepted at par by everybody here (par Mexican, of course), and so credit is fairly stable. At Parral the rebels coined silver money cut of ingots squeezed out of the mining companies, and copper money out of the telephone wires. I'm trying to get hold of some of it. I've seen it and it is beautiful stuff. I had a long talk with Villa today and he promised me that I was to go with him wherever he went, day or night. He is the most natural human being I ever saw—natural in the sense of being nearest to a wild animal. He says almost nothing and seems so quiet as to be almost diffident. His mouth hangs open and if he isn't smiling he's looking gentle. All except his eyes, which are never still and full of energy and brutality. They are intelligent as hell and as merciless. The movements of his legs are awkward—he always rode a horse—but those of his hands and arms are extraordinarily simple, graceful and direct. They're like a wolf. He is a terrible man—not one of his staff daring to question his orders—and he is the absolute dictator here. . . . It's all as romantic as can be.[26]

The quotation reveals Reed's vision of a Mexico governed by Villa: Romantic, arcadian, and utopian at the same time. Reed traveled to Mexico at a crucial time in the history of journalism, in terms of the business of war and the press. Among the types of journalists and the genres they cultivated, war correspondents and their influence on public opinion were highly regarded. Richard Harding Davis (1864–1916) was a paradigmatic case. One of the most celebrated turn-of-the-century journalists, Davis was accused of mixing the papers he worked for (the *New York Journal*, the *New York Herald*, and *Scribner's Weekly*) up in the Spanish-American War in Cuba and WWI. Davis's sensationalist writings forged what came to be known as the yellow press and provoked distrust among certain governments toward some war correspondents. Yellow journalism gave fame to Davis and his employer, William Randolph Hearst, owner of the largest media chain in the United States. Davis's Romantic style popularized war and helped catapult the fame of future presidents such as Theodore Roosevelt and his Rough Riders in the Spanish-American War. The Rough Riders were a group of "cowboys" from the American West and "bluebloods" from the East Coast recruited by Roosevelt for the first volunteer cavalry regiment in the Spanish-American War. In Davis's telling, the Rough Riders displayed heroism, adventure, bravery, and virility in war.

Precisely because of the importance of the media industry for the war, Roosevelt maintained relationships with both Davis and Reed. An enthusiastic and unconditional supporter of Davis, Roosevelt was more ambivalent about Reed, who severely criticized US policies during WWI and the Mexican Revolution. I have already mentioned differences between Roosevelt and Reed about American intervention in Mexico.

New York Times, December 14, 1913.

Although Reed had similar differences with Davis, he nonetheless regarded the latter as a model. Reed questioned Davis's patriotic approach to war reporting, but both journalists shared a way of romanticizing characters, adventure, and action. The press thus grew more robust with its correspondents, many of whom were hired precisely because they were famous fiction writers like Jack London and Ernest Hemingway, to name just a few.

The quotation above, with its Romantic vision of society as governed by Villa ("it's all as romantic as can be"), is characteristic of Reed's portrayal of Villa to public opinion and the government in the United

With Villa in Mexico

We have commissioned John Reed, the brilliant fiction writer and poet, to represent the METROPOLITAN *at the front during the terrible fighting in Mexico. Mr. Reed left New York a few days before this writing and joined Villa's army. We shall begin the publication of his articles in an early issue.*

Here follow some extracts from his personal letters written a few hours after his arrival on the scene. Although not intended for publication, these pen pictures are too vivid to be lost.

JUAREZ, December 21, 1913.

"The army, about 2,000 horsemen and 500 infantry, were drawn up in a great hollow square two ranks deep, completely surrounding that immense plaza in front of the race track. They were in all stages of attire, of course, but much more uniform than the federals at Ojinaga. About two-thirds of them had blue denim suits (overall stuff), and the rest more or less khaki. But every soldier had a different bright-colored handkerchief around his neck, and a different colored sarape strapped on his saddle—all colors, vivid and faded, and mottled like leopard skins.

"Their faces were strongly Indian, for the most part, very dark—there were small boys not fourteen years old, I should guess, too—but their riding boots were magnificently varied, some reaching to the hip, and ornamented down the sides with buckles like silver dollars. They rollicked around like kids, stealing rides on street-cars, making football rushes at each other and rolling over and over on the ground in piles of twenty to fifty, shouting and singing and eating peanuts. I never saw such a happy-spirited crowd.

"Then came the general. At the bugle they jumped on their well-fed, nervous little horses (peaches) and stood as nearly at attention as they knew how. They formed in fours, and at the sound of a cracked bugle they loosened their reins, lashed with their quirts, leaned over and yelled in their horses' ears, and burst into a wild charge like a clap of thunder. I never saw anything like it. Two thousand nondescript, tattered men, on dirty little tough horses, their sarapes flying out behind, their mouths one wild yell, simply flung themselves out over the plain. That's how the general reviewed them. They had very little discipline, but gosh! what spirit! And of course that kindled them still more. Not satisfied with that, they began to shoot into the air as fast as they could, on the run, with a reckless disregard for where the bullets went. They z-z-z-m-m-med over our heads, but a lot we cared. It was ten times as thrilling a sight as the cuirassiers charging at Longchamps. These were wild men, well fed, clothed, armed and mounted, volunteers instead of conscripts like the Federals. A great bunch, believe me. And what pageant material!

CHIHUAHUA, December 26, 1913.

"This is more wonderful than Italy. It is the last word in charm. Chihuahua is an exquisite place. It's set in the middle of a tawny desert, more brown and savage—much more—than anything around Presidio or El Paso. There are jagged mountains all around—big ones in the distance, and the town is really most like a jewel in the center of all this. Its outskirts are of brown adobe huts, and from there toward the center of the city the color gets brighter until in the center all is white, light red, pink and light blue stone and wash. There are the most astonishing golden yellow and mosque-like white churches. The cathedral is one of the most beautiful I have ever seen. It is soft yellow-brown rock, of incredibly soft color and texture, elaborately and crudely carved with arabesques and gigantic primitive angels and popes all over the façades.

"There is absolutely no danger here. Villa rules with a rod of iron, and the town, to all appearances, is just as it was in times of peace. Villa runs the electric light plant, the telephone, the street-cars, the brewery, and almost every public utility. Every night the band plays in the plaza, and the soldiers and señoritas parade around in groups of four.

"The constitutionalist currency, of which I send you a sample, is flooding the town—but it is accepted at par by everybody here (par Mexican, of course), and so credit is fairly stable. At Parral the rebels coined silver money cut of ingots squeezed out of the mining companies, and copper money out of the telephone wires. I'm trying to get hold of some of it. I've seen it and it is beautiful stuff.

"I had a long talk with Villa today and he promised me that I was to go with him wherever he went, day or night. He is the most natural human being I ever saw—natural in the sense of being nearest to a wild animal. He says almost nothing and seems so quiet as to be almost diffident. His mouth hangs open and if he isn't smiling he's looking gentle. All except his eyes, which are never still and full of energy and brutality. They are intelligent as hell and as merciless. The movements of his legs are awkward—he always rode a horse—but those of his hands and arms are extraordinarily simple, graceful and direct. They're like a wolf's. He's a terrible man—not one of his staff daring to question his orders—and he is th' absolute dictator here. The 'Viva Madero' that I heard northward dies away when it approaches the Governor's palace.

"It's all as romantic as can be. All hours of the day and night the street is suddenly filled with armed horsemen, jingling silently along, from no one knows where. At night lanterns are set in the street and you're challenged at every corner by armed sentries. The headquarters of General Villa and of Terrazas, the Secretary of State, are in two magnificent private houses, owned by the Terrazases and Creels, where the most splendid dinners and drunken balls take place."

Metropolitan, February 1914.

States. War correspondents forged the political careers of their presidential candidates. Reed did so with Villa, presenting him as a "wild man" in the arcadian, Gothic, and utopian style.

Pancho Villa, the "Wild Man"

The interviews Villa gave to Reed should be seen in the context of the journalistic creation of political characters for a national and international public. For example, *Pancho Villa: Retrato autobiográfico, 1894–1914* is the facsimile transcription of five notebooks belonging to Manuel

Bauche Alcalde (1881–1929), a reporter, literary critic, and official in the Maderista army. Bauche Alcalde's notebooks consist of interviews with Villa that were intended to be published at the time but were not published until 2003. Nonetheless, it has been pointed out that Villa's biographers referenced the notebooks much earlier: Elías Torres (*Vida y hechos de Pancho Villa*, 1975), Ramón Puente (*Villa en pie*, 1935), Federico Cervantes (*Francisco Villa y la revolución*, 1959), and Martín Luis Guzman (*Memorias de Pancho Villa*, 1954). As textualized in the *Retrato*, Pancho Villa did not choose the bandit life. Fate and victimization had thrown him to it. Thus, the narration sought to confer the legitimacy of the leader, divorced from the demonized vision of the bandit.[27]

The *Retrato autobiográfico* was conceived at the same time as *Insurgent Mexico*. The search for legitimacy in the nation with Bauche Alcalde as mediator was part of a broader international project, as Reed's book shows. Reed traveled and wrote about Villa during the battles of Gómez Palacios and Torreón—victories against Huerta that led to Villa's break with Carranza.

In *Insurgent Mexico*, Villa acquires characteristics that deepen another entrenched myth in the West, the myth of the natural, primitive man. For Reed, Pancho Villa was the "wild man," which made him the popular, natural-born leader: "He could not allow vast extensions of land to be granted to the rich and not the poor. The complex structure of civilization was new for him. You had to be a philosopher to explain anything to Villa: His advisors were only practical men."[28] From the beginning, Reed set Villa in opposition to civilization. What Villa was unable to understand sprang from his deep ignorance of civilized corruption. Villa is thus situated in the "place-myth" of the purity of the natural world, a type of arcadia where men are innocent and therefore question Western values. For Reed, Villa was a fascinating discovery, the object of observation in a laboratory in which the "experiment" consisted of placing a new species in a foreign habitat: "It is fascinating to watch him discover new ideas. Remember that he is absolutely ignorant of the troubles and confusions and readjustments of modern civilization."[29]

Nonetheless, these confusions were no obstacle for Villa's relationship with his troops. Reed remarks that, Villa, "He has the knack of absolutely expressing the strong feeling of the great mass of the people" and that "The common soldiers adore him for his bravery and his coarse, blunt humor."[30] His openness and frankness were the virtues that legitimized him as a natural-born leader—unlike the other generals, including Madero and Carranza, politicians from powerful landowning families who, despite their support for the revolutionary cause, knew well the diatribes of cabinet politics.

Like the paintings by Piero de Cosimo in which the savage man is half animal, *Insurgent Mexico* presents Villas as a centaur, a warrior on horseback who relied of intuition and intimate knowledge of the terrain to develop a completely original method of fighting: "On the field, too, Villa had to invent an entirely original method of warfare, because he never had a chance to learn anything of accepted military strategy."[31] Even the bloody executions attributed to him were justified, Reed insisted, by a natural morality that favored the dispossessed:

> As far as I could see, the Rules of War didn't make any difference in Villa's original method of fighting. The *colorados* he executed wherever he captured them; because, he said, they were peons like the Revolutionists and that no peon would volunteer against the cause of liberty unless he were bad. The Federal officers also he killed, because, he explained, they were educated men and ought to know better. But the Federal common soldiers he set at liberty because most of them were conscripts, and thought that they were fighting for the Patria. There is no case on record where he wantonly killed a man. Anyone who did so he promptly executed—except Fierro.[32]

In this economy of crime, assassinations and executions follow an implacable logic that pardons the soldiers forced by fate to fight. Pancho Villa is not only a primitive man—the "wild man" mix of Robin Hood and Tarzan—in whom the innocence and incorruptibility of "nature" resists civilization. His leadership of the masses is natural because Villa himself is the people. This exaltation of nature is the other face of the Villistas' bloody executions by firing squad. Still, the executions seem to follow a natural logic; their only leak was Fierro, the executor of violence whom Villa held in high esteem.

Although he led an army, Villa's greatest dream was to abolish the military and redistribute land. Reed reports him as saying, "It would be magnificent, I think, to help make Mexico a happy place."[33] Villa's dream, beyond the violence of the revolution, is utopian. Here we see how the "place-myth" operates in Reed's imaginary. On the one hand, Villa's Mexico is extemporal, separate from the civilizing chronology of the West, and assumes arcadian qualities. On the other hand, Reed regards Villa's Mexico as a utopian "place-myth" projected into the future. Villa's Mexico will be: 1) anti-military (although how "evil," to return to Jameson's phrase, that is arms, are going to disappear in the postrevolutionary society is not clear); 2) the dream of the agrarian revolution, the egalitarian redistribution of land and the communal organization of production and commerce; and 3) the dream of Mexico as a place of happiness. Comparing him with Carranza, who, Reed notes, "avoids any promise to resolve the land question," Reeds says of Villa:

Being a peon, and feeling with them, rather than consciously reasoning it out, that the land question is the real cause of the Revolution, acted with characteristic promptness and directness. No sooner had he settled the details of government of Chihuahua State, and appointed Chao his provisional governor, than he issued a proclamation, giving sixty-two and one-half acres out of the confiscated lands to every male citizen of the State, and declaring these lands inalienable for any cause for a period of ten years. In the State of Durango the same thing has happened and as other states are free of Federal garrisons, he will pursue the same policy.[34]

Here again, Reed insists that Villa is a man of action, not of reflection. His decisions aimed to benefit the vulnerable. In his analysis of the representation of the primitive man in Renaissance painting, Roger Bartra discusses the paintings of Piero di Cosimo to show how the satyrs, centaurs, and nymphs are presented in a double posture—they are brutal and violent and once tender, sensitive, and amorous.[35] In *The Death of Pocris*, *A Hunting Scene*, and *The Return from the Hunt* (ca. 1450), "wild men" are represented in this double posture.

This double facet of the wild man is helpful to understand Reed's description of Villa: just but implacably violent; intuitive in his affective relationship with his soldiers but methodical (despite being self-taught) in war. Interestingly, Villa is an armed man who dreams of a society without arms and the happiness of a peaceful postrevolutionary Mexico. Reed thus rearticulates a deeply rooted mythical image in Western history. As Bartra points out, "the wild men of Europe zealously guard the secrets of Western identity. Their presence has faithfully accompanied the advances of civilization."[36] He concludes that:

> The image of the wild man, which served during the Middle Ages as means to affirm the contrasting idea of civilized humanity, came to be used in the modern ages as a metaphor for understanding movement and change, for contrasting the great historical space that separates civilized from natural life. Modern Thought used the savage in a tragic and ironic manner to adopt a distance from civilization, whether for purposes of criticism or in order to establish a basis for the values of civil government, without, thereby, giving up the possibility of using this myth to explore the labyrinths of being and its castles within.[37]

Villa thus appears as a natural man who remains faithful to his principles—innocent and incorruptible. Unlike the educated, elite Venustiano Carranza, whom Reed described as senile, arrogant, and manipulated by his underlings, Villa did not yield to political pressures to change his course.

For Bartra, the controversy over Renaissance humanism was characterized by the redefinition of the savage man as inherently good despite his ferocious appearance as represented by Piero di Cosimo's paintings. Noting how the New World man undergirded the redefinition of the "wild man" myth, Bartra examines the writings of the Jesuit José de Acosta. In the *Natural and Moral History of the Indies* (1589), Acosta comments on the natural man's inclination toward the demonic, which explains his paganism, and addresses the controversy between Las Casas and Ginés de Sepúlveda. In Bartra's reading, Las Casas, like Acosta, argues for the essential humanity of the inhabitants of the New World in *Apologetica Historia*. The quest for spirituality led New World peoples erroneously to worship pagan gods, which is why they can and should be Christianized. Like Las Casas, Reed draws on the version of the noble savage (the readaptation of the wild man myth) and seeks to distance it from versions adopted by newspapers like the *New York Times* that associate Villa's otherness with brutality and evil in order to legitimize the invasion of Mexico. Unlike Las Casas, though, Reed does not use the noble savage myth to justify his indoctrination in civilization but rather to predicate his self-determination.

The figure of Villa as a wild man allows Reed to propose a model of the revolutionary hero, one with which Reed himself identified. The Romanticism of the "wild man" uncontaminated by civilization undergirds Reed's public figure as ever young, faithful, and committed to the original ideal of revolution. Reed's untimely death, in the early years of the Soviet revolution, contributed to the myth of "Reed" the young idealist. The figure of Reed tied to Villa places another layer of mythic imagining of a Mexico that he struggled to construct in *Insurgent Mexico*. One of his contemporaries wrote of him:

> By temperament he is not a professional writer or reporter. He is a person who enjoys himself. Revolution, literature, poetry, they are only things which hold him at times, incidents merely of his living. Now and then he finds adventure by imagining it, oftener he transforms his own experience. He is the one of those people who treat as serious possibilities such stock fantasies as shipping before the mast, rescuing women, hunting lions, or trying to fly around the world in an aeroplane. I can't think of a form of a disaster which John Reed hasn't tried and enjoyed. . . . He is many men at once, and those who have tried to bank some phase of him, to regard him as writer, a correspondent, a poet, a revolutionist, or a lover, lose him. There is no line between the play of his fancy and his responsibility to fact; he is for the time the person he imagines himself to be.[38]

Mexico and Russia: Comedy and Epic, or Two Ways to Narrate the Revolution

John Reed had covered domestic conflicts in the United States, mostly around worker and union uprisings, but his career as a foreign war correspondent only began with his trip to the Mexican Revolution. *Insurgent Mexico* has a clearly comedic tone, adding another aspect to his stories of arcadia with highlights of the festive and carnivalesque. However, comedy yields to epic in his dispatches from Russia. Between the two works, on his way to Petrograd, Reed wrote *War in Eastern Europe*, a book that was transitional both temporally and stylistically.

In *Insurgent Mexico*, before joining the march of the Villista troops, Reed advanced toward his encounters with the Maderista or Constitutionalist troops of other generals such as General Urbina. The narration is mostly descriptive and explores the conditions of the peasant soldiers and the idiosyncrasies of Mexicans. In these first chapters, Reed portrayed the Mexican peasants in a Romantic and idealized light, without relinquishing the power that his camera—and by extension his role as a journalist—wielded among the troops and, even more, among the revolutionary leaders. Usually in a festive fashion, Reed comments on the exaggerated warrior poses they assumed for the camera.

Only in chapter 11 does Reed finally declare that, in the mode of Richard H. Davis, he has "something to tell." The close relationship between journalism and the "adventure" of war becomes clear and Reed mocks his own bravery. Retreating from Gómez Palacio as the counterrevolutionary "Colorado" troops advanced, Reed narrates his fearful flight in an episode he titles "The Retreat of the Mister":

> Juan Vallejo was already far ahead, running doggedly with his rifle in one hand. I shouted to him to turn off the high road, and he obeyed, without looking back. I followed. It was a straight path through the desert toward the mountains. The desert was as bald as a billiard table here. We could be seen for miles. My camera got between my legs. I dropped it. My overcoat became a terrible weight. I shook it off. We could see the *compañeros* fleeing wildly up the Santo Domingo road. Beyond them unexpectedly appeared a wave of galloping men—the flanking party from the south. The shooting broke out again— and then pursuers and pursued vanished around the corner of a little hill. Thank God the path was diverging from the road!
>
> I ran on—ran and ran and ran, until I could run no more. Then I walked a few steps and ran again. I was sobbing instead of breathing. Awful cramps my legs.

> I ran. I wondered what time it was. I wasn't very frightened. Everything still was so unreal, like a page out of Richard Harding Davis. It just seemed to me that if I didn't get away I wouldn't be doing my job well. I kept thinking to myself: "Well, this is certainly an experience. I'm going to have something to write about.[39]

The writing-experience relationship arises amid the profusion of emotions provoked by war, terror, panic, and excitement. The interpretation is literary and the reference to Davis is hardly coincidental. A war correspondent needed to pen a page-turner and Reed's addition of humor makes the story even more attractive. His material is the extreme life-and-death experiences narrated not in fiction but with the force of journalism. The reporter constructed himself as a witness and a protagonist in the very events he was documenting.

In this respect, it is worthwhile to interrogate the relationship that the correspondent has with danger and the closeness of death. Reed's narrative speaks of an extreme proximity, of everyday dealings with soldiers and battles. The editors at *Metropolitan Magazine* valued his stories and featured them on the most prominent pages. Nonetheless, when Reed leaves the *Metropolitan* and travels to Russia with private funding, the magazine published "My Experiences with War Correspondents," by James Keely, longtime editor at the *Chicago Tribune* and the *Chicago Herald*. Keely noted how the golden age of correspondence had yielded to a journalism of reports and "cables" with official government information. In a "war of silence," nations at war were unwilling to divulge their plans and strategies. For Keely, "The special war correspondent" at the front "to-day almost belongs in the dodo class—that is as a vital asset of the business of newspaper reporting he is practically extinct. His passing began a number of years ago and the cataclysm in Europe marks his finish."[40] Reed in Mexico was the type of correspondent that, for Keely, had its swan song in WWI: "In the good old days, the War Correspondents were a great factor in the world. They told the story of the war, they made and unmade generals, placing the laurels of victory on some brows and snatching them from others. They wrote history and made it, too. Their life was one of adventure, thrill and no little peril. They helped to create reputations for newspapers and in doing so carved for themselves no inconsiderable niches in the hall of fame. Personal ingenuity, enterprise and nerve were vital factors in those good old days."[41]

To get close to battles, Reed had to earn the trust of the revolutionary soldiers through a constant negotiation with leaders, troops, and locals. Foreign journalists were viewed with suspicion. At the beginning of his journey, Reed was about to be shot as a spy. The matter was resolved with *sotol*, a nonhuman force with which the soldiers tested Reed because "no Porfirista could drink so much sotol at once."[42] Reed narrates the episode in which he proves with sotol that not only he is not a spy, but that he is also as masculine as the soldiers, despite being a gringo.

> "Aye, meester!" they shouted. "Here comes meester on a horse! *Que tal*, meester? How goes it? Are you going to fight with us?"
>
> But Captain Fernando at the head of the column turned and roared: "Come here, meester!" The big man was grinning with delight. "You shall ride with me," he shouted, clapping me on the back. "Drink, now," and he produced a bottle of *sotol* about half full. "Drink it all. Show you're a man." "It's too much," I laughed. "Drink it," yelled the chorus as the Tropa crowded up to see. I drank it. A howl of laughter and applause went up. Fernando leaned over and gripped my hand. "Good for you, *compañero!*" he bellowed, rolling with mirth. The men crowded around, amused and interested. Was I going to fight with them? Where did I come from? What was I doing? Most of them had never heard of reporters, and one hazarded the opinion darkly that I was a Gringo and a Porfirista, and ought to be shot.
>
> The rest, however, were entirely opposed to this view. No Porfirista would possibly drink that much *sotol* at a gulp. Isidro Amayo declared that he had been in a brigade in the first Revolution which was accompanied by a reporter, and that he was called *Corresponsal de Guerra*. Did I like Mexico? I said: "I am very fond of Mexico. I like Mexicans too. And I like *sotol, aguardiente, mescal, tequila, pulque*, and other Mexican customs!" They shouted with laughter.[43]

The reporter needed to understand local codes that associated alcohol with virility and, in this case, loyalty to the revolutionary cause. A traditional beverage from Chihuahua in northern Mexico, sotol was a man's drink. Journalists, former president Porfirio Díaz, and women were on the other side. Effeminateness was a sign of weakness attributable to the enemy and drinking alcohol was a display of gender. Since Reed understood this code, he is able to emerge triumphant. Still, he tries to keep the soldiers guessing. "It's too much," he says at first, playing with the stereotypes they had formed about him, only to contradict them with actions that highlighted his masculinity. With this victory, Reed the reporter gets the soldiers to respond to the question that runs through the whole book: "What are you fighting for?"

> Captain Fernando leaned over and patted my arm. "Now you are with the men *(los hombres.)* When we win the *Revolucion* it will be a government by the men,—not by the rich. We are riding over the lands of the men. They used to belong to the rich, but now they belong to me and to the *compañeros*."

"And you will be the army?" I asked.

"When the *Revolucion* is won," was the astonishing reply, "there will be no more army. The men are sick of armies. It is by armies that Don Porfirio robbed us."

"But if the United States should invade Mexico?"

A perfect storm broke everywhere. "We are more *valiente* than the Americanos—The cursed Gringos would get no further south than Juarez—Let's see them try it—We'd drive them back over the Border on the run, and burn their capital the next day . . . !"

"No," said Fernando, "you have more money and more soldiers. But the men would protect us. We need no army. The men would be fighting for their houses and their women."

"What are you fighting for?" I asked. Juan Sanchez, the color-bearer, looked at me curiously. "Why, it is good, fighting. You don't have to work in the mines . . . !"

Manuel Paredes said: "We are fighting to restore Francisco I. Madero to the Presidency." This extraordinary statement is printed in the program of the Revolution. And everywhere the Constitutionalist soldiers are known as "Maderistas."[44]

After registering the anti-militarism of the Villistas, Reed heard the revolutionaries' opinion on the United States. In response to the question of why the revolutionaries were fighting, Reed was able to report that they were not fighting merely to end of the domination of the wealthy. The revolutionaries were fighting for a series of causes that were at once immediate (avoiding work in the mines) and idealist (restoring Madero's presidency). Considering the exploitation of mine workers, the former seems reasonable: as least as far as booty is concerned, the ethics of war were superior to the ethics of mines. The latter is anachronical for, by then, in 1914, Madero was already dead. The misinformation that circulated among the revolutionary troops was a testament to the troops' indoctrination but also to their loyalty toward the revolutionary leader who launched the struggle.

Reed understood that his objective was to cover the advances of Villa's army in the north and interview Francisco Villa himself. Although *Insurgent Mexico* is a journalistic chronicle penned by a foreigner, it is useful to include the book, as critics such as Juan de la Cabada have suggested, within the collection of texts on the Mexican Revolution. Reed's text contributes several aspects to the writing of the revolution, making his characters into literature and, at the same time, creating a textual space of legitimacy for one of the revolution's grandest leaders, Pancho Villa. Nonetheless, compared to Mariano Azuela's novel *The Underdogs*,

Reed diverges from the narrative of the revolution by presenting a diversity of reasons to fight. In Azuela's case, the revolutionaries, totally ignorant of national affairs, fight for booty or revenge.[45] Reed, in contrast, recorded a polyphony of revolutionary voices and reasons.

Furthermore, the presence of foreign, and even Mexican, reporters in revolutionary campaigns was neither coincidental nor isolated. Reed was one of many correspondents. Richard Davis himself covered the invasion of Veracruz during the US intervention. The relationship between war correspondents and soldiers invites critical reflection on the interactions, asymmetries, and the varied effects of the situation on both. For instance, in the attack on federal lines in Torreón, Reed described how the explosion of a grenade provoked different reactions among soldiers and journalists. While a hundred soldiers fled in panic, rushing on their horses toward the rear-guard, reaction among the correspondents and reporters was very "peculiar."

> No sooner had the first shell exploded than someone produced the whisky jug, entirely of his own impulse, and we passed it around. No one said a word, but everybody drank a stiff swig as it came his way. Every time a shell would explode nearby we would all wince and jump, but after a while we did not mind it. Then we began to congratulate each other and ourselves for being so brave as to stay by the car under artillery fire. Our courage increased as the firing grew far between and finally quit altogether, and as the whisky grew low. Everybody forgot dinner.[46]

The correspondents reaffirmed their bravery in contrast to the soldiers. "One American can lick fifty Mexicans! Why, did you see how they ran this afternoon when the shells hit that grove? And how we—hic—we stayed by the car?"[47] Again drink, a nonhuman, in this case whiskey, was associated with bravery and virility. But unlike the sotol of the Mexican soldiers, whiskey did not prove the foreigners' bravery. Rather it generated the illusion of bravery in the face of danger. The two beverages, whiskey and sotol, distinguish nationalities, classes, and professions: whiskey for the foreign correspondents and sotol for the soldiers. But Reed was able to traverse these distinctions, moving between worlds, drinking too much in both. Notably, he did not express judgment. Instead, he let the characters of his story act and speak for themselves, provoking the reader's own interpretations of the correspondents who, ironically, comically, considered their bravery superior to that of the Mexican soldiers.

On his return from Mexico, censured for his supposedly anti-patriotic opposition to World War I, Reed decided to go to Russia where the revolution was about to explode. He embarked in September 1917 and returned to the United States in February 1918 with the manuscript, *Ten Days that Shook the World*. Although he traveled with credentials from the *Masses* and the *New York Call*, these newspapers did not pay for his trip. Funding came from a socialist group who, persuaded by Reed's friends Max Eastman and Eugen Boissevain, donated two thousand dollars.[48] Due to the vicissitudes of censorship and a prison term for alleged espionage, the manuscript was only published in 1919.

From Paterson to *Insurgent Mexico*, Reed became the protagonist of the events he narrated by writing himself into the middle of the action. Directly or indirectly, he was a Romantic hero. In *Ten Days*, however, the multitude plays the starring role. Reed transcribed the massive assemblies, the speeches from the public tribunals of leaders and ordinary citizens. His eye was on the crowd that was everywhere in Petrograd and Moscow. He described the buildings, inside and out, seized by the masses. In the case of the building of the Convent and the Smolny Institute, two hundred yards long and three stories high, with an imperial coat-of-arms on the facade, converted into a convent-institute for the daughters of the Russian nobility under the personal sponsorship of the Tsarina, the revolution seized it and turned it over to the organizations of workers and soldiers. The signs above its hundred enormous rooms that read "Ladies' Classroom" and "Teachers' Bureau" were replaced with ones that said "Central Committee of the Petrograd Soviet," "Union of Socialist Soldiers," and "Central Committee of All Russian Trade Unions," etc.: "The long, vaulted corridors, lit by rare electric lights, were thronged with hurrying shapes of soldiers and workmen, some bent under the weight of huge bundles of newspapers, proclamations, printed propaganda of all sorts. The sound of their heavy boots made a deep and incessant thunder on the wooden floor. . . . Signs were posted everywhere: 'Comrades! For the sake of your health, preserve cleanliness!' Long tables stood at the head of the stairs on every floor, and on the landings, heaped with pamphlets and the literature of the different political parties, for sale."[49]

For Reed, "the depths of Russia had been stirred, and it was the bottom which came uppermost now."[50] The revolution as an allegory of a tremendous geological disruption helps explain why Reed no longer focused his gaze on a person or a political leader such as Trotsky or Lenin, as he had done with Pancho Villa and Carranza. For Reed, "the only reason for Bolshevik success lay in their accomplishing the vast and simple desires of the most profound strata of the people, calling them to work of tearing down and destroying the old and afterward, in the smoke of falling ruins, cooperating with them to erect the frame-work of the new."[51] Of the fragmented speeches that the book features by Lenin, Trotsky, and others, it is clear that the accent is not on the individual leader but rather on the Soviets who represent the desire of the people: for the peasants, land; for the workers, factories; for the soldiers, peace. This is the vision that Reed presents of the Russian Revolution.

Unlike *Insurgent Mexico*, which depicts the leadership of Villa and his alter-ego Carranza, *Ten Days* includes Reed's interviews with Trotsky and Lenin but does not highlight the leaders on center stage in their own separate chapters. The Russian soldiers appear in informal dialogues with Reed, much like the peasant revolutionaries in Mexico. Yet the Russian troops do not joke with the correspondent; they are curious and critical of the American capitalist system, in which the powerful "can buy cities." The soldiers are aware of the corruption scandals in the American legal system and challenge Reed: "And in a free country! Had the people no revolutionary feeling?"[52] Reed has no solid arguments in response and the sense of superiority that appeared toward Mexican soldiers becomes inferiority before the moral strength of the Russians.

This is perhaps one of the few times that Reed appears vulnerable as a writer, a journalist, and an American. The only time he manages to get to the front with a group of revolutionary soldiers, he again is on the verge of being executed as a spy. Within the narration of an adventurous war correspondent, the situation is not unusual. But this time he seems a bit more desperate because language is playing against him; unable to speak Russian, he must rely on French. Furthermore, the Russian soldiers do not know how to read his safe-conduct. The risky situations thus pile up and the traveler's account highlights fear instead of humor and adventure.

Nonetheless, witnessing the revolution, meeting the revolutionaries, and seeing how the revolution changed its protagonists produced a radical change in Reed. It is not Pancho Villa who Reed admires; it's the entire Russian people. At the funerals of fallen revolutionaries in Moscow, Reed exclaims, "I suddenly realised that the devout Russian people no longer needed priests to pray them into heaven. On earth they were building a kingdom more bright than any heaven had to offer, and for which it was a glory to die."[53]

The striking workers in Paterson and Ludlow appeared as innocent children in search of the true nation, and the Mexican soldiers were wild centaurs. Reed moves away from these arcadian images in Russia, where a people have forged the utopia that he had sought first in his own country and then in Mexico. These revolutionaries are neither children nor centaurs. Both are "utopian enclaves," yet Reed's Mexico is written with the joy and playfulness of comedy while Russia is written with the seriousness and excess of epic.

Reed's Impossible Domesticity

In Reed's chronicles, the Mexican utopia contains elements of arcadia and comedy. It is an enclave, like the intentional communities studied by Jameson. Pancho Villa, the revolutionary leader, is at the center of this representation—a wild man, loving and ferocious. He will ensure peace and happiness for his people as long as external agents do not interfere in the struggle. Rising in response to centuries of ancient and modern exploitation of peasants, the revolution follows sociopolitical coordinates that are intrinsic to Mexico and incomprehensible to foreigners. For Reed, therefore, the Mexican Revolution needs to continue its course without US intervention. Yet he fails: he is unable to stop the invasion of Mexico with his writing. Nonetheless, his chronicles give a firsthand take of the revolution—his dialogues with peasants, interview with Villa, and stories of adventure and danger at the battle front—and solidify the characteristics of the genre of war correspondent. He created a powerful cross between history and fiction and established the business of narrating war in journalistic sensationalism.

Identifying the oikos in a traveler such as Reed is difficult. Although his biographers, and certainly the prize-winning 1980s movie *Reds*, celebrate him as a Romantic and patriotic hero, in fact the reading of his chronicles shed light on his constant critique of war, the United States, and the capitalist system. His death in Russia and his burial in the Kremlin speak eloquently of his ideological landscape, his openness to and acceptance of other utopic worlds—of his impossible domesticity.

Chapter 5

Gabriela Mistral in Mexico

Teacher, Mother, and Saint

Gabriela Mistral's stay in Mexico marks a fundamental shift in the life and career of the Chilean poet. The trip led her to abandon Chile forever. From the time of her departure in 1922 until her death in New York in 1952, she only returned to Chile three times. During this voluntary expatriation, Mistral built her career as an internationally recognized poet, educator, and cultural ambassador. Her appointment as lifetime consul for the Chilean government in 1935 made her a permanent foreign national. She would travel and live in Europe (Spain, Portugal, Italy), Latin America (Guatemala, Mexico, Brazil), and the United States (Los Angeles, New York). In 1945, her fame outside of Chile earned her the Nobel Prize in Literature, making her the first Latin American to receive the distinction. Her life, like the lives of other writers featured in this book, was marked by travel. Her trip to Mexico was a journey of initiation.

Mistral arrived in Mexico by invitation of the secretary of education, José Vasconcelos. During her stay from 1922 to 1925, she became an integral part of the postrevolutionary educational reform and a leading figure in Latin American education. Amid women educators' struggle for social and economic recognition, Mistral accentuated the role of women in Mexican education through a powerful ideological sign: the teacher as mother and virgin. I argue that this ideology of mother and virgin contradicted the struggle of women professionals although it did facilitate acceptance of the social role of female teachers. Within the history of pedagogy and the role of professional women in Latin America, Mistral's trip to Mexico is crucial. She wrote pages on the subject while regarding the educational reform initiated by Vasconcelos as part of a utopian social project to be constructed, as a work in progress.

For Mistral, Mexico is a place-myth, in the sense that it is a place where major social change can happen. As it was for Reed, Mexico in her view is a "utopian enclave" being built through the public schools. Schools, for her, are the laboratory of modernity in Mexico, where the female teacher takes on a leading role. Nonetheless, the educational "experiment" cannot be delimited and controlled in ways that Mistral and Vasconcelos imagined. The female labor force and its demands for legislation that supported reproductive rights in the work place constituted one of several excesses that challenged the model of the celibate teacher officially promoted by Mistral. Still, they were excesses that sprang from Mistral's exaltation of women in the designs of the modern nation. It is interesting to see Mistral's incongruences that reflect the excesses in the utopian enclave. She is in favor of women, but she is not a feminist; she is religious, but anticlerical; she favors the teaching of Spanish and the eradication of Indigenous languages, but during her time in Spain she opposed the imposition of Castilian Spanish in Latin America. To develop my arguments on these points, I will analyze Mistral's writings on Mexico compiled by Pedro Pablo Zegers B. in *Gabriela y México* and in *Readings for Women*, a text prepared by Mistral during her years in Mexico as part of her work for the Secretariat of Education.

Vasconcelos's invitation is an enigma for some observers. Mistral was not, at the time, a poet of international fame. Her works circulated in magazines, but her first book of poems, *Desolación* (published in New York by the Instituto de las Españas in USA), only appeared in the same year as her trip to Mexico. Nonetheless, as scholars have noted, Mistral did already have a fruitful career as an educator in Chile. In 1921, she became director of the Liceo #6 de Señoritas in Santiago. Travel was not new to her. Her profession had made her into a migratory subject. As a rural teacher and school administrator in Chile, she had moved from her native Elqui Valley to La Serena, then to Barranca, Traiguén, Punta Arenas, and Temuco, among other places. She held varied positions without having a degree in education, which led detractors to criticize her appointment as director of the *liceo* in Santiago. Nonetheless, her poetry gained a wide audience due to its use in pedagogical exercises. Official primary-school textbooks featured her *rondas* and children's poems. Manuel Guzmán Maturana's five *Libros de Lectura* (1916–1917), the most important textbook collection at the time, featured more than fifty of her works.

Mistral's intensive correspondence further suggests why Vasconcelos invited her. Throughout her career, she had carefully managed public relations, exchanging letters with the most renown writers and intellectuals of the Spanish-speaking world—Pablo Neruda, Victoria Ocampo, Miguel de Unamuno, Eduardo Barrios, Alfonsina Storni, Juan Ramón Jiménez, José Ortega y Gasset, and many more. In the decade before

Vasconcelos's invitation, Mistral had developed literary friendships with Amado Nervo, Antonio Caso, Alfonso Reyes, and other prominent members of the Ateneo de México, which advocated for humanistic and popular education.[1] After meeting her in Chile, the poet Enrique González Martínez suggested that Vasconcelos, also a member of the Ateneo, bring her into Mexico's pedagogical reform process.[2]

Considering these networks and academic contacts, Vasconcelos's invitation is less surprising. Indeed, Mistral was received as a celebrity in Mexico. Moraga Valle notes that when she arrived in the port city of Veracruz in July 1922, together with the educator Amantina Ruiz and the sculptor Laura Rodig, she was received by Diego Rivera, Roberto Montenegro, Alfonso Reyes, and a group of intellectuals and artists representing Vasconcelos. Paula Guillén, a professor in the normal school and Vasconcelos's collaborator in the organization of popular libraries, was commissioned to facilitate Mistral's activities in Mexico. The press followed her every step, and she took advantage of the coverage to explain the reasons for her voyage. Her statements projected the mythical and utopian visions of Mexico shared by many travelers: "For me . . . Mexico is one of the American countries that inspires the greatest interest, not only for its traditions, its art, and for its admirable artists, but for its spirit of renewal and progress. I believe that, since the time of Sarmiento in Argentina, no one had begun education reforms such as those in Mexico."[3]

Vasconcelos and Mistral developed a relationship of mutual admiration, exemplified by the founding in 1923 of the Gabriela Mistral School. Their admiration sprang from deep ideological agreement around miscegenation, religion, and Hispanism. Both understood teaching to be a sacred, civilizing mission, though Mistral emphasized the social aspect of education that would find more resonance in the socialist education policies of President Lázaro Cárdenas a decade later than in Vasconcelos.

The Educational Crusade and Rural Schools

Mistral joined Vasconcelos because she believed that his work was visionary. Under the direction of the recently created Secretariat of Education, led by Vasconcelos, public education had a national scope for the first time. Previously, only Mexico City had public education programs; the rest of the country, especially rural areas, was under the tutelage of the Catholic church. The Constitution of 1917 radically changed this by federalizing and secularizing education. Vasconcelos's educational reform project was central to the formation of the postrevolutionary citizen. To establish a new nation from the "ruins" of the revolution, Vasconcelos sought to develop and implement an educational system that homogenized citizens according to the ideal of a mestizo nation.

With his landmark 1925 book *The Cosmic Race*, Vasconcelos stands as the ideologue of miscegenation. In his view, miscegenation, education, and nation all go hand in hand.

After serving as director of the National University, Vasconcelos became the secretary of education. Between 1921 and 1923, he successfully pushed for an unprecedented 50 percent increase in the education budget. Funds went to new schools, buildings, and teacher training. The Secretariat was divided into three departments: Education, Libraries, and Fine Arts. The library department published books compiled by Mistral, such as the 1924 *Classic Readings for Children* and *Readings for Women*. Vasconcelos used Fine Arts to link education and art, promoting muralism and popular art. The department resurrected the San Marcos academy and the National Conservatory and founded the symphony orchestra.[4] Educational programs emphasized not only books and schools but also lectures, concerts, and courses. Vasconcelos insisted on the need to bring art and culture "down" to the people. He launched agricultural schools and educational programs that sought to retain the humanistic ideal that Vasconcelos had embraced in the Ateneo.

Both Vasconcelos and Mistral linked the humanism of the Ateneo to the vision of teaching as an "apostolic crusade." Their humanism conjoined with Catholic Hispanism to form an implicit messianism. Teachers were to be "true missionaries, like Vasco de Quiroga, Molina, and Bartolomé de Las Casas; [they] should preach the gospel of teaching among the unprotected; and make the educational program a 'holy crusade' against ignorance."[5]

The application of this educational messianism to rural areas in Mexico was unprecedented. During Vasconcelos's term, a mestizo Hispanicism permeated the mission, predicated on aesthetic universalism manifested in a characteristic gesture: "the distribution of thousands of copies of the classics to peasants who had only recently learned to read and write."[6] This "holy crusade" for education expected Indigenous people to join the nation through the assimilation of European culture. Here the book-objects circulated outside of their designated routes, which helps explain the contrasts between Mexico City and the marginal rural areas.

Whether this program reflected the needs of rural schools is an open question. For Raby, these "missionary teachers" whom Vasconcelos sent to the field were the ones that oversaw the first rural normal schools. They, not Vasconcelos, pressured congress to allocate resources for the Secretariat of Education's Department of Indigenous Education and Culture. They promoted the idea of a rural school adapted to the material needs of the peasantry and later developed a "creative and original philosophy of rural education."[7]

Mistral had her eye on rural schools as well. Upon her arrival in Mexico, she chose to be part of the "cultural missions" in the countryside. Her writings on the agrarian school project her utopian ideal: "The small agrarian republic these children have created will point the way to the economic regime and the roads to prosperity; [these children] will not have the hatred of wealth that only arises when man has nothing of his own to defend or love under the sun."[8] She adds: "I did not throw myself into a river of fantasies; rather, I feel, for the first time in my life, what this small experience of children means for the big social problems. When education is incarnated in deeds and not mere garrulous verbiage, I have seen its strength for the economy. There have been times when the mass of schoolchildren who work the land, with good sense and high intuitions, have seemed to me a true republic, and I have felt intoxicated by great faith."[9]

School thus becomes a utopian enclave; the agrarian school becomes an allegory of the nation. Mistral sees Mexico as "myth-place," upon which travelers project their wishes, fears, anxieties, and utopic ideas.[10] The educational reform was integral to the utopia-building process. Following the revolution, the cultural and educational project to be created in Mexico constituted, in Ernst Bloch's terms, a "new spatial totality with intentional communities."[11] Schools were fundamental to the formation of the new citizen and the new nation that would rise from the rubble of the revolution.

Despite the shared principles of humanism and Catholic Hispanism, Mistral's utopian project of educational reform emphasized agrarian schools and action pedagogy over the classical curriculum promoted by the secretary of education. Her views aligned more with Dewey's theory of "school of action," in vogue in Mexico at the time, according to which practical activity should drive learning. This was a pedagogical application of the philosophy of pragmatism. Dewey's technical, practical vision incorporated concepts of child psychology to adjust learning to the economic needs of the industrialized world.

In Mexico, Moisés Sáenz, a disciple of Dewey at Columbia University, adapted this practical pedagogy to rural Mexico. Schools were to have garden plots and teach crafts such as pottery, basketry, carpentry, and textiles. There were to engage directly with the community and function as the center of the social life. Nonetheless, theory did not match the needs of peasants. Caudillismo and clientelism still dominated the countryside; agrarian reform, the central pledge of the revolution, remained unfulfilled. Most of the peasants who were part of the rural schools did not own land. Raby notes that, in the 1920s, the agrarian schools represented more utopian desire than actual social change. Failure was inevitable. Despite their revolutionary potential, rural schools could not upend social hierarchies or address the unequal distribution of land. Many teachers succumbed to apathy or turned to radicalism.[12]

It is useful to recall Ernesto, the teacher in Rosario Castellanos's famous novel *Balún Canán* (1957), although the story takes place years later. Peasants who worked on a hacienda owned by César, the father of the novel's protagonist, demanded a school, in keeping with federal law, and a teacher. César designates Ernesto, an unqualified drunkard who does not speak the local Maya language and beats the children. The ensuing tension shows the difficulties of implementing federal laws in isolated rural areas far from the gaze of the central government. As the novel suggests, opposition by landowners hindered President Lázaro Cárdenas's radical reforms in land and education a decade after Mistral's visit. The frustrated dreams of education lead the Chamula Indigenous people in the novel to revolt.

> The first day Felipe (the Chamula leader) arrived to see what the class was like. He sat on the floor with the children who smelled of cheap glitter and polished cleanliness. Ernesto swallowed nervously. He resented Felipe's presence as that of a witness, like that of the judge in front of him. But he had to teach the class anyway. He was sure that when he wanted to speak, he would have no voice and that everyone would laugh at the ridiculous job he was going to do. Taking out a copy of the *Bristol Almanac*, which he carried in the pocket of his trousers, he began to read. With great astonishment his voice matched the words and he could even raise it and make it firm. He read, hastily, pronouncing poorly, making mistakes. He read horoscopes, jokes, and the lives of saints. The children stared at him in amazement, their mouths open, without understanding a word. For them, Ernesto could have read the *Almanac* or any other book. They did not know how to speak Spanish. Ernesto could not speak Tzeltal. There was no possibility of understanding between the two. Upon finishing the class, Ernesto approached Felipe with the hope that he had realized how useless the ceremony had been and sure he would demand his resignation. But Felipe seemed very satisfied that the law was being fulfilled. He thanked Ernesto for the favor he gave them and promised that the children would be punctual and applied. The children remained attentive, amazed by the show that was unfolding before their eyes. But then they started to get distracted and misbehave. They rubbed shoulders and assumed a hypocritical immobility; they laughed, huddled behind their broken palm hats; they made rude noises. Ernesto forced himself, with an enormous effort, not to lose patience. Since the law did not set the number of class hours, Ernesto abbreviated them as much as possible.[13]

Castellanos shows the multiple interests and disagreements involved in the struggle to implement rural schools after the revolution. State officials, landlords, teachers, Indigenous villagers, and the church all converge in the school—the powerful space that defined access to citizen rights and the modernity of social change. In the context of extreme marginality and feudalism, the figure of Ernesto underscores the problems with the federalization of education and the actual scope of regulations formulated by the national government.

Together with land and political freedoms, the creation of schools was one of the earliest demands of the revolution. However, despite educational reforms and the expansion of schools envisioned in the Constitution of 1917, which declared primary education free of cost and secular, it was only when Obregón became president and Vasconcelos secretary of education that a policy of educational federalization was established and the creation of rural schools began in earnest.[14] As I noted above, the Secretariat of Education was founded in 1921, but Vasconcelos, as director of the National University in 1920, had already launched a literacy campaign that called on intellectuals and professionals to volunteer as teachers. Likewise, Vasconcelos advocated for changes in article 73 of the constitution to establish a federal educational policy in which authority over primary schools would go from local to national officials. Despite opposition to secular and free education by the church and landowners, by 1924, when Vasconcelos left the secretary position, there were one hundred missionaries and some one thousand rural schools.[15]

From Vasconcelos's tenure, national rural normal schools were created to train teachers. The cultural missionaries sent by Vasconcelos played an important role in the schools since they traveled to rural areas to recruit local teachers and establish schools. Gabriela Mistral was active in this regard. The rural question was intrinsically related to concerns about agriculture, rural industry, and integration of Indigenous people into the nation. Language was often a barrier since 16 percent of the rural population spoke only native languages. For Vasconcelos, the only solution was to abandon native languages and bring the Indigenous fully into Hispanized Mexican culture.

The fundamental problem was not only that liberal or Hispanicized education had little validity for peasants, but also that schools could not transform the cultural life of the countryside if the economic and social conditions of the peasantry did not also undergo a transformation. Dominant groups of landowners and local leaders continued to oppose such a transformation. As Castellanos's novel shows, landowners in regions like Chiapas fought against rural schools even in the era of Lázaro Cárdenas ten years later.

The Feminization of Education

Beautiful and strong the land is in which you were born . . . you are the ally of the earth, you must provide the arms that collect the fruits and the hands that weed the cotton. You are the collaborator of the earth, and that is why she bathes you with grace in the light of each morning.

Mexican mother: vigorously claim for your child what existence owes to the beings who are born without asking to be born. For him you have the right to ask for more than anyone, and you must not let your clamor rise from other mouths. For him, ask for sunny and clean schools; ask for joyful parks; ask for the great artificial fountains and the festivals of the images in the book and in the educating cinema; demand laws that cleanse the illegitimate child from shame and that do not cause him to be born a pariah and live as a pariah in the midst of the other happy children, laws that deliver welfare services [and] regulate your work and that of the children who are exhausted in the brutal work of the factories.

For this you can be daring while remaining prudent; your word will not be grotesque, it will receive sanctity and send divine shivers among the multitudes who hear it. You have the right, mothers, to sit among the teachers, to discuss the education of your children, and to tell them their mistakes until they are amended . . .

Mexican woman: Latin blood is rocking on your lap and there is no destination bigger and bigger than yours at this hour.[16]

Many educated, upper middle class, urban women came of age during the Porfiriato, when incipient feminist groups began to demand equality. Many of these women studied in normal schools and coalesced around the magazine the *Mexican Woman*. Its founder, Dolores Correa, wrote *Humble Life, or Memories of a Teacher* (1911).[17] During Mistral's stay in Mexico, two meetings were held by women who pursued moderate feminism. The Pan-American Feminist League sponsored the "National Convention of the School of Commerce and Administration of Women in the National University of Mexico" from March 20 to 26, 1923. The second was the International Feminist Congress's "Women for the Race," organized by the League of Iberian and Hispanic American Women at the Mining Palace on July 5 and 6, 1923. Strikingly, Mistral does not appear in the list of attendees. She does not appear to have participated in these groups. Unlike the feminism of upper-class, educated women in Mexico, her ideology regarding women's education was anti-liberal and religious.

The quote that begins this section speaks of the preeminent role women were to play in educational reform, of the ideal of the "telluric" women who embodied earth and nature. However, this feminine primitivism becomes a feminist call to citizen agency: "Ask, demand with your own voice" and "you have the right." Still, to think of this discourse as feminist would be misguided. Mistral brought together two tendencies of Mexican educational reform: on the one hand, a conservative ideology that envisioned the female teacher as a virgin mother and, on the other, the broad social and labor participation of women. Women's "natural inclination" to raise children supposedly made them the most suitable candidates to be teachers. Thus, the figure of the teacher did not contradict the traditional and domestic role of "mother" despite female teachers' increased engagement in the labor market. In an illuminating work, "Women Teachers of Postrevolutionary Mexico: Feminisation and Everyday Resistance," Oresta Lopez notes that:

> During the period marked by an expansion of rural education in Mexico from 1924 to 1940, many young women were entering and leaving careers in teaching. They were hired as assistants to male professors and paid lower salaries, even though they had equal or greater training than men. Women were also controlled through regulations that prohibited them from marrying and having children while they were employed by the government. Thousands of letters and documents stored in the historical archives of the Ministry of Public Education offer evidence of the discreet but constant struggles women teachers endured trying to attain equality with their male colleagues. At the same time, these women were also trying to gain reproductive rights.[18]

Since the end of the nineteenth century, feminist organizations had begun opening women's access to education and careers in such fields as teaching, which had traditionally been the domain of male teachers. Mistral undoubtedly made important contributions to the leading roles that women assumed in the educational reform that followed the Mexican Revolution. However, as Oresta López demonstrates, women teachers continued to occupy second-rate roles, especially in rural areas. They received lower pay and risked losing their job if they became pregnant. Schools that hired women continued to value virginity and celibacy. Undoubtedly, as "teacher, mother, and saint" and the "teacher of America," Mistral and her celibacy reinforced this image.

Oresta López points out that legislation between 1867 and 1917 gave women the opportunity to receive and impart education, especially in normal schools. However, laws did not consider the reproductive rights of women, and the prevailing liberal discourse affirmed the model of a celibate or childless female teacher. During this period, discourse naturalized the notion that women were biologically more intuitive, less authoritarian, and therefore, more apt to work with children. The stereotype derived from Rousseau and Johann Pestalozzi (1746–1827), whose works *How Gertrude Teaches Her Children* (1801) and *Book of Mothers* (1803) were translated and published in Mexico and remained popular throughout the twentieth century. Pestalozzi maintained that an educator's intuition was fundamental to childhood development. Following Rousseau's notion of the *bon savage*, he proposed a nonauthoritarian rural education for poor children.

After the revolution, women's participation in the educational workforce increased significantly. Yet, even exposed to greater dangers in remote or rural schools, women were still paid less than men. Rural teachers in general came from less favored social classes; female teachers often experienced gender-based violence that left them extremely vulnerable. Moreover, they were assigned less prestigious tasks within the educational hierarchy. Although the Secretariat of Education favored co-ed schools, its position regarding female teachers remained ambivalent. Women only saw changes in wage and labor discrimination after 1933, when, for example, they obtained the right to maternity leave. However, Oresta López's study of rural teachers in the Valle de Mezquital shows that schools continued to prefer celibate or sterile women. Female teachers had to keep their marital status a secret to obtain their positions.[19]

Women's access to education and teaching urges us to think about how class and race permeate Mexico and Latin America. Scholarship on the educational crusades of postrevolutionary Mexico has largely overlooked rural teachers. On the one hand, the figure of the teacher as mother and virgin envisioned by Mistral and postrevolutionary educational philosophy facilitated acceptance of women in education. On the other hand, the same figure continued to reproduce stereotypes (women as intuitive and nature-linked, maternal and virginal at the same time) that hinder the struggle for parity and reproductive rights in the postrevolutionary period. In *Readings for Women*, the Secretariat of Education publication that she compiled, Mistral notes:

> The increasingly intense participation of women in the liberal and industrial professions brings an advantage: economic independence, an indisputable asset; but it also brings a certain detachment from the home, and, above all, a loss of the sense of motherhood. In the old woman, this sense was deeper and more alive, and therefore I find the best of women in the past. They seem to me more austere than those of today, more loyal to the true ends of life; I think this should not change. For me, those old values are eternal. For me, the form of female patriotism is perfect motherhood.[20]

Mistral thus assigns women their place in the nation: the home, the raising of children, the new citizens. Teachers should be an extension of this figure; school should reinforce the home. That is why Mistral is happy when the school that Vasconcelos builds in her name is called the " Gabriela Mistral School-Home." It is no coincidence that the first text in *Readings for Women* is by the Victorian writer John Ruskin (1819–1900), who described the ideal woman as the "Angel of the home." A few years later, Virginia Woolf (1882–1941) rightly called on women to exorcise the ideal in order to achieve the true liberation of professional women.[21]

Privately lesbian, Mistral never married, but she always had female companions on her travels and in her domestic life. She never had a stable home. As a cultural ambassador for Chile, she lived in Europe, Central America, Brazil, and the United States. She had an adopted son, Yin. There are poems by Mistral that indicate queerness and dissidence toward the "traditional" woman that she advocated for elsewhere. In the postrevolutionary nation that increasingly brought women into the workforce, it is paradoxical and extraordinary that, as Licia Fiol-Matta points out in *A Queer Mother for the Nation*, Mistral envisioned the traditional mother as the model for true female patriotism.[22]

Education and Religion

Mistral's spirituality is a remarkable aspect of her writings on Mexico. Although Christianity predominates her thinking, Mistral shared with Vasconcelos a Buddhist spirituality. She was also affiliated with the theosophical school of Madame Blavatsky. Fabio Moraga Valle points out that by 1913 her collaboration with *Nueva Luz*, a magazine of the Teosófica Destellos Lodge, marked a close connection to theosophy that distanced her from Catholicism.[23] Mistral was a religious woman. For her, the teacher was a priest, education was a religious mission. She found the rural educational "crusades" particularly attractive. "The teacher must be the priest of the new religion of the fatherland," she wrote in 1917, "the school its temple and the book its ritual."[24] In her 1919 "Prayer of the Teacher," Mistral exclaimed, "Lord, You who were a teacher, forgive me for teaching, for bearing the name of teacher that You brought to earth. . . . Put in my democratic school the radiance that hung over your circle of barefooted children."[25] As an advocate for religious education, Mistral experienced the contradiction of working for a revolutionary state that expressly prohibited religious teaching in schools. The postrevolutionary secular federalization of education collided with the church and its power in education. How could Mistral reconcile her religious ideas and the teaching of the Bible with the now secularized institution of the school?

In response to whether Mexican schools should include images of Christ, Mistral wrote "The Image of Christ in School." Her approach to teaching the Bible draws on the ideals of the revolution, as well as Western ideals and the modern canon. She highlights aspects of the Bible that seem appropriate for the new, modern, revolutionary school in Mexico. She talks about the Belgian socialist and Catholic school, where the teaching of history, economics, and literature reflected Christian social parameters. "The Belgian Catholic school, the most remarkable I know, follows the social question with a fidelity of tact and gives its students the Christian norms to solve it."[26] She adds: "The social doctrine of the Christian school must be democratic, because the Gospel is full of passion for the poor, loaded with charity that goes much further than the so-called justice of our labor codes. In any book, the law was more effusively popular than in the Gospel and the poor have never received more absolute exaltation than those our Lord gave them."[27]

So, returning to the question of whether the image of Christ should be featured in schools, Mistral response that Christ should be considered one of the liberating heroes of the universal revolution. According to Mistral, he crushed the Roman Empire and the imperial tyranny that prevented men from loving a sublime God and that forced them to love "grotesque and vulgar" gods. And even more, he left a "new literature in his parables and the Sermon on the Mount."[28] For Mistral, coursing through the New Testament "is a milk of superior beauty that had never been savored before, and not a single page of this exalted word can be found in Roman literature as it is found in the mouths of the Saint Mark and Saint Matthew."[29]

Amid this movement from social ideology to aesthetics—from liberating hero to a "literature of parables of superior beauty"—Mistral seeks to place the Bible on the required reading list of the Mexican Revolution, not only because of its ideas but because of the loftiness of its aesthetic form, its quality as literature. Far from grotesque, unclean, or "low" literature, the Bible is elevated, linked to a sublime God.

Including the Bible in the postrevolutionary curriculum had significant political and ideological implications. In his essay "Canonical and Non-Canonical: A Critique of the Current Debate," John Guillory analyzes the relationship between the canon and the education system. Guillory begins by questioning the autonomy of the aesthetic value of canonical works above their representational value of inclusion of groups supposedly represented by canonical works (Homer, Shakespeare, Eliot, Austen). He asks whether these works and authors homogeneously represent the values of "Western civilization." The canonical texts are not necessarily repositories of cultural values (or religious value, which is what Mistral thinks but does not say). Guillory seems inclined to believe that the inclusion of a text in the canon is almost always justified more by its literary value than its moralistic or dogmatic value—the kind of legitimization that Mistral gives to the Bible. However, following Walter Benjamin, Guillory argues that:

> Canonicity is not a property of the work itself but of its transmission, its relation to other Works in a collocation of Works; and this is true even when that relation is the intentional object of aesthetic production. Whatever the relation of the work to its initial audience, it must certainly have other relations as canonical work, and these are the relations mediated by the form of the canon. The failure to make this distinction is the condition of every invocation of tradition, the supposed reproduction of cultural values by the monuments of culture. Yet if canonical works do not in themselves reproduce values, it is significant–even integral—to the real social process of reproduction that they are thought to do so. The real social process is the reproduction not of values but of social relations.[30]

Guillory analyzes the example that R. R. Bolgar gives in his book *The Classical Heritage and Its Beneficiaries*. Bolgar looks at the importance of teaching Greco-Roman literature in the provinces of the Roman Empire, particularly works in literate Latin that depicted urban life in early days of the empire, before it was contaminated by the vulgarity of commerce and administration. For Guillory, the importance of the transmission of these works was that they were in high Latin; they distinguished the elite from provincial groups who lacked the necessary linguistic and symbolic cultural capital. The canon did not reproduce aesthetic values, he argues, but asymmetrical social relations

Linguistic codification underscores how the educational system regulates access to cultural capital objectified in the canon. Through the cultural and linguistic legitimation of the Bible taught in Spanish—the language of the mestizo—Mistral followed Vasconcelos's ideology of miscegenation, in which the language and culture of the whitewashed mestizo go together. For her, language and culture come together in the religion of the European conqueror. In her essay on the Indigenous languages of America, she maintains that:

> The missionaries knew before anybody else that to learn the local dialect was to hunt the Indian with his own honey, and they began not only to learn but to teach it to some of the brave soldiers; and no one afterward has given more attention to the formidable linguistic knot that is indigenous language. Incorporation and common business language was one and the same for the missionaries. Although in other aspects missionaries treated the indigenous

people like children, they believed they were capable and worthy of handling a European language; it is only later that *indianistas* informed us, somewhat tragically, that indigenous people are incapable of attaining such dignity, and that it is unfair to force them in this regard. . . . The plan of the missionaries was to communicate with the indigenous people in both Spanish and their native tongue until the students had enough skill in Spanish. . . . Now, Vasconcelos teaches the same thing to teachers in rural areas: to maintain the dialect as a transitional measure; to charitably and courteously speak with the children initially in Tarasco or Tarahumara, but only in the beginning of the relationship . . . then to require them to learn Castilian.[31]

The debate that Mistral waded into over the inclusion of the Bible and Spanish language teaching was no small matter. It was *the* question debated by Mexican intellectuals and pedagogues. Raby notes that the doctrinal indigenist school (represented, for example, by Alfonso Toro's widely used 1926 textbook *Compendium of the History of Mexico*) considered the Spanish Empire in Mexico to be a product of evil. However, several prominent intellectuals, such as Antonio Caso, Moisés Sáenz (undersecretary of Education of 1925–1930), and Rafael Ramírez (director of the Cultural Missions from 1927 to 1935) were convinced that the colonial and creole legacy could not be erased and that Indigenous languages had to disappear. The only way to bring the Indigenous into the modern nation was through assimilation to the language and the dominant mestizo—essentially Hispanic—culture.[32] The most radical defender of this position was Vasconcelos, whose *Brief History of Mexico* recognizes only two heroes: the conquistador Hernán Cortés and the revolutionary leader Francisco I. Madero. In his autobiography, Vasconcelos acknowledged that in 1922 he had insisted that the sole purpose of the Department of Indigenous Education and Culture was to prepare Indigenous people to enter ordinary schools by giving them rudimentary Spanish.[33]

The school program was clearly about integration and assimilation. Echoing Vasconcelos's integrationist curriculum, Mistral insisted that aboriginal languages were incapable of expressing the Indigenous in modern life. "The mestizo, definitely proud to speak Spanish, wants nothing to do with Mayan or Quechua and dispatches them into the mountains, showing the same contempt for them that he shows for all Indigenous customs."[34]

The Bible, the book of the colonizer, is inseparable from the Castilian language. The alliance between the Spanish missionaries, the mestizos, and the language of sophistication that schools reproduce as a system of accreditation and hierarchy was manifest. Mistral adduces two eminently modern aspects of the Bible to justify its entrance into schools: aesthetic value and the Gospels' revolutionary social conscience. The strategy is to compare Catholic teaching and the Bible with the socialist model of the Belgian school, a model of prestige for revolutionary Mexico. For Mistral, the entry of the Bible into the school canon is the tacit reproduction of what Guillory calls the reproduction of social relations. Mestizos and white criollos occupy the position of privilege over the natives. This is evident in Mistral's writings on religion, conquerors, and language. In her defense of the language of the mestizo, Mistral aligns herself with Vasconcelos's vision of miscegenation that highlighted the mestizo's European quality.

By assuming this defense of the mestizo's language, Mistral certainly aligned herself with Vasconcelos's proposed mestizaje, which, as many have noted, celebrated the European aspects. What I want to highlight is how Mistral constructs the "Bible" object for its inclusion in the school canon, tying it to religion, to the classics, and especially to the Spanish language.

Yet, Mistral's defense of the teaching the Bible in Spanish should not be conflated with total adherence to Hispanism. Mistral was very critical of Spaniards, as became acutely clear during her stay in Madrid as consul (1933–1935) following her trip to Mexico. "It was not a mystery to anyone," Julio Saavedra Molina notes, "that the poet professed little sympathy for the Spaniards."[35] Ciro Alegría, Mistral's friend and author of *Gabriela Mistral íntima* confirmed it much years later. Alegria recalled a conversation with Mistral in her Santa Bárbara house in which she criticized the influence of the Spanish conquerors in America.[36] Not even the editor of her first book of poems *Desolación* escaped her criticism. For Mistral, "This archigode could not digest the palpable fact that we still have mestizos and Indians."[37] Ana Caballé notes a comment that Mistral added to the colophon of *Petrópolis* that came with the 1945 reissue of *Ternura*:

A Spanish colleague sometimes mocked the creole effort to force popular poetry, causing a birth by will, or an abortion. I listened with interest: a Spaniard always has the right to talk about the business of the language that he gave us and whose line he holds in his right hand, that is, in the most experienced. But what do they want us to do? Much of the Spanish is no longer useful in this world, where people, habits, birds, and plants are so different from those on the peninsula. We are still your clientele in the language, but many now want to take possession of the New World. The enterprise of invention will be grotesque; repeating from beginning to end what came in the caravels will be too. Someday I must respond to my colleague about the tremendous conflict between being faithful and being unfaithful in a verbal colony.[38]

Mistral was very critical of the Hispanism of the imperial language, especially regarding her writings and work with editors. The racial discrimination she felt in Madrid made her tenure as a consul an ordeal. She criticized the Spanish government in letters to friends, compromising her job as consul. Once again, the contradiction between public figure and private person, which characterized her life, arises.

Saint Gabriela Mistral

After Gabriela Mistral became the first Latin American writer to receive the Nobel Prize for Literature in 1945, her books sold widely. Now, her poems are read less and less. The once common practice of elementary school children reciting poems from *Ternura* has been gradually disappearing. Nonetheless, her sanctified image as the "teacher of America" persists. In a 1956 hagiography that highlights Mistral's spirituality, Benjamín Carrión called the Chilean poet "Saint Gabriela Mistral" and "mother of all the children of the world."[39] Although Mistral stood out as a teacher and administrator in Chile, it was her participation in the postrevolutionary educational reforms that catapulted her as a woman educator.

Secretary of Education José Vasconcelos invited Mistral to Mexico during an intense and opportune moment, when the Mexican nation was rising from the ruins of revolution. Mexico needed to be reinvented; the peasants needed to become citizens. Vasconcelos had assumed the task through schools, art, and culture. Mistral not only contributed to this mission, but also embraced it with the idealism of someone who believed she was helping build a utopia that was becoming real.

Vasconcelos and Mistral coincided in their predilection for humanistic teaching and classical authors. Following their similar criteria, Gabriela Mistral compiled anthologies that were published by the Secretariat of Education, such as *Readings for Women* (1924). Despite its vocation toward the poor, the school of Vasconcelos did not embody the ideals of agrarian reform; his Hispanist miscegenation was a linguistic and cultural horizon.

Mistral's role was to train teachers and mothers, providing them with a model of citizenship at a time when the female workforce was channeled toward education. Female teachers gradually occupied the place previously assigned to the male teacher. But this change required a state discourse that authorized women's role as educators and labor legislation that, however haltingly, put women on equal footing with men. This was the context into which Mistral entered.

Since the late nineteenth century, feminist organizations and national legislation had been expanding women's access to education and careers such as teaching. Nonetheless, women, especially in rural areas, continued to occupy second-class roles, with lower pay and greater vulnerability. From 1924 to 1940, a period marked by the expansion of rural education in Mexico, many young women entered careers in education. Despite training that was equal or superior, they worked as lower-paid assistants to male teachers. Regulations prohibited female teachers from marrying or having children while they were government employees. Thousands of letters and documents stored in the historical archives of the Secretariat of Public Education are evidence of women's discreet but constant struggles to achieve equality and obtain reproductive rights.[40]

Undoubtedly, Mistral's celibacy reinforced the teacher-mother-saint image of female educators preferred by the state. As recent research has shown, Mexican and Latin American officials misinterpreted Mistral's celibacy by excluding her queer and homosexual identity. The asexual and virginal image that the Mexican state advocated for Mistral was more convenient for the holy crusade of education.

Nonetheless, the Mexican reality—with a peasant school without deep agrarian reform, crusades of ideologized teacher missionaries, Indigenous children unable to read the Bible in Spanish—spilled beyond the myth that Mistral projected in her writings. Furthermore, the virgin teacher was an unsustainable model without legislation that protected labor and reproductive rights. The utopian or mythical images are constructed; but they are also contradicted in travel narratives.

Chapter 6

Antonin Artaud in Mexico

The Economy of Failure

The next three chapters, on Antonin Artaud, the Beat generation, and Roberto Bolaño, return to the topics addressed thus far—the agency of objects, utopia, and impossible domesticity—but with an emphasis on failure, as practice and discourse, in travel writing and literature. Failure permeates travel writing. Perhaps the most outstanding example is Álvar Núñez Cabeza de Vaca's *Naufragios*. For nine years, from 1527 to 1536, after Spanish ships sank and his expeditionary group fell apart, the lost and naked traveler walked from Florida to Texas. During this journey, interpreted by some as a pilgrimage, different Indigenous nations made Álvar Núñez a slave, a merchant, and a healer. Yet his failure was a victory to the extent that his direct contact with Indigenous peoples, from a position of inferiority, led to firsthand knowledge of the nations he visited. Once rendered narration, this knowledge was useful for imperial mapping, surveillance, and exploitation. As one of the most enthralling stories of the conquest and the colonization of the Americas, it also represented economic gain in terms of symbolic goods. The travelers studied in these next three chapters adhere to a similar economy of failure in which material loss yielded symbolic gain.

Artaud did not convince the Mexican authorities to respect peyote use among the Tarahumara. On his return to Europe, he was interned in several psychiatric institutions and died in one. Traumatized by electric shocks, stripped of his possessions and his writings, he continued to write, up to the last day of his life, about his trip to Mexico. In this chapter, I read Artaud's failure in the light of queer theory, drawing on *The Queer Art of Failure* (2011) by Jack Halberstam and *The Promise of Happiness* (2010) by Sara Ahmed. This theoretical approach is also informed by what Pierre Bourdieu calls the "rules of art," in which poets and writers marginalized or expelled from the canon—that is, creators who have "failed" in their particular moments—reproduce the tradition of rupture with the status quo that is expected and sought in the artistic field. They thus become reproducers of a practice that capitalizes on the failure and marginality of the *poète maudit*—expelled, albeit usually only momentarily, from the consecrating circuits of their profession.

Antonin Artaud, Spaces of (Un)happiness

Before his trip to Mexico in 1936, Antonin Artaud wanted nothing more than to come into contact with the elemental life of the cosmos. He had begun to study eastern religions and the cultures of ancient Greece and India three years earlier. With a solid idea of how to reach his goal, he wrote to Jean Paulhan from Paris on July 19, 1935, and discussed his desire to travel to Mexico to help Mexicans return to the civilization that had existed before the arrival of Hernán Cortés. His plan was to explore the magical forces that remained alive but submerged in Indigenous Mexican cultures. These hidden forces persisted in their religious rituals, and an "immediate" rediscovery of culture could bring them to the surface. Culture, he argued, was not in books, paintings, statues, or choreographies; rather, it was in the "nerves and the fluidity of nerves."[1] Unlike André Breton and other French travelers, Artaud entered deep into the Mexico of the Tarahumaras where he would confirm his ideas about the "theater of cruelty" and "theater and its double."

Artaud's ideas reproduced Eurocentric stereotypes of "otherness," which cast Mexico as an idealized, primitive place, the healing destination of pilgrims, but only superficially. Artaud was diagnosed with schizophrenia and interned for several years in psychiatric institutions; his precarious mental state helped feed a metaphorical image of the unconscious Europeans projected upon the "dark" zone of civilization, like "Mexico." Nonetheless, such a reading overlooks the risks he assumed as a traveler. Like a character from Borges, he embraced otherness in order to become it. Like an illuminatus, he risked the disintegration of his identity.[2] Artaud was not only conscious and critical of European ethnocentrism, he was also unhappy in Europe, where he felt like an exile, a man without a country. The failure of his theatrical works had left him, economically and socially, in ruins. In "Mexico and Civilization," one of the talks he gave in Mexico City, he argued that: "The Indian blood of Mexico holds an ancient secret of race, and before that race is lost, the force of this ancient secret must be seized. . . . Mexico today copies Europe and yet, for me, European civilization should seize Mexico's secret. The rationalist culture of Europe has failed, and I have come to the land of Mexico to search for the roots of a magical culture that may still ripped from the Indigenous soil."[3]

In this chapter, I will study Artaud's travel experience in Mexico as represented in *Les Tarahumaras*, published by L'Arbalete in 1955. The book contains essays, letters, and notes Artaud wrote during his trip in 1936 and a decade later. The latter texts are clearly mediated by memory, drugs, and electroshock therapy. Some critics argue that the most "trustworthy" texts, in terms of description of his experiences with the Tarahumaras, were published in the 1930s in Mexico; these texts include "The Peyote Dance," "The Mountain of Signs," the three articles published in Spanish in *El Nacional* ("Le Pays des Rois-Mages," "Une Race-Principe," and "Le Rite des Rois de l'Atlantide"), and the 1937 article in *Voilá*, "La Race des hommes perdus." Nonetheless, what I want to bring to light is Artaud's relationship with the objects of his trip, specifically peyote and the signs of passage, the talismans that he interpreted as "magical" and of a prelinguistic reality, which was the reality that theater needed to liberate.

For Ahmed, the happiness of objects is determined by the social value assigned to them and by proximity: we want to be close to objects we associate with happiness and far from those we reject, objects we do not want to see, hear, taste, and so forth. Objects affect us in intentional and affective fashions: "To be affected 'in a good way' thus involves an orientation toward something as being good. Orientations register the proximity of objects, as well as shape what is proximate to the body. Happiness can be described as *intentional* in the phenomenological sense (directed toward objects), as well as being *affective* (having contact with objects)."[4]

In Artaud's voyage, the intentional and affective relationship with objects from the Tarahumara culture not only motivates the desire to travel; it also shaped the very travel experience, the memory of which remains in even his final writings. Artaud's relationship with magical objects sprang from his notion of theater and its double. The conception was diametrically opposed to anthropology and to the discourse of national modernity. The later texts that Artaud wrote about Mexico in the Rodez mental institution reveal submerged aspects of the psyche that are more critical of conventional discourses, more destabilizing, than the texts that Mexican newspapers published during his trip.

Furthermore, the talks he gave and the essays he published during his trip in the 1930s were mediated by a need to please his sponsors. If they seem more "trustworthy," it is because they aligned with disciplines such as anthropology and artistic trends such as surrealism. Before leaving for Mexico, Artaud had met with the editors of *Paris Soir*, who promised to commission an essay on Mexico and to give him an advance of five or ten thousand francs if he agreed to travel on an official mission. Artaud contacted Jean Paulhan and Jean Marx from the Quai d'Orsay to request credentials to travel on an official French mission, which would also open doors in the Mexican government. He also wrote the French Ministry of Foreign Relations and the Ministry of Education. After three months, his trip was deemed an official mission. Jaime Torres Bodet, then cultural attaché for Mexico in France, worked diligently for Artaud's mission and waved the visa fees for entering Mexico. Torres Bodet also contacted writers and other figures in Mexican cultural circles who could grant Artaud access to national newspapers and conferences.[5]

Theater and Its Gods

In an open letter to the Mexican government published in *El Nacional Revolucionario* during his stay, Artaud argued that the Indigenous sacred rites and dances (which he had yet to encounter but would soon see in his trip to the Tarahumara lands) were the most beautiful forms of theater; indeed, they revealed the living force of the universe. Artaud's obsession was to rediscover theater's relationship with a super-sensorial world, to find communication beyond language, and in his talks on theater, Mexico appears as the place where channels to nature's hidden forces remained open.

His search had begun with the Balinese theater in France, which definitively shaped his vision of theater. The accentuated gestures of the actors, the music, the sounds, the presentation of costumes, objects, and bodies in scenes where linguistic text, as such, was inexistent—these were the elements that opened theater to its most pure form. In Artaud's visions, this theater was a channel for metaphysics, a physical language based on signs instead of words. Artaud's examination of Balinese theater prefigured his concept of theater and its double:

> A kind of terror grips us as we contemplate these mechanized beings, whose joys and sorrows do not really seem to belong to them but rather to obey established rites that were dictated by higher intelligences. In the last analysis, it is certainly this impression of a Life that is higher and prescribed that impresses us most in this spectacle, which is like some rite that one might profane. And it has the solemnity of a sacred rite—the hieratic quality of the costumes gives each actor something like a double body, a double set of limbs—and the actor stiffly encased in his costume seems only the effigy of himself. . . . An impression of inhumanity, of divinity, of miraculous revelation is also created by the exquisite beauty of the women's headdresses.[6]

Derived from the Balinese theater, the idea that theater, as well as its objects and its signs, could connect humanity to pure forces of the cosmos was put to the test and deepened by the Tarahumara peyote ritual in

Mexico. There, Artaud found evidence for his theory on the "theater of cruelty" and "theater and its double." Three years before his trip to Mexico, "theater and its double" had already occupied an important place in Artaud's theory. The first "theater of cruelty" play was "The Conquest of Mexico," written in 1933. In a letter to André Rolland de Renéville dated January 22, 1933, Artaud wrote that the script for *The Conquest of Mexico* revealed his physical conception of theater of cruelty. Here, cruelty was not what "we can practice to each other by cutting up each other's bodies, by sawing away at our personal anatomies," but rather the cruelty of the consciousness that "we are not free. And that the sky can fall on our heads. And that the theater has been created to teach us, first of all, that."[7] For Artaud, theater of cruelty was experienced in the skin, in a sensorial and prelinguistic terrain.

At first glance, *The Conquest of Mexico* does not seem to be a play. It reads like a surrealist poem. But, for Artaud, theater should be pure poetry: "Beneath the poetry of texts there is poetry pure and simple, without form and without text."[8] At a plot level, the piece not only revives the brutality of conquest and colonization; at the same time, it also erodes the notion of European superiority over New World cultures. The play sets Christianity against ancient religions such as that of the Aztecs. But beyond any explicit topics, Artaud sought to rescue the absolute commotion (scream-torment) and the words (sounds) that employed telluric forces to "represent wonder" and metaphysics.[9]

Ideas around "theater and its double" took definitive shape during the transatlantic journey from Europe to Havana, the first stop before arrival in Mexico. In a letter to Jean Paulhan dated January 25, 1938, Artaud wrote from the ship:

> Dear friend: I think I've found the apt title for my book: *Theater and Its Double*. Since theater duplicates life, double life, true theater has nothing to do with Oscar Wilde's ideas about art. That title would respond to all the doubles of theater that I believed to have found so many years ago—metaphysics, the plague, cruelty, the reservoir of energies that Myths constitute—which men no longer embody but which theater does. I understand that double as the grand magical agent of which theater in its forms is but a figuration waiting to become transfiguration. On stage, the union of thought, gesture, and act is reconstituted. And the double of theater is the real, *unutilized* by men of today.[10]

As we have seen in previous chapters, since José Vasconcelos's tenure in the Secretariat of Education, the postrevolutionary Mexican state had been promoting and sponsoring cultural visits and activities. During the administration of Lázaro Cárdenas, foreigners such as exiles from the

Spanish Civil War were granted political asylum in Mexico, as well. Unlike Artaud, the work produced by travelers during this period fit well within the institutions of European and North American art and culture. Here I am referring to Soviet poets and filmmakers such as Vladimir Mayakovsky and Sergei Eisenstein, novelists like D. H. Lawrence, Malcolm Lowry, and Ramón del Valle-Inclán, photographers Tina Modotti and Paul Weston, founders of surrealism like André Bretón, and the Soviet Leon Trotsky. As for contemporary theater, Artaud's vision did not align with contemporary Mexican theater, such as the company of Margarita Xirgu in 1922 and 1936 and before that the company led by the Argentine actress Camila Quiroga in 1922 and 1924.

Although he was representing an official mission, Artaud had little contact with Mexico's most prestigious theater organizations, which included the Teatro de Orientación directed by Celestino Gorostiza, the Teatro de la Universidad directed by Julio Bracho, and the Comedia Mexicana (precursor to the Comedia Nacional de Teatro). Similarly, other figures in dramaturgy such as Salvador Novo, Carlos Díaz Dufóo, and Catalina D'Erzell do not seem to have attracted Artaud's attention. He was looking for the deeper theater of the Tarahumara ritual practices.

Despite his limited interactions with the contemporary world of Mexican theater, Artaud gave three conferences in French at the Simón Bolívar hall, sponsored by the Department of Social Action of the National Autonomous University of Mexico as part of his official mission. The conferences were: "Surrealism and Revolution," on Wednesday, February 26; "Man against Destiny," on Thursday, February 27; and "Theater and the Gods," on Saturday, February 29. Artaud discussed his discrepancies with Marxism, which had led to his separation from surrealism in 1926 and distanced him from the policies of Lázaro Cárdenas. Nonetheless, more than Marxism, his talk criticized the revolutionary government's abandonment of Mexico's deep roots in favor of European modernity:

> You may know that there is an immense phantasmagory in Europe, a sort of collective hallucination around the Mexican Revolution. It is but a step from imagining Mexicans of today wearing the dress of their ancestors, actually carrying out sacrifices to the sun upon the stairs of the pyramid of Teotihuacán. I assure you I say this only slightly in jest. In any case, we have heard of the grand theatrical reconstructions on that same pyramid and have believed that there was in Mexico a well-defined anti-European movement, and that the Mexico of today sought to establish its Revolution upon the return to the pre-Hispanic tradition. In a word, it is believed that the Revolution of Mexico is a revolution of the indigenous soul, a revolution

to conquer the indigenous soul such as it existed before Cortés. The survey for which I was commissioned rested on this point. Well, the revolutionary youth of Mexico do not seem to be to be much concerned with the indigenous soul. And here is where the drama arises. [11]

Artaud refrained from openly criticizing the government, perhaps because he was traveling on an official mission. Furthermore, as we shall see, he hewed closely to anthropological descriptions of the peyote ritual. During these months, he engaged more with children's theater in Mexico, especially the pedagogical-cultural puppet shows that the Cárdenas administration encouraged to expose children to traditional Mexican folklore. The fact that this theater was a vehicle of state ideology was plainly clear to Artaud. Still, he noted that the ideas of the Mexican Revolution were not univocal. What fascinated him was not the unified principals of the state vision, but rather the strength and dynamism of its agents:

> I was honored to be invited by the Department of Fine Arts, directed by Muñoz Cota, to the Congress of Children's Theater as a delegate of the French Revolution. I have seen that the Revolution of Mexico has a soul, a live soul, a demanding soul, which Mexicans themselves are unsure of where it might take them. This is the pathos of the revolutionary movement of Mexico. The young Mexico goes forward, determined to remake the world without hesitation, in order to reconstruct that world, before any transformation. Ask the young revolutionaries of Mexico and no one will respond in same way, but in this chaos of opinions the best proof of the Revolution's dynamism. . . . I have seen as much in this Congress of Children's Theater, which deemed to entrust me with a "conference" on the dynamism of puppet shows.[12]

Artaud and Breton

Although he was traveling under official credentials, one remarkable aspect of Artaud's journey, which distanced him from André Breton and other surrealists who came to Mexico, was his trip to the Tarahumara lands in the mountains of Chihuahua. He traveled under the most precarious conditions, without friends, suffering withdrawals from heroine, and with barely enough money to hire a guide and travel 750 miles north, first on train and then on horseback.

For his part, Breton came to Mexico for a four-month stay as a cultural envoy of the French government. The objective of his trip was to meet with Trotsky, a mission the Mexican Communist Party did not look kindly upon. This is perhaps why some of Breton's talks were canceled due to low turnout. His most outstanding presentation addressed the Buñuel film *Un Chien andalou*. The talk was reviewed favorably by Xavier Villaurrutia, of the "Contemporáneos" group, and less favorably, due to Breton's relationship with Trotsky, by the poet Efraín Huerta. In her study of surrealism in Latin America, Melanie Nicholson notes that Breton's work was already well known in Mexico (Torres Bodet published a muddled review of *Nadja* in the October 1928 issue of *Contemporáneos*). However, surrealism was still not an avant-garde European school that Mexican artists sought to imitate.[13]

Breton's main purpose was to meet with Trotsky, but the surrealist imaginary had already conceived of Mexico as a mythical place, in part thanks to Artaud's earlier visit. Breton's journey was different, though. He met with outstanding artists and visited the monumental Mexico of archaeological sites and museums. Artaud similarly gave talks that were later published in newspapers, but his trip was a spiritual search, an experimentation with peyote in far-away northern Mexico. Artaud viewed surrealism's alliance with politics with scorn. His focus was to discover in Mexico the relationship between dreams, objects, and esoteric beliefs, which had alienated him from European modernity. He returned to France with the memory of an original experience, a memory that was later distorted by mental illness, drugs, and his confinement in psychiatric institutions.

When Breton returned to France, much like Humboldt and other naturalists and ethnographers, he brought several Mexican "treasures" and a series of impressions that reinforced his original fantasies about Mexico. These impressions appear in his essay "Souvenir du Mexique," which nurtured the European surrealist imagination from 1938 on. Published in the May 1939 issue of *Minotaure*, "Souvenir" featured a cover illustration by Diego Rivera and photographs by Manuel Álvarez Bravo. The essay begins with the metaphor of the maguey plant and compares Mexico to the regenerative cycle of life and death: "Red earth, virgin earth impregnated by the most generous blood, a land where the life of man has no price, always as willing as the maguey, before disappearing from the gaze that expresses it, to be consumed in a flower of desire and danger."[14] Breton highlighted a fascination about two aspects of Mexico: the surrealism inherent in Mexican culture and arts and the revolutionary spirit.[15] His comments in an interview with Heliodoro Valle about Mexico as the "surrealist place par excellence" are emblematic.[16] On the revolution, "Souvenir of Mexico" notes: "At least there remains in the world one country where the winds of liberation have not yet fallen. Those winds in 1810, in 1910 irresistibly roared in the voice of all the green organs that emerge from below the tormented sky: one of the first phantoms of Mexico is made of those giant chandelier-type cacti from which a man with a rifle emerges with fire in his eyes."[17]

The objects Breton transported formed part of a cycle of accumulation of art and knowledge about Mexico in the metropole. He returned to Paris with ceramic figures, retablos, masks, Day of the Dead skeletons, photographs by Álvarez Bravo, etchings by José Guadalupe Posada and paintings by Frida Kahlo. Some were shown at the Renou et Colle Gallery in Paris in 1939 in the "Mexique" exhibit. Scholars have examined how cultural and art magazines expressed interest in the non-European cultures of Oceania, Africa, and pre-Columbian Latin America and how artists frequented the Trocadero Ethnographic Museum. James Clifford's study of ethnographic surrealism is crucial to understanding the alliance between ethnography and avant-garde art, the collection of objects (of ethnography and art), and their exhibition in museums. Clifford argues that this alliance changed European ideas about art and man.[18]

Clifford points out that "the accumulation of possessions, the idea that identity is a kind of wealth (of objects, knowledge, memories, experience), is surely not universal." In the West, "collecting has long been a strategy for the deployment of a possessive self, culture, and authenticity."[19] However, what is interesting about the accumulation and exhibition of objects transported by ethnographic surrealist travelers in European museums and galleries is the singular way in which they are decontextualized, juxtaposed, and gathered as collage. Indeed, before 1930, the Trocadero Museum was a "jumble of exotica." Magazines like *Documents* and *Minotaure* asked, "What belongs with what? Should masterpieces of a sculpture be isolated as such or displayed in proximity with cooking pots and ax blades?"[20] The surrealist ethnographers asked similar questions as they composed and decomposed "natural" hierarchies in each culture. Their principles of classification, valorization, and exhibition questioned Western aesthetic values, canons of normalcy, distinctions between high and low culture, as well as the supposed neutrality of ethnographers or artists who valued objects from foreign and domestic cultures. The surrealist ethnographers followed Lautréamont's famous definition of beauty as "the chance encounter of a sewing-machine and an umbrella on a dissecting table."[21]

Breton applied these principles in a review of Frida Kahlo's work and later in the "Mexique" exhibition in Paris. In his review Breton focuses on "What Water Gave Me" (1938), which Kahlo painted during his visit to Mexico.[22] The painting has the characteristics of a destabilizing juxtaposition of hierarchies; water adds to its oneiric symbolism. For Breton, the painting was proof of surrealism's universalism:

What should be my surprise and happiness to discover, on arriving in Mexico, that its art, conceived in complete ignorance of the reasons that have pushed me and my friends to act, is flourishing with the final expressions of surrealism in its plentitude? In the current point of development of Mexican painting—which, since the early nineteenth century, has best managed to escape all foreign influence, the most deeply pregnant with its own resources—I have rediscovered in the other extreme of the world that same spontaneously springing question: What irrational laws do we obey, what subjective signs allow us to move at each instant, what symbols, what myths are powered in such an amalgam of objects, in what plot of evens, what sense should be attributed to the device of the eye that makes us apt to go from visual to visionary power? The painting that Frida Kahlo de Rivera was then completing—What Water Gave Me—unwittingly illustrated the phrase I put in another time into the lips of Nadja: "I am the thought upon the bathtub in the room without mirrors." Frida Kahlo de Rivera's art is a ribbon around a bomb.[23]

The "Mexique" exhibition was founded on the same decontextualizing and de-hierarchical principle. Kahlo interpreted Breton's attitude as neglectful. But the goal of ethnographic surrealism was not to tell a linear or complete story, much less give lessons on art and culture. From this perspective, the collage of retablos, handicrafts, photographs, and paintings make sense. For Frida, what the surrealists exhibited about Mexico was "bullshit," or in her own words, "mamarrachadas."[24] She was expecting an exclusive exhibition of her work, a repeat of the individual show she had had months earlier in New York. For her, "Mexique" displayed a colonializing attitude that threw her art together with everything that was chaotic. Although the exhibit sought to transcend classifications, by labeling all these snapshots as "Mexico," the West's other, it still succumbed to Orientalist exoticism.[25]

Despite Frida's negative impression of the show, she still interacted with such famous painters as Yves Tanguy, Picasso, Kandinsky, and Duchamp. Diego Rivera's autobiography mentions the commotion Frida caused in Paris. Kandinsky, moved by the paintings, hugged her and kissed her on the cheeks and forehead in front of all the attendees. Picasso wrote to Rivera that "Neither Derain nor I or you could paint a head like Frida Kahlo."[26] In her documentation of Kahlo's biography, Elizabeth Fuentes Rojas notes that "Frida caused as much impact with her work as with her physique and semi-precious stones, to the point that her bedazzled hand appeared on the cover of *Vogue* magazine and her Tehuana dress inspired Schiaparelli's Madame Rivera dress."[27] Still, Frida Kahlo's opinion of the surrealists and the Parisian intellectuals in

general remained terrible. In a letter to Nick Murray, her Hungarian-
American lover, she wrote:

> You have no idea how deployable these people are. They make me sick.
> They're so damn "intellectual" and fucked up I can't bear them anymore.
> It is truly too much for my character. I'd rather sit on the floor of the To-
> luca market and sell tortillas than have to deal with these "artistic" bitch-
> es of Paris. They sit for hours in the "cafes" warming their precious asses
> and speaking nonstop about "culture," "art," "revolution," and this and that,
> thinking they are gods of the world. I've never seen Diego or you wasting
> time on stupid gossip and "intellectualism" which is why you are truly *men*
> and not filthy "artists." Fuck! It was worth the trip just to see why Europe is
> rotting. Because all these people, good for nothing, are the cause of all the
> Hitlers and Mussolinis. I'd bet my life that I will always hate this place and
> its people as long as I live. There is something so false and unreal in them
> that drives me crazy.[28]

Frida's association of Parisian intellectualism with a supposed lack
of virility and the rise of fascism and Nazism is striking. Her trip oc-
curred in the context of imminent war. The vision of a decrepit Europe
in the interwar period was strong in the Americas, where works such
as *The Decline of the West* by Oswald Spengler (1918–1923) were widely
read. The exile of Spaniards in Mexico during the Spanish Civil War
further confirmed the notion that Europe was no longer the model to
follow.[29]

Breton's relationship with Kahlo and Artaud's relationship with
María Izquierdo prompt reflection on how the two surrealist intellectuals wielded colonial masculinity. Mexican women served, as they have
so often, to projected visions of primitivism that could justify white,
male, and European superiority. Breton projected onto Frida the ideals
of surrealism, arguing that she had developed a surrealist aesthetic in
isolation, without knowledge or influence from Europe. He therefore
concluded that surrealism was universal, that Europe had discovered a
true art form. Artaud rejected all European influence in María Izquierdo's art; he believed that Mexican art needed to liberate itself from European "contamination and become purely "Indian." Yet, Artaud avoided
discussing surrealism in Izquierdo's art; unlike Breton, he did not need
to legitimize surrealism's universal status. For Artaud, Izquierdo's art
needed to preserve the authenticity that would return art to its origins,
to the connection with nature and primitive gods—something that surrealism lacked. This art, the art of Mexico, would regenerate humanity.
In "The Painting of María Izquierdo," Artaud writes:

I have come to Mexico looking for indigenous art, not imitations of European art. And well, imitations of European art, in all its forms, abound; truly Mexican art is not to be found. Only the paintings of María emanate truly Indian inspiration. That is, amid the hybrid manifestations of contemporary painting in Mexico, the sincere, spontaneous, primitive, disquieting painting of María Izquierdo had been for me a revelation. Nonetheless, I hasten to clarify: this painting is spontaneous, but not pure: here and there, in certain works, direct influence from European modern art can be found. This is the danger: it could be said that, the more that María Izquierdo's art evolves, the more it will be influenced by the modern techniques of Europe and, in certain canvases, even by the spirit. This is all the more lamentable . . . but the spirit of the Indian race speaks so strongly in her that even unconsciously she repeats its voice.[30]

Behind the naked virgins weeping at the crucifix in Izquierdo's paintings, Artaud found an amalgam of contemporary Mexican civilization: a pagan Catholicism that fused the Latin cross of Christ with the ancient geometrical palaces of Uxmal, Mitla, Palenque, or Copán. When he spoke about María Izquierdo, Artaud was not speaking about surrealism, but he did speak of dreams and the capacity to perceive objects oneirically. In his view, the only possible way to know objects was to overcome the state of consciousness that separated men from things and arrive at a state of complete unity with the object. This type of art granted access to the relationship between dreams and objects:

If it is through objects that the Senses are known, then it is through dreams that objects are known. In a waken state, all that exists is dead; and objects do not discover their shape. Sleep is needed for them to begin to speak. If there was a time in which things spoke without being asked to, then only a man of the current era will believe that such a time pertains to the past. . . . But he who says unity says knowledge, for to "know" is to "resurge with"; and in dreams, the shapes of moving things have, together with their own unique properties, the properties of all the other objects. For objects do not form what is real, but they are in what is real, traveling; and in dreams, it is the properties of the objects that travel; and, transmitting their force to one another, they show us the entirely of reality.[31]

Only in dreams was it possible to approach things in their unity and totality. This was the "primitive spirit" that tore down the barriers that separated the consciousness of objects: "If everything is in everything, only the primitive spirit has allowed human consciousness to enter into the variety of objects via the metamorphosis of an object."[32] In this sense, Artaud repeated the same ethnographic surrealist question studied in

Breton and in publications like *Documents* and *Minotaure*: What principles of classification unify objects and establish their relationships?
For him, nonrational, nonhierarchical criteria communicate magically
through dreams, in the authentic "primitive" thought, which leads to the
extreme axiom of "the chance encounter of a sewing-machine and an
umbrella on a dissecting table."

Although Artaud urged her to maintain an air "uncontaminated" by
European influences, Izquierdo combined surrealist and Mexican aesthetics throughout her career. Her family had Indigenous heritage, but,
like Frida Kahlo, she grew up in a middle class, traditional Mexican
criolla milieu.[33] Her education at the National Academy of Arts (where
Diego Rivera recognized her in 1928 as the only student with any special
talent) is a testament to her connection to social circuits that were hardly marginalized from modern influences. The essentialism that Artaud
projected on to María Izquierdo is clearly problematic and ethnocentric,
even if its motivations differed from those that generated Breton's admiration of Kahlo.

Just as Breton did with Kahlo, Artaud took to Paris some thirty of
Izquierdo's paintings to be exhibited in the Galerie Van den Berg in
Montparnasse in early 1937. Most of these works have since disappeared.
What happened to them is unknown. Some may have been confiscated
and destroyed after Artaud was institutionalized in 1937; they may also
have been destroyed in World War II, or seized in private collections.
There is no remaining copy of the show's catalogue, but judging from
Artaud's opinions on Izquierdo, it is very plausible that her work was
exoticized with essentialist visions of "Mexican otherness." According
to the artist's daughter, Izquierdo donated her paintings to Artaud so
that her work would become known in Europe. But she also wanted to
contribute to his medical treatment and detoxification.[34]

Artaud's friendship with Izquierdo reveals Izquierdo's independence
from official circles of Mexican art and the group of famous muralists
(Rivera, Siqueiros y Orozco). Breton did not meet Izquierdo during his
visit, for example. Years later, in 1945, the Ministry of Culture cancelled
her commission to paint a mural in the Zócalo, the city's central plaza,
after the muralists threatened a boycott. Despite the international recognition Izquierdo received in exhibitions in Paris, New York, Lima, and
elsewhere, the muralists jealously objected that a woman without mural
experience should be in charge of a mural in the Federal District government building, one of the sites most prized by the most famous painters.
Only Diego Rivera had been commissioned to paint in the buildings
along the Zócalo. As Nancy Deffebach remarks in "What Sex Is the
City: Izquierdo's Aborted Mural Project," had the project gone forward,

María Izquierdo would have provided a different gender perspective of the construction of postrevolutionary Mexico, for her work diverged from the vision of the central masculine hero in Rivera's work.[35]

Artaud's Writings on the Land of the Tarahumaras

During his trip, and for more than twelve years after, Artaud published several articles about his experience in the land of the Tarahumaras. The first, "Voyage of the Land of the Tarahumaras," appeared in *El Nacional Revolucionario* in Mexico City in October 1936, soon after Artaud's return from Chihuahua. The first section of the essay is titled "The Mountain of the Signs" and the second, "The Peyote Dance."[36] Many of Artaud's articles on the Tarahumaras were published in important French magazines like *La Nouvelle Revue Française*. The first of these, "The Mountain of the Signs" appeared in 1937; he wrote the last, a poetic piece titled "Tuguri," in the Ivry-sur-Seine clinic two weeks before his death.

Artaud's trip was existential and mythical, but the only way to pay for it was by publishing his travel notes and ethnographic observations. It is often overlooked that travelers who wrote about their trips subsisted on payments from publications. The accumulation of knowledge in the metropolis (Latour) does not only come from the transfer of objects from the periphery to the metropolis, where they are exhibited and studied in centers of calculation, but also from transformation and reduction of scale that renders such objects mobile, stable, and susceptible to transfer and accumulation. Narratives and their publication make objects mobile and travel experiences transferable in paper form. This is why Artaud's narratives were published first in Mexico City and then in Paris.

After the original appearance of "The Mountain of the Signs" in *El Nacional Revolucionario*, it was reproduced in the August 1, 1937, issue of *La Nouvelle Revue Française*, together with "The Peyote Dance," under the title of "A Voyage to the Land of the Tarahumara." In "The Mountain of the Signs," the first of his published texts on the Tarahumaras, Artaud addressed "the geographic extension of a race."[37] For Artaud, the culture-nature separation was irrelevant in the Tarahumara world. He noticed repeating signs in the mountains—boulders that projected the same shadow of an animal head devouring itself, rocks in the shape of a woman's breast, the phallic symbol of three stones on the tip of a boulder, four holes upon its exterior face. Artaud acknowledged that someone might object that these were merely natural shapes; however, he rejected that this "repetition" was random. "And what is even less natural, is that the Tarahumara repeat the same forms of their land in their rituals and dances: These dances were not born randomly; they respond to the same secret mathematics, the same intention of the subtle game of numbers to which the whole sierra responds."[38] This "secret mathematics" was the principle of the kabbalah, which Artaud described as the "music of numbers" that reduced the material chaos to explained and ordered principles in the "type of grandiose mathematics": "Science also gives numbers: 2,5,3,4,7,12, when it explains the rhythm by which atoms order themselves to form bodies."[39]

For Artaud, the physical constitution of the world of the Tarahumaras reflects this mysterious rhythm of numbers. In the journey through the mountain, he sees crosses, triangles in dual beings that face each other. Artaud then recalled that the Knights of the Round Table, the Rosy Cross of the mystical route of the Holy Grail, had used similar symbolism disguised as science. Artaud thus connected his previous readings and collected knowledge to the experience in the land of the Tarahumaras. Although esoteric, his discourse did not, at that time, arise from clinical dementia or mental illness. Something similar happens with his knowledge of European painting. In his second essay, "The Land of the Wisemen," Artaud remarks, "Where have I said that it is not in Italy, but in Mexico, when the painters before the Renaissance have taken the blue of their landscapes and the profound perspectives with which they decorate their Nativities."[40] For Artaud, the pre-Renaissance painters were also initiated into a secret science and were not moved only by religious spirit. The nativity paintings by Piero della Francesca, the Luca de Leyde, the Fra Angelico, and Piero di Cosimo also manifested a preoccupation with the essential, with the "primitive explosions" of nature. He continues: "In the Tarahumara mountain, everything speaks of the essential; that is, of the principles according to which nature was formed: man, the storms, the wind, the silences, the sun."[41]

"The Rite of the Kings of Atlantis" can be read in the same light. There, Artaud refers to the study of the movement of the sun and its scientific veneration represented in the mathematically oriented pyramids and altars among civilizations that, like the Maya, had deep understandings of astronomy:

> Once one realizes that the astronomical tribute to the Sun has been universally revealed by means of signs, and that these signs are the same ones that belong to an ancient, perfect science, that the absurd European language has named universal esotericism; and once these same signs—the handle-cross, the swastika, the double cross, the great circle with a point in the middle, and the twelve zodiac signs—abound in the Orient, as they do in Mexico, in temples and manuscripts that I have never seen in nature like I have in the Tarahumara Mountain; once one knows all this and enters, suddenly, in

a country that is literally filled with these kinds of signs; and once one finds it in the gestures and rites of a race; and once the men, the women and the children of this race carry them embroidered on their blankets, the spirit feels disturbed, as if had reached the source of a mystery.[42]

In this account, Artaud claims to have seen, at the bottom of the Sierra Tarahumara, the ritual of the kings of Atlantis as described by Plato in *Criticism*. Plato describes the people of Atlantis as a race of magical origin. The Tarahumaras, whom Artaud considered to be their direct descendants, continued to practice the magical rites.[43] Like the kings of Atlantis, the Tarahumaras gathered at sundown before a sacrificed bull, which they cut into pieces and left only the head of as the sun set. Inebriated from the blood they drank from large jars, they sang a somber melody. Regarding the specific Tarahumara rite, Artaud references the dance of the "matachines," which the Tarahumaras performed with flowers, accompanied by violin, guitar, drums, bells, and iron staffs. According to Artaud, it was a Spanish dance adapted by the Tarahumaras.

The Peyote Dance

Artaud describes his twenty-eight days in the Sierra Tarahumara as an experience of willful desperation. Although weakened in mind and body, he persisted in his search for revelation and healing:

> It required, of course, an act of the will for me to believe that something was going to happen. And all this, for what? For a dance, for a rite of lost Indians who no longer even know who they are or where they come from and who, when you question them, answer with tales whose connection and secret they have lost.

> And after twenty-eight days of waiting, I now had to endure, throughout one long week, an incredible comedy. All over the mountain there was a hysterical coming and going of messengers who were presumably being sent to the sorcerers. But after the messengers had left, the sorcerers would arrive in person, amazed that nothing was ready. And I discovered that I had been tricked.[44]

Artaud found several obstacles. According to him, as a white man, the spirits had abandoned him. Further, the Tarahumaras did not have enough *tesgüino*, the alcohol they drank to prepare for the rituals. Another obstacle was the local charlatans who passed themselves off as true shamans to foreigners. All this delayed Artaud's arrival to the peyote ritual. When the ritual was finally at hand, Artaud describes the preparation of the circle, the crosses, the fire, the dancer who enters and exits the

circle as though deliberately advancing upon evil: "He immerses himself
in it with a kind of terrible courage, in a rhythm which above the Dance
seems to depict the Illness."[45] He noted that no other man dared to enter
the circle. Birds who strayed into the circle would fall dead, the fetuses
of pregnant women would rot. Artaud counted the *ten* crosses in the
circle and the *ten* mirrors, the *three* sorcerers upon a wooden beam, the
four priests ("two *Males* and two *Females*"), the dancer, and himself, the
European for whom the rite was executed. Peyote root was placed in a
hole at the feet of each sorcerer. Artaud describes the roots as "hermaph-
rodites" since they represent the male and female in Nature ("peyote has
the shape of man and woman copulating"). In the hole, on a wooden
bucket or dirt dumped upon the hole, which resembles the globe, the
sorcerers "grate the mixture or the dislocation of the two principles, and
they grate them in the Abstract, that is, in the Principle. Whereas below, these two Principles, incarnated, repose the Matter, that is, in the
Concrete."[46] With triangular gestures that strangely cut perspectives in
the air, the sorcerers reestablished the lost relationship with the cosmos. During the ritual, the priests urinated, farted, and defecated with
great roars. To prepare, they spent three years in the mountain and then
carefully guarded the secrets they learned. These priests, like actors in
a theatrical piece, were the vehicles that connected the hidden forces in
"theater and its double."

Artaud experienced the peyote ritual as an initiation, similar to the
crucifixion, in which he must suffer and die in order to resuscitate in a
new life:

> On the ground, so that the rite would fall on me, so that the fire, the chants,
> the cries, the dance, and the night itself, like a living, human vault, would
> turn over me. There was this rolling vault, this physical arrangement of cries,
> tones, steps, chants. But above everything, beyond everything, the impres-
> sion that kept recurring that behind all this, greater than all this and beyond
> it, there was concealed something else: The Principal.
>
> I did not renounce as a group those dangerous dissociations which Pey-
> ote seems to provoke and which I had pursued for twenty years by other
> means; I did not mount my horse with a body pulled out of itself, which
> the withdrawal, to which I had abandoned myself, deprived henceforth of
> its essential reflexes; I was not that man of stone whom it required two men
> to turn into a man on horseback: and who was mounted on and dismount-
> ed from the horse like a broken robot—and once I was on the horse, they
> placed my hands on the reins, and they also had to close my fingers around
> the reins, for left to myself it was only too clear that I had lost the use of
> them; I had not conquered by force of mind that invincible organic hostility

in which it was *I* who no outworn imageries from which the Age, true to its own system, would at most derive ideas from advertisements and models for clothing designers. It was now necessary that what lay hidden behind this heavy grinding which reduces dawn to darkness, that this thing be pulled out, and it *serve*, that it serve precisely by my *crucifixion*.

To this I knew that my physical destiny was irrevocably bound. I was ready for all the burns, and I awaited the first fruits of the fire in view of a conflagration that would soon be generalized.[47]

In his studies of peyote, anthropologist Carlo Bonfiglioli attempts the ritual in ways that confirm and expand Artaud's description. Bonfiglioli acknowledges the Norwegian researcher Carl Lumholz, the prominent anthropologist whose 1902 essay "Unknown Mexico" was the first to address the subject and bring the peyote dance ritual to the attention of the international scientific community. Bonfiglioli also follows the work of Merrill and Guillén and Martínez on the concept of the soul and illness that can be treated with *jíkuri* (jíkuri, or peyote, is ciguri in Artaud's writings). Similar beliefs exist in northern Mexico and throughout Mesoamerica:

1. All human bodies are governed by a certain number of souls, big and small, that guarantee psycho-physical wellbeing.

2. A part of a person's souls, or of the souls' components, leave the body briefly, for example, during sleep, drunkenness, or sex, but returns to its place; but if it fails to return, the body becomes sick. Prolonged absence can lead to death.

3. Failure to return can be attributed to beings who work against people, such as sorcerers (*sukurúame*), certain plants or animals, swirls of wind, the dead, a type of stone known as *sukiki*, and other less important beings.[48]

When this happens, one must secure the return of souls through a ritual healing, *la raspa* or "the scraping," in order to repair the damage inflected and restore the state of the soul. Another aspect noted by both Artaud and Bonfiglioli is the importance of numbers (especially three and four) in the gender and the souls that govern bodies. In Tehuerichi and other Tarahumara communities, it is commonly said that "a man is worth three and a woman is worth four," that is, men have three souls and women have one more because they procreate.

The anthropologist also notes that the Tarahumaras believe that the universe has seven stories—three above, three below, and one, the earth, in between. The numerical agreement between the stories and the total values attributed to men and women is too important to be coincidental. Bonfiglioli argues that it should be considered an expression of the structural unity between certain characteristics of the body and of the cosmos. For Bonfiglioli, the three levels of the daytime sky are associated with God (the sun) and with masculine power. The three stories beneath earth are associated, in the mentality of an agricultural people, with the feminine virtues of procreation, the earth and the mother. It is important to recall that, in the ritual, the shaman ascends and descends with a staged or spiraled instrument. The scraping thus unites the world above with the world below, that is, the seven levels of the cosmos.

For Artaud, peyote united the feminine and masculine sexual organs. Artaud describes the movement of the scraping because the healing depends on the reestablishment of harmony and unity of the cosmos: "the tool is more than a musical instrument: it is a cosmic stairway—that is, a road ascending and descending—whose steps would be depicted as notches. . . . When the sipáwame rubs the sticks—an action that is accompanied by song—what is activated is the traffic of divine influences between heaven and earth, expressed by movement and sound." [49] The healing of the sick consists of restoring the unity between the body and the cosmos through the shaman's movement. Bonfiglioli, following Levi-Strauss, discusses the symbolic cause of peyote's healing powers; in the ritual, the shaman reconstructs the causes of the problem "through a retroactive trip into the problem." The sick person becomes conscious of conflicts and, via the shaman's mouth, accepts them just as he believes in the result of the shaman's victorious struggle. In this act of belief, it is highly important that the other members of the community also believe.[50] Artaud submits himself to belief in the ritual to heal himself.

The ritual described by Artaud in 1936 is, as we have seen, very similar to that described by Bonfiglioli, who, in turn, follows the classic study by Lumholtz, Artaud's predecessor.[51] Artaud's "Peyote Dance" is an introspective text of the experience of the ritual, but it is also a descriptive text that coincides with descriptions by anthropologists who studied the subject. Nonetheless, the texts written in Paris in the 1940s, more than a decade after his trip to Mexico, reflect the fluctuations of an unbalanced psyche. Artaud wrote these texts in different hospitals where he was confined without adequate food, subjected to shock treatment, and without his notes or earlier writings, which had been confiscated by hospital authorities. The passage of time, added to his mental instability, reveals different aspects of the trip to the land of the Tarahumaras as it was presented in the texts of the 1930s.

Written in 1943 in the Rodez psychiatric hospital and according to the confessions of Dr. Gaston Ferdière, "The Peyote Rite" discusses an annual ritual carried out by the Tarahumaras that is entirely different from the healing ritual described in the 1937 "Peyote Dance." Artaud describes a ritual without any ill persons, only the priest and his assistants, a man and a woman who are ordered to copulate by the priest after ingesting peyote. Artaud wrote that it was during this ritual, not in the healing ceremony described in "Peyote Dance," that he tried peyote and discussed its effects.

With some pain, Artaud narrated the distrust that the priest had, not in peyote as a divine force that brought man closer to the Truth, but rather in himself, the priest, as an effective intermediary between peyote and the men of the community. Artaud noted the Tarahumaras' progressive distance from peyote as a result, largely, of the role of the state and the extension of national schools that aimed to eradicate cultures considered to be obstacles to the advancement of Mexican modernity: "The Mexican government does the impossible to take the peyote away from the Tarahumaras and prevent them from surrendering themselves to its effect, and the mission of the soldiers sent to the mountain is to prevent its cultivation. At the moment I reached the mountain, I found the Tarahumaras desperate due to the recent destruction of a peyote field by Mexican soldiers."[52]

Why did Artaud not discuss how the state and the schools threatened Tarahumara rituals in the articles he published in the 1930s? The most plausible hypothesis is that the Mexican government would not have looked fondly on such criticism from a traveler on an official mission. At other times, though, Artaud criticized the Mexico government's clearly Westernizing *mestizaje* and advocated for a return to pre-Hispanic cultures. The government had prohibited the peyote ritual since it was seen as a barrier to the Tarahumaras' integration into the nation. Artaud met with a schoolteacher in the sierra who insisted that "when they take peyote, they disobey us."[53] In the abovementioned essay, Artaud volunteered to act as an intermediary. He tried to convince the teacher and the authorities to allow the annual peyote ritual: "What would you do if you were facing a war involving the return of Mexico to Native Indian culture, if by taking action you would be provoking a civil war? Meanwhile, and from that point on, it would be necessary to authorize this celebration if you wanted the Tarahumaras to be faithful, and it would be necessary to give the tribes the ability to gather together in order for them to have a favorable impression of you."[54]

In *The Peyote Effect*, Alexander Dawson notes that peyote causes disobedience and indiscipline. Unlike recreational drugs that nullify the agency of the subject, the effects of peyote are empowering.[55] Artaud, recognizing the importance that peyote had for Indigenous peoples, advocated for its use with their communities. For Dawson, who did not study Artaud, this would be a type of racialization of peyote, aligned

with the functionalist or relativist anthropology of Franz Boas, Bron-
islaw Malinowski, and A. E. Radcliffe-Brown, who held that cultures
had their own inner workings.[56] For Artaud, peyote was constitutive of
the inner workings of the Tarahumara culture.

"The Peyote Rite" is a palimpsest. On the one hand, it seems to belie
his earlier texts such as "The Peyote Dance" where Artaud hewed closely
to established anthropology. In a later postscript, he declared that he
had written "The Peyote Rite" a year after being interned in the Rodez
hospital where he was isolated after being confined for seven years in
other psychiatric institutions and subjected to systematic and daily poi-
soning. Although the postscript represents his first reattempt at healing,
it is a confusing text. He notes that "The Peyote Rite" was written in
the "stupid" mental state of convert whom the "sorcery of cheap priests
[*clerigalla*], taking advantage of momentary weakness, maintained in a
state of servitude."[57] He later repudiated the many religious, especially
Christian, referenced in a letter to his new editor, Henri Parisot. In this
same line, another essay, "And Is in Mexico," discusses how witchcraft
had marked his life for the worse: every time he spoke of witchcraft, his
doctor applied shock treatment; he insisted that his psychiatrist Ferdière
was under a spell; and the Indigenous tried to keep him from the Sierra
Tarahumaras through witchcraft and masturbation.

The Lost Amulet

With his trip to the land of the Tarahumaras, Artaud attempted to experience, in his very body, ideas about theater and its double—theater
that, through objects and nonlinguistic signs, could recreate and connect humanity to the submerged spiritual forces united in reality, his
metaphysics. The narration of his experience with the peyote dance in
the 1930s seems to have confirmed his theories. The Tarahumara priests,
like actors, were channels who connected reality and the spirits. For Artaud, the practice had remained untouched by Western influence and
therein lay its healing powers. Nonetheless, a decade later, when Artaud
no longer discussed theater and his theories, he continued to talk about
his experiences in Mexico. The trip and its narration were, for Artaud, a
lifesaver to which he clung in an effort to maintain his sanity. Stripped of
his personal possessions, his manuscripts, his mental health, what kept
him afloat was the memory of his trip to Mexico.

This memory is epitomized in the nostalgia for a magical object that
marked his journey from the beginning and that was confiscated by
hospital authorities. Before setting foot in Veracruz, during a layover in
Havana on January 30, Artaud attended a Vodun ritual. In *Les Nouvelles
Révélations de l'être* (1937), Artaud describes a fetish, a prophetic object

with magic powers, he received from an Afro-Cuban shaman: the sword of the missionaries with three hooks and seven rope loops. In a letter from Rodez, dated December 10, 1943, Artaud wrote to Henri Parisot:

> It happens that from September 1937 to the present date, I have been arrested, imprisoned in Dublin, deported to France, interned in Le Havre, transferred from Le Havre to Rouen, from Rouen to Sainte-Anne in Paris, from Sainte-Anne to Ville -Evrard, from Ville-Evrard to Chezal-Benoit and from Chezal-Benoit to Rodez. All my belongings were seized by the police and all my papers were lost. I have absolutely nothing I had: a certain number of manuscripts, a portfolio and, above all, a 12 cm high sprat of Toledo, tied with three hooks and given to me by a black from Cuba.[58]

Artaud recalled the fetish in one of his final writings as one of the objects ripped from him by doctors and nurses in the asylums where he was interned after his trip. The fetish appears inextricably associated with the space and his experience with the Tarahumaras, as an obsession and a sign of loss, but also as hope for healing, much like the peyote ritual and its narration. In this sense, what was considered a fetish becomes a good luck amulet. The recurrence of Artaud's Mexico trip thus transcends experience as an unfinished and insufficient story that is unable to impose discipline on the object or the subject of the narrative. The objects resist domesticity.

Chapter 7

The Beats in Mexico

Vagabond Poets William Burroughs and Jack Kerouac

The frontier favors poetic experimentation. Poets and writers have long journeyed to liminal zones, far from the metropolis with its literary institutions and political regulations. We need only recall Arthur Rimbaud's trip to Africa. This sort of "orientalism" or exoticization of geographic frontiers as mythical spots of creation and experimentation, joined with adventure narratives, sheds light on the Beat generation's experience in Mexico. My purpose here is to read the journey to Mexico (and elsewhere in Latin America) as a journey of youth, of non-heteronormative masculinities, of vagabond poets in conflict with their origins, their oikos. These poets did not adhere to the happiness that flows from success or to domestic bliss.[1] For the Beats, the oikos is defined furthermore amid the promise of vanquishing US superiority in World War II. I propose therefore to problematize the traveler's "imperial gaze," which assumes an asymmetrical power relationship between the traveler-observer and the people and places observed. One acceptation of the name "Beat"— hit, mistreated—forces us to rethink the dimensions of power wielded by these travelers within and beyond the United States. In the discursive plane, the definition of the Beat generation was disputed within the American mainstream, which expressed incomprehension and rejection. In 1959, two years after the publication of *On the Road* by Jack Kerouac, John Clellon Holmes wrote to Allen Ginsberg that:

American College Dictionary sent me their big square definition of the "Beat generation," and wanted to know if I would revise, emend or make a new one. Theirs was awful, "certain members of the generation that came after World War II who affect detachment from moral and social forms and responsibilities, supposedly due to disillusionment. Coined by Jack Kerouac." So, I sent in this: "Beat generation, members of the generation that came of age after World War II–Korean War who join in a relaxation of social and sexual tensions and espouse anti-regimentations, mystic-disaffiliation and material-simplicity values, supposedly as a result of Cold War disillusionment. Coined by JK.[2]

In his social-constructionist theory of space Rob Shields emphasizes the significance of liminal or marginal spaces and the imaginary geography of space.[3] Such an imaginary geography becomes independent from the social practices that constitute it and configures a repertoire of images and mythical narratives that influence the reception and perception of a given space, beyond and despite any experiential registry of such places, or rather, an imaginary around the space that shapes how it is experienced. In this discursive production around space, these places are defined in opposition to other places in a symbolic system in which they form part of binaries such as nature-civilization, center-periphery, social order-carnivalesque space. An emotive order and codified geography—half topology and half metaphor—are inscribed in them. My reading of the Beat generation in Mexico operates according to the logic described by Shields, with an imagined US-Mexico binary, in which travelers define each term by opposition. In this sense, it is useful to recall this binary as an economic relationship, in which the home or point of departure defines and evaluates the travel experiences. As Georges Van Den Abbeele explains in *Travel as Metaphor,* "The economy of travel requires an *oikos* (the Greek for 'home' from which is derived 'economy') in relation to which any wandering can be *comprehended* (enclosed as well as understood)."[4]

Nonetheless, in my reading, the objects—mostly drugs—with which travelers interact during their journey, and the sexual encounters they experience, impose an excess on this economy of the oikos by resisting classification and domestication. The Beats' fragmented, sensorial, flow of consciousness writing allows the incommensurability of cultural encounters to seep through this porousness. Many members of the Beat generation passed through Mexico. Burroughs settled in Mexico City first with his wife Joan Vollmer after failing to grow marijuana on a California farm. Soon, his friends from the group visited him, among them Jack Kerouac and Allen Ginsberg. Later, when Burroughs lived between Africa and Europe, Neal Cassady, Ken Kesey, Gregory Corso, Ray Brenser, and his wife Bonnie arrived in Mexico. Bonnie's book *Troia: Mexican Memoirs* narrates the couple's tragic adventures in Mexico, where she had to prostitute herself to maintain her husband and daughter. Toward the end, Ray is deported for drug possession and their daughter is given up for adoption.[5] Mexico meant a suspension of social rules for the Beats, but the less-regulated access to drugs, sacred hallucinogens, and non-heteronormative relationships also constituted a place of tragedy.

To understand the existential and literary posture of the Beats and their relationship with Mexico, it is necessary to contrast it with the environment in which it emerged and which it opposed: post–WWII American politics and society. In *The Typewriter Is Holy: The Complete, Uncensored History of the Beat Generation,*[6] Bill Morgan argues that the Beats questioned the foundation of traditional American society by proposing a lifestyle based on individual freedom, freedom of expression, sexual freedom, and the right to use and experiment with drugs. Some took the lifestyle to its ultimate consequences. The Beats thus opened the way to the countercultural movements of the 1960s and '70s.

The Beats repeatedly had to face the legacy of McCarthyism in literary censorship. On June 3, 1957, the San Francisco police arrested Lawrence Ferlinghetti, owner of City Lights bookstore and publishing house, for publishing *Howl and Other Poems* by Allen Ginsberg. The press covered the book's censorship and the attack on civil liberties. The courts ruled in favor of Ferlinghetti, setting an important precedent for the freedom of the press. Shortly after, Grove Press was able to publish *Lady Chatterley's Lover* by D. H. Lawrence, *The Tropic of Cancer* by Henry Miller, and other works.

Political hostility, together with literary and social censorship, shaped the Beat generation. Years before the Ferlinghetti trial, Burroughs traveled to Mexico to escape arrest for different reasons. From the beginning, the Beats were associated with crime and murder. Although they did not call themselves Beats yet, the first members of the group, who lived in Joan Vollmer's cheap apartment near Columbia in New York, witnessed the murder of one of their own, David Kammerer, by another member of the group, Lucien Carr. These young writers formed close friendships with ex-convicts, such as Neal Cassady, drug dealers, and all kinds of petty delinquents. There was a fascination for life in legal marginality, where writing and transgression coexisted as allies. Drugs and weapons led to the arrest and trial of Burroughs in New Orleans and his legal instability led him to seek new destinations—Mexico being the first. Around 1949, William Burroughs emigrated to Mexico City as a fugitive with his wife Joan Vollmer and their two children. As is well known, it was in Mexico where Burroughs shot Vollner's face in a William Tell game while both were under the effects of narcotics. Burroughs began to write his novel *Junkie* in Mexico City.

It is important to understand the Beats' trip to Mexico in the context of the Cold War and the cultural changes related to post–WWII

American triumphalism and its promises of happiness. Such changes included technology and its effects on the arms race and multiple other social dimensions, the consolidation of the United States as a rich and powerful country, the forging of political scientists, and high degrees of professionalization among the middle classes. The Beats were a product of this society, against which youth were rebelling in the 1950s (with the Beats) and more radically so in the 1960s with the hippies, the Black Panthers, and other civil rights movements. In *Cold War American Literature and the Rise of Youth Culture*, Denis Jonnes argues that one cause of this rebelliousness was the strong humanities foundation in university education that did not correspond to the demands of a technological society. As a result, professionals ill-equipped for the new labor demands became unhappy critics.[7]

Jonnes studies the deep internal contradictions in American society that led to a radical youth culture such as that of the Beats. Youth who rebelled against a constantly expanding militarized society, a powerful government, and a bureaucratic and corporate educational system took to heart the ideals—such as freedom—that had led the United States to fight fascism and Nazism. On January 6, 1941, Franklin Delano Roosevelt had clearly articulated the principles of liberty in his "Four Freedoms" speech. Two of these fundamental freedoms were the freedom of expression and religion, which derived directly from the American Bill of Rights. Both freedoms were conceived as universal rights that went beyond the United States. The American "mission" was to guarantee them anywhere on the planet. Roosevelt gave this speech only a few years before his successor, Harry Truman, approved the use of atomic bombs on Hiroshima and Nagasaki. Jonnes points out that 70 percent of the American population approved of the making of the atomic bomb.[8] The United States thus reaffirmed its power in global polices, not merely in the economy of Western Europe, but also in the occupation of the Philippines, Japan, and its control of the Pacific Ocean and the Mediterranean Sea. Freedom was imposed with repression and violence within and beyond the United States.

Although much of the American society believed that the atomic bomb was necessary to protect the "American way of life" and the safety of Americans, the government failed to inculcate the same belief among the youth. Government publications such as the *United States Civil Defense* emphasized in 1950 the role of the American family in war: "Every person and every community has a part to play in the civil defense program."[9] Also in 1950, Richard Gerstell's book *How to Survive an Atomic Bomb*, written and published with support from the secretary of defense, suggested that "everyone in the family ought to have special jobs to do in case of attack."[10] Young people, perceived as potential sources of dissidence and a threat to the protection of the nation, were seen as "outsiders" in this family and social model.

Not everyone happily assimilated the ideology of the arms race and the economy that sustained it. Under the Soviet threat during the Cold War, the American government increasingly repressed individual liberties in and beyond the United States, liberties that it proclaimed at the same time as a mission. But there was more. The youth of the post–WWII power enjoyed what their parents only had seen in their later years: a world of infinite possibilities that sprang from the economic superiority, however contradicted and hijacked by the government's need to neutralize and destroy any suggestion of difference. American youth knew about and wanted everything, but they could do little. According to Jonnes, an increasingly wide gap grew between young people and the mainstream of American society: "Having been raised in the heady, affluent, America-can-do-it-all atmosphere of the early Cold War, growing number of America's youth would be determined to realize the promise of freedom—for themselves and for their peers—the US had championed around the world."[11]

In the apocalyptic environment of the Cold War, produced by the fear of the atomic bomb, the strength of religion and spirituality grew in American culture. After WWII, amid an unprecedented economic boom, religion unified the country against the "Godless" Communist community. Religion revived the myth of American exceptionalism: "Never before had so many Americans belonged to, attended, or associated themselves with religious institutions. The heightened popularity of Billy Graham's evangelical crusades, Fulton Sheen's television series *Life Is Worth Living*, and Norman Vincent Peale's self-help spirituality contributed to and reflected a postwar "turn to religion." Contemporary observers used terms like *religious revival* and *theological renaissance* to describe the sudden insurgencies of patriotism and faith."[12]

In *The Fifties Spiritual Marketplace*, Robert Ellwood describes the ideology of the Beat generation as part of an "underground" religious economy.[13] For the Beats, religion was more a way of being than an institutional practice; more than a conservative ideology, religion was a destabilizing force: "Together, the Beats set out on a journey toward utopia, their destination being ever-elusive America of absolute freedom."[14] Following Shields's spatial binaries, in which a mythical place is defined in opposition to what it is not, or following Van Den Abbeele's notion that the economy of the oikos determines the value of the journey, the Beats imagined Mexico as the place where dreams of freedom could become reality, unlike and in opposition to the United States. It was a lawless place, far from the norms of a puritan and militarized society. It was also the refuge of the fugitive, a sort of "badlands." According to conventional definitions, "badlands" are deserted territories of infertile and hard soil. Yet I prefer the definition in Kevin Hetherington's *The Badlands of Modernity*, where such places are described as "heterotopical," that is, places where the coordinates of time and space are altered in order to yield less regulated modes of existence.[15]

Burroughs, the Magical Plant, and the Laboratory

Roberto Bolaño refers to Burroughs as a lighthouse author of his generation (as we shall see in the following chapter), a key reference for those who understand literature as courage and horror:

> For some people of my generation, William Burroughs was the unmoving man, the chunk of ice that never melted, the eye that never closed. They say he had his worldly vices, but I believe him to be a saint to whom the vice-ridden of the world came because he was too polite or imprudent to shut the door. Literature, from which he lived during his final thirty years, interested him, but not too much. In this, he resembled other classic Americans who focused their efforts on observing and experiencing life. When he spoke of his readings, one had the impression that he was recalling imprecise eras of stints in jail. . . . He traveled the world: his vision of the planet is perhaps one of the most desolate of the century. . . . His observations on certain hard drugs makes him kin to the great creators of hells, except that in Burroughs there is not moral or ethical intention, only the description of unmoving abyss, the description of a process of endless corruption. Language, he said, is a virus that comes from the outside, that is, an illness, against which he struggled during his whole life.[16]

In 1949, Burroughs traveled to Mexico where he killed his wife. Despite the crime, or perhaps because of it, his stay in Mexico was not definitive. In 1953, he began a three-month journey through Colombia, Ecuador, and Peru; subsequently, he went into exile in Tangier, Paris, and London. Following the publication of *Junkie*, when he no longer faced criminal charges, he returned to New York as a renowned author. His *Everything Lost: Latin American Notebook of William S. Burroughs* complements *The Yage Letters* to Allen Ginsberg (published in 1963 but written in 1953 during his South America trip). The entries in the *Notebook* go from mid-July to early August of 1953, covering his trip to Panama, Mexico City, stops in the Guatemalan city of Talara, Tapachula, short stays in Veracruz, the Gulf of Mexico, Merida, and Yucatan. His notes capture dramatic or critical moments in his trip and reveal that he traveled with a lover, AG. Religion and the pursuit of spirituality through drugs were important aspects of his trip to Latin America. Burroughs distinguished sacred hallucinogenic drugs from hard drugs. Although he consumed both, the aim of this trip to Mexico and South America was to experiment and study the effects of the sacred drugs. In *Naked Lunch*, he explains the difference between sacred and profane drugs.

> Junk is the mold of monopoly and possession. The addict stands by while his junk legs carry him straight in on the junk beam to relapse. Junk is quantitative and accurately measurable. The more junk you use the less you have and the more you have the more you use. All the hallucinogen drugs are considered sacred by those who use them—there are Peyote Cults and Bannisteria Cults, Hashish Cults and Mushroom Cults—"the Sacred Mushrooms of Mexico enable a man to see God"—but no one ever suggested that junk is sacred. There are no opium cults. Opium is profane and quantitative like money.[17]

The Beats' experimentation with drugs was scientific as well as religious. I am therefore interested in studying the journey toward and the search for *yage* (or *ayahuasca*) in light of the metaphor of the laboratory. Kevin Hetherington adds the idea of the laboratory to Shields's definition of the liminal place or place-myth, following Bruno Latour: "Spaces like the laboratory are socially and technically constructed, contested, heterogenous, partial, contingent and deferred. They act as important nodes, obligatory points of passage for the development of new modes of ordering."[18] The idea is simple when we think that experimentation of liminal places is substantial much like laboratories. With scientific aspirations, Burroughs travels and lives in Mexico and South America to experiment and understand the effects of hallucinogenic plants.[19] For Burroughs, experimentation with these herbs yields a deeper understanding of reality, a truer and more primitive vision of reality, removed from rational normativity. In this sense, Burroughs is like Humboldt, studied in the first chapter, and other naturalists. Like them, Burroughs tested nature with his own body in order to reach a more perfect knowledge of human and non-human qualities. Mexico and South American were a grand laboratory, where the very body of the traveler became an instrument of measurement. His discoveries notwithstanding, Burroughs did not attain Humboldt's status in the scientific community. But the community of young artists who linked poetry to extreme experiences professed deep admiration for Burroughs, the eldest of the Beats.

Like every laboratory, the space of experimentation required certain freedoms and isolation, specific regulations and protocol. These regulations allow the experiment to become a scientific discovery. Latour's text on the fermentation of lactic acid, discovered by Pasteur, sheds light on the linguistic mechanisms at play in scientific travel narratives. Latour compares, on the one hand, the yeast that causes lactic fermentation to Cinderella and, on the other, Pasteur to the prince who rescues yeast from the discredit to which theories of chemistry had supposedly condemned it. Pasteur wrote this first text to demonstrate that lactic yeast was a live organism. More than a simple chemical reaction, fermentation was the result of the actions of a microorganism. In this text, Pasteur discusses the thorough observation to which he submitted the yeast and acknowledges the difficulty of distinguishing it from other substances. He describes its appearance and behavior in minute details because he understood that other scientists would doubt its existence; indeed, he integrates his detractors' arguments within his discussion. Pasteur thus becomes the shining "prince" and emerges as the hero of the story.[20] To further validate his perspective, Pasteur subjected the yeast to multiple tests, measurements, transformations, and transferences before granting it a place as a known living organism in the taxonomy of natural history. Pasteur carefully designs tests so that the yeast (this nonhuman) will behave as an actor. Pasteur knows that if his experiments manage to demonstrate that yeast is a live organization, the discovery will bring prestige and credibility within academic circles. Although he tells a story—as Latour notes, every experiment is a story and scientists are storytellers—his experiment will be subjected to supervision by his colleagues who will decide if the experiment is anything more than a text. If the experiment is endorsed by his colleagues, Pasteur will win a medal; but if the experiment fails to reach the standards of credibility, Pasteur will be nothing more than a writer of fiction.

The story of yeast also illustrates what Latour calls the "blood flow of science," the multiple connections between supposedly "extra-scientific" areas that, in fact, are inherent to the practice and the very constitution of scientific objects such as industrial applications, political uses, and alliances with colleagues and more general audiences. The interesting aspect of the Pasteur's description of his yeast experiments, as retold by Latour, is that every experiment requires translation into narrative, even within the scientific community. Likewise, Burroughs's experiments with the hallucinogenic effects of local plants formed part of a narrative in his travel journal and letters to Allen Ginsberg. Less spiritual or surrealist than Artaud's, this narrative responds to a political-scientific motivation: just as Pasteur had done with yeast, before it was classified in scientific taxonomies, Burroughs endeavored to free drugs from discredit and criminalization in his society. For Burroughs, the struggle to decriminalize drugs was as constant as his iron will to detoxify himself whenever he needed to recover balance with sanity.

Burroughs carefully details the effects of yage: dizziness, cramps, spins, violent and sudden nausea, blue flashes, the inability to walk, heaviness of his feet; "an uncontrollable mechanical silliness took possession of me."[21] In *Latin American Notebook*, Burroughs confirms, after Colombia, the importance of his trip to Peru. In scientific terms, after the fashion of Humboldt, he corrects and verifies his initial hypotheses about yage: "I made subsequent discoveries about yage in Peru in view of which earlier conclusions are completely invalid."[22] In this sense, Burroughs was not so different from other naturalists. Indeed, he began to research yage in the University of Colombia, which he describes as a heterotopic place where multiple social levels interact. In a January 25, 1953, letter from Colombia to Allen Ginsberg, he wrote:

> Next day I went to the University to get information on Yage. All sciences are lumped in the Institute. This a red brick building, dusty corridors, unlabeled offices mostly locked. I climbed over crates and stuffed animals and botanical presses. These articles are continually being moved from one room to another for no discernible reason. People rush out of offices and claim some object from the litter in the hall and have it carried back to their offices. The porters sit around on crates smoking and greeting everybody as "Doctor." In a vast dusty room full of plant specimens and the smell of formaldehyde, I saw a man looking for something he could not find with an air of refined annoyance. He caught my eye. "Now what have they done with my cocoa specimens? It was a new species of wild cocoa. And what is this stuffed condor doing on my table?" The man had a thin refined face, steel rimmed glasses, tweed coat and dark flannel trousers, Boston and Harvard unmistakably. He introduced himself as Doctor Schindler. He was connected with a U.S. Agricultural Commission. I asked about Yage. "Oh yes," he said, "we have specimens here. Come along and I will show you," he said taking one last look for his cocoa. He showed me a dried specimen of the Yage vine which looked to be a very undistinguished sort of plant. Yes, he had taken it. "I got colors but no visions." He told me exactly what I would need for the trip, where to go and who to contact. I asked him about the telepathy angle. "That's all imagination of course," he said. He suggested the Putumayo as being the most readily accessible area where to I could find Yage. I took a few days to assemble my gear and dig the capitol. For a jungle trip you need medicines; snake bite serum, penicillin, enterovioformo and aralen are essentials. A hammock, a blanket and a rubber bag known as a tula to carry your gear in.[23]

The objects that Burroughs finds are in constant movement, as they were for Humboldt: "crates and stuffed animals and botanical presses" are carried from one office to another "for no discernible reason." The scene recalls the disorder, the "queer messiness,"[24] of the nonhumans, their resistance to discipline, classification, and laboratory delimitation. Like the naturalist travelers, Burroughs details the preparations for his expedition. He lists the necessary instruments—"medicines; snake bite serum, penicillin, a hammock, a blanket and a rubber bag known as a tula"—and his consultation with scientific experts like Dr. Schindler from Harvard.

The above quotation helps us to retrace the Burroughs's steps in South America. He knows he cannot underestimate the knowledge of foreign botanists in Colombia and local shamans. His letters express deep aversion for Colombian officials, the federal forces in the civil war, as well as the official and popular cultures in Colombia in general. He is only truly interested in learning about and experimenting with yage. The letters reveal the adventure and danger Burroughs faces to reach his goal. Even more vulnerable than Humboldt and other earlier naturalists, he embraces the rhetoric of the body subjected to the "agency" of nature: "Bogota is high and cold and wet, a damp chill that gets inside you like the inner cold of junk sickness. There is no heat anywhere and you are never warm. In Bogota more than any other city I have seen in Latin America you feel the dead weight of Spain sombre and oppressive. Everything official bears the label Made in Spain."[25]

The local guides cause suspicion and conflict for Burroughs, as they did for Humboldt. However, unlike Humboldt, also a queer subject, the Beatnik writes an openly homosexual erotic story. Although the sexual adventures are a source of frustration, Burroughs relates them with humor and irony:

> On my way back to Bogota with nothing accomplished. I have been conned by medicine men (the most inveterate drunk, liar and loafer in the village is invariable the medicine man), incarcerated by the law, rolled by a local hustler (I thought I was getting that innocent backwoods ass, but the kid had been to bed with six American oil men, a Swedish Botanist, a Dutch Ethnographer, a Capuchin father known locally as the Mother Superior, a Bolivian Trotskyite on the lam, and jointly fucked by the Cocoa Commission and Point Four). Finally, I was prostrated by malaria. I will relate events more or less chronologically.[26]

For Burroughs, the guides are "the pests all over South America."[27] Critics' analyses of fictional or documentary travel narratives tend to omit the local guide or pathfinder, perhaps because they assume that the figure is there only for money or some other material compensation. Although the pathfinder is an important agent in travel narratives, as the chapter on Charnay showed, the figure is usually overlooked or its presence is explained in terms of the asymmetrical power relationship with the traveler. Yet it is impossible to avoid mentioning fictional and legendary examples such as the wise Virgil in Dante Alighieri's *Divine Comedy*, La Malinche, or the type of gaucho known as *baqueano* ("pathfinder") in *Facundo: Civilization or Barbarism* (1845). Burroughs's description demystifies the legendary figure; far from ignoring the pathfinder, he subjects it and himself to criticism. He demystifies the supposedly sexually ascetic behavior with which naturalists or religious travels tend to identify in their narratives, especially in relation to their guides. He mocks the ethnographers and botanists, merchants, and missionaries. Even the allusion to the "Bolivian Trotskyite on the lam" appears to predict the death of Che Guevara in Bolivia.

Burroughs's Latin American experience was a failure. Therefore, his writings constitute what Ahmed calls the archive of unhappiness and he fails in ways described by Jack Halberstam in *The Queer Art of Failure*.[28] Despite the promising success of *Junkie*, the notes of his travel through Latin America reveal a desperate man. Burroughs does not hesitate to reveal his negative and derogative opinion of Mexico and South America: "I hate Mexico, whole fuckin hemisphere . . . ; Everything is detestable to me. Mexico, the rain, everything. Allerton. His sweetness is a fraud."[29] Mexico and South America seem like a black hole that swallows people, especially his lover. With the presence of Allerton in his letters, the trip becomes a search not only for experience with ayahuasca but also persecution of his lover. For Burroughs, the Latin American trip is a journey of loss, not only of his loved one, but also of youth and everything he valued. Everything disintegrates in Latin America.

> I see the SA trip a disaster that lost me everything I had of value. Bits of it keep floating back to me like memories of a day time nightmare. Slow traps. The Mercado Mayorista reveals full gap and indifference by very fact of tolerance. What is wrong with SA. Disintegration into component parts. The nightmare fear of death and age, you feel every day as something lost, your flesh ages before your eyes like a speed up movie, Control is growing like a cancer, a proliferating Tumor of stupidity. People just disappear. Like in the Mayorista. You never see them again. Angelo. Here at night people swarm out and walk round and round the square. The Indians are sad and Beaten by the great meaningless country. The New World is a lack a yearning ache of despair. Deprivation and shrinkage. The fish caught in the shrinking pond. Dream. I was in Mexico City and everywhere I looked such an ache of memories of Allerton and people who have gone away. I could not stay there. I must go now. Angelo sweet and sad, has gone.[30]

Burroughs's phrase "disintegration into component parts" describes his writing style as well as his experience. It is the fragmented, intense language of someone struggling to capture emotions and sensations without articulating them. His style heightens the emotions and the thoughts that spring from his trip and the search for his lover. The absence of conjunctions between phrases translates the agonizing subject who effectively seems to be under the effects of hallucinogens, dreams, or agony.

The journey begins with the company of his lover "M" (Lewis Marker), who later is fictionalized in the pseudonym of Allerton. Burroughs writes in his notes about the "Time-Gap between me and M. love him like a 4-year-old child, with a child's unconditional intensity."[31] He repeats the travel narrative trope of search and loss, thus reproducing a mythical topic of the journey or the pilgrimage. Like other travelers in the New World, especially the Andalusian traveler Alvar Núñez Cabeza de Vaca, Burroughs loses his youth, his money, his health, and his friendships. Yet, he continues to search, first for ayahuasca (or yage) and then for Allerton, or both at the same time. The search drives his trip. Like Cabeza de Vaca, Burroughs interacts with locals and submits to the power of the "doctors," guides, and government officials. Burroughs is a foreigner, alone, sick, in love, and weakened in Mexico and South America. Like the travelers of the next chapter, on Roberto Bolaño, Burroughs travels looking for a lost person. Bolaño's poets look for Cesárea Tinajero, and Ulises Lima travels to Israel to look for his true love, Claudia. Likewise, Burroughs becomes a traveling detective, deciphering clues that take him to Allenton, whose real name was Mike: "Checked in Hotel and went straight to Tato's. No use asking Pepe for info. He wouldn't know where anybody was. I was looking for one person. M. Like in a dream I had several times."[32]

Mexico in On the Road by Jack Kerouac

Sal Paradise, the protagonist in *On the Road* (1957), travels to experience the United States in depth. But the travelers in the novel also go to Mexico. Sal decides to cross the United States from east to west, passing through the places that define, in his imagination, American geography, history, and society. As his biographers have noted, Kerouac had a deep affinity for US history. His westward trip reflected the mythical perception of the frontier during the conquest of the "far west." This narrative of historical conquest and supremacy of the white man coincided with the American triumphalist attitude following WWII. Nonetheless, for Denis Jonnes, the critic cited above, *On the Road* goes beyond the mythical westward journey and reaches the subject's discovery of being, autonomy, and self-actualization.[33] In this sense, it is a novel about growth in which the search for personal autonomy and adventure coincide with the image of the pioneers who conquered the frontier. It is an "attempted return" to the primitive, the "glamour" of the frontier, for which Dean Moriarty, Sal's traveling companion, acts as an Adamic archetype. Jonnes notes that the spontaneity, mobility, and sensuality that Sal acquires at his side makes Moriarty "a powerful and redemptive figure—'a new kind of American saint'—whose dynamism and instinctive knowledge of America promise an emancipation and regeneration of the self."[34]

Interestingly, Dean Moriarty does not conform to the familiar values that the postwar national unit proclaimed. Jonnes offers an allegorical reading of Dean Moriarty's family situation, stating that his orphan-ness, together with his father's abandonment, are a manifest rejection of the American culture that predicated the values of national security on family unity.[35] The character's reluctance to commit to monogamous relationships and to accept his paternity points in the same direction. In this sense, the characters from *On The Road* also form part of Ahmed's archive of unhappiness, an archive inhabited by texts that oppose domestic bliss.

Seeing the character of Dean Moriarty in light of resistance to conventional family patterns illuminates the novel's gender relations, in which the female characters are seen as the incarnation of these family values and national unity. In an encounter with Galatea Dunkel in San Francisco, during Sal and Dean's second visit there, the women, led by Galatea, put Dean "on trial" because before arriving, Dean's wife Camille had told Galatea that Dean had abandoned her and their daughter:

> They all sat around looking at Dean with lowered and hating eyes, and he stood on the carpet in the middle of them giggled—he just giggled. He made a little dance.... I suddenly realized that Dean, by virtue of his enormous series of sins, was becoming the Idiot, the Imbecile, the Saint of the lot. "You have absolutely no regard for anybody but yourself and your damned kicks. All you think about is what's hanging between your legs and how much money or fun you can get out of people and then you just throw them aside. Not only that but you are silly about that. It never occurs to you that life is serious and there are people trying to make something decent out of it instead of just goofing all the time." That's what Dean was, the HOLY GOOF.[36]

In Sal's description, the women unfairly and publicly humiliated and demoralized Dean in what is described as an "emasculation" scene. Sal sees that all Dean could do was repeat "yes, yes, yes": "He was BEAT—the root, the soul of the Beatific. What was he knowing? He tried all in his power to tell me what he was knowing, and they envied that about me, my position at the side, defending him and drinking him in as they once tried to do. Then they looked at me. What was I, a stranger, doing on the West Coast this fair night?"[37]

The quote is significant for several reasons, chiefly because of the mention of the Beat generation. The novel confirms Kerouac's understanding of the term: the Beats were mistreated and abused by a society that neither understood nor tried to assimilate them; at the same time, they were saints. The quote, furthermore, reveals the links of masculine brotherhood, or male bonding. In her pioneering studies on homoerotic relationships, Eve Sedgwick calls these relationships "homosocial" in order to return to friendship the potentiality of desire among men who consider themselves heterosexuals: "To draw the 'homosocial' back into the orbit of 'desire,' of the potentially erotic, then, is to hypothesize the potential unbrokenness of a continuum between homosocial and homosexual—a continuum whose visibility, for man, in our society, is radically disrupted."[38] The complicity between Sal and Dean and the deep admiration the former had for the latter provoke unease among the female characters. Kerouac admired his friend Neal Cassidy for several reasons, among them the adventurous life and transgressions of an ex-convict.

Kerouac also admired the colloquial manner in which Cassady narrated his adventures, highlighting small details that in Neal's style became interesting. This fluid fashion of narrating experiences constituted one of Cassady's characteristics that Kerouac found most attractive. In *On the Road*, Kerouac takes the experiment with this literary style to an extreme. The novel was inspired by the "non-stop" prose style of Cassady's "Great Sex Letter." As Weinrich notes: "*On the Road*'s composition is legendary. Not only was the book a stylistic departure, written on a roll of teletype as one huge sentence grammatically *exclamation* (in the manner of Melville's *Moby Dick*) as if every moment was a simultaneous highest high and lowest low, describing the antics of two travelers across the vast body and expanse of America in a fast car; it was a thematic departure as well, with its refrain of 'Everything is collapsing.'"[39]

It is not only the women, wives of the Beats, who try to assimilate them.[40] It is also the police who stop them during their trip. Money troubles do their part as well. These examples add up to the point that critics coincide in seeing the novel's development as a progression toward disillusionment. The trip that had begun as a search full of possibilities ends up showing nothing more than disenchantment. The proof is that Dean never finds his father at the end of the novel. He travels to the frontier, the quintessential symbol of American, where he ends up a failure. The United States makes the Beats into the mistreated and misunderstood. This is why they decide to go to Mexico: "Behind us lay the whole of

America and everything Dean and I had previously known about life, and life on the road. We had finally found de magic land at the end of the road and we never dreamed the extent of the magic . . . 'This road,' I told him, 'is also the route of old American outlaws who used to skip over the border and go down to old Monterrey, so if you'll look out on that graying desert and picture the ghost of an old Tombstone hellcat making his lonely exile gallop into the unknown, you'll see further.'"[41] The quotation combines the orientalized image of Mexico as a magical place with the history of the American outlaws who similarly were unable to find a place in the United States and sought refuge—the return to the maternal womb prior the law of the father—in Mexico, but who were, on the other hand, a constitutive part of the American history and literature of the Far West and the cowboys. By identifying with outlaws, Kerouac situates the long-term literature of delinquency and adventure of the United States within his literary narration.[42] Kurt Hummer notes that:

> Kerouac and Burroughs were arrested in August 1944 as material witnesses for the murder of David Kammerer by Lucien Carr. Burroughs was arrested again in 1946 for forging prescriptions in New York. He moved to Texas and was arrested for indecent exposure in 1948. After moving to Louisiana, he fled an impending court appearance for drug possession in New Orleans and settled in Mexico City. In September 1951 he accidentally shot and killed his wife and, when his lawyer fled after becoming himself a potential murder suspect, Burroughs broke his probation by leaving Mexico and eventually made his way to Tangier. While only sixteen, Gregory Corso was sent to prison for robbery in 1947. Ginsberg was arrested in April 1949 as an accomplice to theft and avoided prison by being sent to the Columbia Presbyterian Psychiatric Institute, an experience that would inspire his masterpiece "Howl." In the 1950s, Herbert Huncke, who had been in and out of jails as a youth, was in and out of New York State Prisons. Neal Cassady, who as a teenager was supposedly arrested ten times and served over a year in jail, was arrested for possession of marijuana in April 1958. So, to some degree the Beats' attraction to outlaws can be explained by empathy for those who found themselves on the wrong side of the law. But the Beats' attraction to the outlaw as a symbol had much more to do with the politics of Cold War than with their lives of crime. Despite their penchant for lawlessness, the Beats were not revolutionaries calling for an end to the American way of life. They demanded that America live up to its promises of freedom and democracy. As Beat art scholar Lisa Phillips asserts, "They knew that you could love your country and still be a rebel."[43]

By explaining the mythical image of Neal Cassady as the inspiration for Dean Moriarty in Kerouac's *On the Road* and for the "secret hero" in several of Ginsberg's poems, Gary Snyder says that, "what got Kerouac and Ginsberg about Cassady was the energy of the archetypal West, the energy of the frontier, still coming down. Cassady is the cowboy crashing."[44] Cassady's name itself evokes the heroic cowboy Hopalong Cassidy and the famous outlaw Butch Cassidy. In the imagination of Kerouac and Ginsberg, fed by the Westerns on the radio and movies the 1920s and '30s, Cassady was the avatar of the American frontier.[45]

The fusion of the virtuous cowboy and the outlaw hero seems paradoxical, but both figures have similar codes of honor. The good cowboy defends laws he recognizes as just while the outlaw, like Robin Hood, violates laws he sees as unjust. Both satisfy the audience's expectation that the hero will do the right thing. The Beat movement promoted this rebellious position as a survival tactic in a world where the radicalism of both Cold War powers was equally dangerous. The rebel is situated outside this schema, consciously or unconsciously, but in any case, his posture is political in its nonconformism. The rebel may not have a solution but nor is he willing to be part of the problem. Crossing the border means for Dean and Sal leaving behind the life of the mistreated and launching into adventure:

> We bought three bottles of cold beer—*cerveza* was the name of the beer—for about thirty Mexican cents or ten American cents each. We bought packs of Mexican cigarettes for six cents each. We gazed and gazed at our wonderful Mexican money that went so far, and played with it and looked around and smiled at everyone. Behind us lay the whole of America and everything Dean and I had previously known about life, and life on the road and we never dreamed the extent of the magic. "*Think* of these cats staying up all hours of night" whispered Dean. "And think of this big continent ahead of us with those enormous Sierra Madre mountains we saw in the movies, and the jungles all the way down and a whole desert plateau as big as ours and reaching clear down to Guatemala and God knows where, whoo! What'll we do? What'll we do? Let's move!" We got out and went back to the car. One last glimpse of America across the hot lights of the Rio Grande bridge, and we turned our back and fender to it and roared off. . . . "Now, Sal, we're leaving everything behind us and entering a new and unknown phase of things. All the years and troubles and kicks—and now *this!* So that we can safely think of nothing else and just go on ahead with our faces stuck out like this, you see, and *understand* the world as, really, and genuinely speaking, other Americans haven't done before us? The Mexican war. Cutting across here with canon."[46]

The quote shows Dean as the quintessential poet, traveler, and philosopher. They arrive in Mexico thanks to him. He underscores the discovery of Mexico as a place where a new life can be invented, where it was possible to leave behind the years as mistreated subjects and wade into the country imagined from Western movies: "We're leaving everything behind us and entering a new and unknown phase of things."[47] In a certain sense, Dean reproduces the orientalist gaze that thinks of Mexico as tabula rasa, where circumstances of the social environment do not affect biography, because society as such does not exist—it only exists as an imaginary space, where Mexicans and their history are thought to be part of the landscape without agency. Dean nonetheless distances himself from the gaze of American conqueror by pointing out that Americans did not see Mexico in the same way during the US-Mexico War. Nonetheless, Sal reminds him that in the American tradition of the Western in Mexico, there were other Americans like the Beats; they were the cowboy outlaws.

In other books, Kerouac often returns to his trip to Mexico, complementing the vision that appears in *On the Road*. In *Lonesome Traveler* (the "Mexico Fellaheen" section), for example, the narrator describes crossing the border and entering into Mexico as a return to infancy, a reminder in good measure of the carnival society studied by Bakhtin and Rob Shields in his book *Places on the Margin*. "Mexico Fellaheen" reads:

When you go across the border at Nogales Arizona some very severe looking American guards, some of them pasty faced with sinister steelrim spectacles go scrounging through all your Beat baggage for signs of scorpion of scofflaw.—You just wait patiently like you always do in America among those apparently endless policemen and their endless laws against (no laws for)—but the moment you cross the little wire gate and you're in Mexico, you feel like you just sneaked out of school when you told the teacher you were sick and she told you could go, 2 o'clock in the afternoon.—you feel as though you just come home from Sunday morning church and you take off your suit and slip into your soft worn smooth cool overalls, to play—you look around and you see happy smiling faces, or the absorbed dark faces of worried lovers and fathers and policemen, you hear cantina music from across the little park of balloons and popsicles.—In the middle of the little park is a bandstand for concerts, actual concerts for the people, free—generations of marimba players maybe, or an Orozco jazzband playing Mexican anthems to El Presidente.—You walk thirsty through the swinging doors of a saloon and get a bar beer and turn around and there's fellas shooting pool, cooking tacos, wearing sombreros, some wearing gungs on their rancher hips, and gangs of singing businessmen throwing pesos at the standing musicians who wander up and down the room.—It's a great feeling of entering the Pure Land, especially because it's so close to dry faced Arizona and Texas and all over the

Southwest—but you can find it, this feeling, this fellaheen feeling about life, that timeless gayety of people not involved in great cultural and civilization issues—you can find it almost anywhere else, in Morocco, in Latin America entire, in Dakar, in Kurd land.—There is no "violence" in Mexico, that was a lot of bull written up by Hollywood writers or writers who went to Mexico to be "violent."[48]

In *Places on the Margin*, specifically in the chapter "Ritual Pleasures of Seaside Resort: Liminality, Carnivalesque, and Dirty Weekends," Rob Shields studies the journey to Brighton on the English southern coast in the eighteenth and nineteenth centuries in ways that, despite the differences, shed light on the Beats' travel experiences in Mexico. The interesting aspect of the comparison is how a place of distension can mix with a zone of marginality and delinquency, where laws become lax, and take on characteristics of a ritualized destination and journey. Following Victor Turner and Arnold Van Gennep, Shields argues that these trips to the margin are moments of discontinuity in the social fabric that generally lead to a religious experience. They are journeys of transition during moments of changes in stages or life cycles. English travelers went to Brighton seeking the therapeutic benefits of the "maritime cure" (ocean air and bathing) in Victorian England. The trip to the coast involved a relaxation of clothing and customs, a moment of liberation from the normative codes and practices of everyday life. As a beach and a frontier, Brighton (at the southern edge of England, within sight of the continent) constituted a liminal place since from the early nineteenth century it was a territory in which the beaches were still not delimited by private property, where the absence of rational production of the land and industry differentiated it from places known to be "civilized." Brighton was a place of "extraordinary" vacations, a liminal temporality, or time out.[49] Brighton was a place not of production but of consumption.

Following the Russian theorist Mikhail Bakhtin, Shields situates Brighton in the space and temporality of the carnival, with its disrupted hierarchies and bodies that resist the morality of codes. For Shields, furthermore, carnival "is the occasion for the enactment of alternative, utopian social arrangements."[50] Brighton's long association with the carnivalesque consolidated its reputation in the English imaginary as a place free of restrictions. Toward the end of the nineteenth century, Brighton had become a place favorable to delinquency as well as the weekend destination for adulterers. It was the space of the "love affair."

This idea is key for understanding Mexico's place in the Beat imaginary. For both Kerouac and Burroughs, Mexico was a place of escape, where social, judicial, and sexual norms were laxer. Mexico was a vacation spot. For Burroughs, Mexico, and by extension South America, was a place favorable to experimentation not only with drugs but also non-heteronormative love and sexual consumption. For Kerouac, the brothel occupies a place in the narration of northern Mexico in *On the Road* and a prostitute appears as the protagonist in *Tristessa*, another novel about Mexico.

The sex-consumption relationship in Kerouac's narrations of Mexico reaffirms this idea of a "vacation spot" with relaxed customs. The first part of *On the Road*, for example, describes Sal's relationship with Terry, a young Mexican woman traveling through Southern California whose family works in the grape harvest. Sal describes their encounter in a bus in Los Angeles: "Without coming to any particular agreement, we began holding hands, and in the same way it was mutely and beautifully and purely decided that when I got to my hotel room in LA she would be beside me. I ached all over for her; I leaned my head in her beautiful hair. Her little shoulders drove me mad; I hugged her and hugged her. And she loved it."[51]

After falling in love instantly, Sal begins to question Terry's intentions. Paranoid, he associates her with nonexistent pimps. Still, the desire to stay together prevails and they decide to return to New York as a couple. First, they harvest cotton and grapes in California to earn the money for their trip. They spend a brief time in Southern California, where Sal fails as a cotton harvester: "But I knew nothing about picking cotton. I spent too much time disengaging the white ball from its crackly bed; the others did it in on a flick. Moreover, my finger-tips began to bleed; I needed gloves, or more experience."[52] Although he describes the environment and the time as paradisiacal, Sal grows so disenchanted that he leaves for New York without Terry. Terry's Mexican family and friends are described as indolent, happy drunkards. Their constant postponement of plans and endeavors with the word "mañana" begins to wear on Sal's patience and desire to be with Terry: "Sure, baby, mañana" It was always mañana. For the next week that was all I heard—mañana, a lovely Word and one that probably means heaven."[53] Ángel and Fanny Calderón made similar complaints as they sought out the objects that Prescott asked them to bring to Boston from Mexico. The Mexicans responded that they would get the archived documents "mañana." The foreigners expressed frustration and humor with a situation that was clearly a place of resistance to the movement imposed by capitalist accumulation and transfer to the center of calculation.

In *The Rhetoric of Empire*, David Spurr notes that the most important aspect of imperial rhetoric consists of making the other primitive, highlighting features of indolence, irrationality, and eroticism, among others.[54] All these elements appear in the scenes of Sal's life with Terry. Terry offers to help him harvest cotton and grapes, so he won't have to work; she gives him food, room, and sex, but Sal still abandons her. In many ways, this romanticism is no different from that of the imperial travelers of the nineteenth century. There are powerful symbols in imperial travel narratives that reveal the guilty conscious of the white man vis-a-vis the colonized subject and that, at the same time, reflect fear of revenge. In their final nights together, Sal and Terry make love under a tarantula on the ceiling. "Terry said it wouldn't harm me if I didn't bother it . . . I made love to her under the tarantula.[55] The passage coincides with what Tim Young analyzes as "the shock of disruption caused by the discovery of the familiar where it is least expected, and by the intrusion of the strange where it is unexpected and unwelcome, may threaten one's sense of self, especially when one is travelling 'alone' and away from the society in which the circulation of goods is regulated and one's identity is given meaning partly through one's relationship to them."[56]

The combination of the familiar or the known, in this case sex with Terry, with the unknown or the threatening quality of the nonhuman (the tarantula), jeopardizes the integrity of the subject. At the same time, it suggests that modalities of wielding masculine power through sex are unsettled by the threat of the tarantula. This surprising nonhuman introduces a relationship with the traveler that was not codified in the economy of travel and disrupts its certainty. In this sense, the tarantula introduces what this book studies as *queer messiness* in other travelers.

Later, Sal returns to topic of race and, in line with the imperial rhetoric we have been discussing, admits his fascination and rejection for the other, expressed in the image of the tarantula, the desire and the repulsion that Richard Young has described in *Colonial Desire*: "I wished I were a Denver Mexican, or even a poor Jap, anything but I was so drearily, a 'white man' disillusioned. All my life I'd had white ambitions; that was why I'd abandoned a good woman like Terry in the San Joaquin Valley."[57]

Kerouac's characters always return, in one way or another, to Mexico. Sal does so, as we have seen, at the end of the *On the Road*. The return to Mexico appears in other books, such as *Tristessa* and *Lonesome Traveler*, both published in 1960s. *Tristessa* tells the story of platonic love between an American writer and a Mexican prostitute, who is, for him, an emblematic portrait of the Virgin Mary. Through the automatic writing in *Tristessa*, the reader examines the narrator under the effects of morphine, fears, hallucinations, unconnected thoughts, and emotions. Together with Tristessa, the protagonist traverses the spaces of the Mexican underground, the allies, dive bars, illegal drugs, and prostitution.

In the end, he abandons her, when in a moment of enlightenment, he sees her with his friend Burroughs (the character of Old Bull) as two irredeemable beings. For Kerouac, Mexico was a vacation spot of cheap morphine, idealized love for prostitutes and junkies, of the extreme experiences of hell conjoined with the sacred.[58]

Mexico City Blues

Kerouac's poems about Mexico develop two main themes that are deeply connected with his narrative writings. They at once bring him close to and distance him from Burroughs. On the one hand, the theme of primitivism, seen in *Lonesome Traveler* and *On the Road*, appears from the perspective of infancy, the moment of paradise lost, that the poet associates with the songs he heard from his mother. The "Indians songs in Mexico" in *Mexico City Blues* repeat the onomatopoeias and evoke the same deep memories of happiness. As we saw in "Mexico Fellaheen," Kerouac associates Mexico with recreation, a pre-patriarchal instance, where language is pre-symbolic and closer to the semiotic maternal language. The musicality of the "choruses" shows Kerouac's inclination for jazz, where onomatopoeias are linguistic transcriptions of musical instruments like the saxophone, for example, and reverberate on levels different from the rationality of language. The onomatopoeias are also a transcription of the Indigenous languages that the poet hears during his journey through Mexico.

> 12th Chorus
> Indian songs in Mexico (the Folk Chanties of Children at dusk jumprope—
> at Saturday Night power failure—) are like the little French Canuckian
> songs my mother sings—Indian Roundelays—Row Canoe—Ma ta wacka
> Johnny Picotee Wish-tee Wish-tee Negwayable Tamayara Para ya Aztec
> squeaks (ONLY THE MOTHERS ARE HAPPY).[59]

On the other hand, the poems take up the topic of ancestral religiosity that, for the Beats, was a confirmation in Mexico. The Maya and Aztec cultures, especially, prompted reflection on spirituality and ways of reaching through "sacred drugs" a state of connection with the divine. For the Beats, there was a deep connection between spirituality, drugs, and literature:

> 13th Chorus
> I caught a cold From the sun When they tore my heart out At the top of the
> pyramid O the ruttle tooty blooty windowpoopies of Fellah Ack Ack Town

that russet noon when priests dared to lick their lips over my thumping meat
heart—the Sacrilegious beasts Ate me 10,000 million Times & I came back
Spitting Pulque in Borracho Ork Saloons of old Sour Azteca Askin for more
I popped out of Popocatepetl's Hungry mouth.[60]

This chorus visualizes the theme of the eternal return to birth, death,
and resurrection in the digestion of the volcano Popocatepetl's eruption
of pulque after the pyramid priests ate the poet's heart. It is a chant of
apocalyptic drama but also a cycle of life in which human sacrifices and
volcanic eruptions form part of the continuity of being.

For Lardas, there is a marked difference between the Mexico in Kerouac and the Mexico in Burroughs that is worth examining in this conclusion. In *The Bop Apocalypse*, the critic points out that Kerouac (and
Ginsberg) "viewed the inhabitants of Mexico as a fellaheen remnant
who had survived the decline of Civilization and were now living in a
post-apocalyptic age."[61] The poem quoted above can be read in this light;
the cosmic belief that the poet projects upon Mexico and the cataclysms
that embody the cyclic relationship between life and death is evident.
Burroughs, in contrast, believed that Mexico was corrupt beyond redemption, not only because of Western advance but also because of the
authoritarian legacy of the aboriginal ritualistic cultures.[62] Traversed by
the tragic murder of Joan Vollmer and the fruitless search for his lover
Matthew/Allerton, Burroughs regarded Mexico as a place of degradation, decline, brutality, disintegration, the place where an "Ugly Spirit"
had taken him over.[63]

In the Beat imaginary, Mexico was a mythical place, of degradation, apocalypse, redemption, and ritual. Importantly, sight of "home"
is never lost. Mexico was the other face of the United States, American
culture, the prism that mediated the Mexican experience in the economy
of travel.

In this economy of travel, where the oikos is the point of departure
and destination, the mythical construction of the Mexican space becomes
clear. Mexico become a privileged site for a rite of passage, necessary as
transition through life changes (of status, rebellious life stages, or social
conditions of existence like Cold War America). Although these rites of
passage suggest moments of fracture or suspension of social order, they
in fact reinforce the oikos. For Van Gennep, the rites of passage include
three stages: separation, margin, and reinsertion.[64] The journey to this
mythical place constitutes the first two instances of the rite, without
which the final stage would be impossible. This physical separation that
occurs in a marginal place is where the transgressive moment of the rite
is also found, where, as I mentioned, the social norms are suspended or

altered, as is the case of these traveling poets in Mexico and its northern border. From Van Gennep's perspective, these liminal places favorable to the transgression of the rite of passage reinforce the hierarchical order to which the subject will eventually return. This is what happened to the Beats. By the 1990s, the Beats were American cultural icons and their image is still merchandise within the cultural myth of the youth counterculture: "By the 1990s, Jack Kerouac and Allen Ginsberg were wearing khakis for GAP advertisements, and William Burroughs was endorsing Nike. It was a sign: the erstwhile beatnik societal misfits had become cultural icons. They had name recognition; they could sell products, and it had little to do with what they wrote."[65]

Therefore, the space of marginality that the Beats occupied in the 1950s served to reproduce the logic of the artistic field, capitalizing on rupture and transgression—that temporary "unhappiness"—thus making failure into success within the specific coordinates of the field.

Chapter 8

"An Oasis of Horror in a Desert of Boredom"

Mexico in Roberto Bolaño

In a well-known interview on Chilean television, Roberto Bolaño sadly remembered the circumstances of the death of Mario Santiago, the inspiration for Ulises Lima, the famous and eccentric character in *The Savage Detectives*. Bolaño noted that the body of ("by far") his best friend spent several days in the morgue before being identified. Santiago died in the street, surrounded by strangers and alone.[1] Neal Cassady, the outlaw adventurer and friend of Jack Kerouac, also died alone in Mexico. The deaths of both men are obscure, surrounded by enigmas. Cassady had settled in the San Miguel Allende neighborhood of Mexico City with a group of artists and bohemians. One night he left his house near the train station and the next morning his body was found on the tracks, naked, dead from a mix of alcohol and barbiturates. Allen Ginsberg wrote that his friend had died "exhausted and feeling alone and lost."[2] Neal Cassady and Mario Santiago both inspired famous doubles in travel novels. Cassady is Dean Moriarty, Sal's ex-con friend in *On the Road* by Jack Kerouac. Both Dean and Ulises were travel companions and intimate friends of the protagonists Sal and Belano.

These parallels are not coincidental. As *The Savage Detectives* makes clear, Bolaño read the Beat generation. And yet, as often happens with Bolaño, the author reflected on the similarities between his work and that of other writers indirectly or allusively. For example, in his collection of essays *Entre paréntesis*, instead of referring to Kerouac or Cassady, Bolaño makes the object of his reflection William Burroughs, the oldest and perhaps the strangest of the beatniks, who not only lived in Mexico but also killed his wife Joan Vollner there.

The association between Bolaño and the beatniks is hardly novel, and critical discussion of the topic has proved divisive. Those who argue against the association point out that Bolaño, unlike the beatniks, was not addicted to drugs (specifically heroin). His death was in no way caused by alcohol or drugs. For critics and writers such as Carmen Boullosa, the heroin-Bolaño-beatnik connection comes from the American writer Jonathan Lethem's 2008 review of the translation of *2666* in the *New York Times*. Clearly, the "Bolaño beatnik" myth seems to have been created in the United States for the consumption of the American reading public, as Sarah Pollack has noted.[3] Lisa Locascio, in a 2013 essay for the *Los Angeles Review of Books*, addresses the "Bolaño myth":

> Seeking a point of entry to Bolaño's unforgettable prose . . . we repeat the verses of his contradictory legend: He was an alcoholic like Bukowski. He was Alejandro Jodorowsky's protégé. He was a heroin addict. He never did drugs. Hepatitis C, contracted from dirty needles, damaged his liver. He was arrested under suspicion of terrorism in Pinochet's Chile, held in a secret prison, and escaped execution only because the men guarding him turned out to be his high school classmates. He was never in Chile. The prison story is a compensatory fiction prompted by guilt. Naturally a poet, he only began writing fiction to support his family.[4]

Myths aside, there are interesting philosophical and poetic parallels between the Beat generation and the avant-garde movements of the *infrarrealistas* (the *"realvisceralistas"* in *The Savage Detectives*) founded by Roberto Bolaño and Mario Santiago in the 1970s in Mexico. Two testimonies by infrarrealistas included in Mónica Maristain's biography of Bolaño refer not only to the beatniks but also to the surrealists (another movement explored in this book), which suggests a transversal relationship between several writers and travelers in Mexico. The testimonies come from the infrarrealista poets Ramón Méndez and José Vicente Anaya, whom Bolaño renamed Gregory Corso and Antonin Artaud. They discuss the founding and the end of the movement:

> And then we started talking about many things, about the poetry of our time, about young poets in Peru, about the Beatniks, and about what we were doing in what remained of Juan Bañuelos' workshop. And Roberto was getting more excited with the discussion and at the end he was very happy about what we had talked about. We left his house around dawn and he told us, "You guys are the Beatniks. You [Mario Santiago] are Allen Ginsberg and you [Méndez] are Gregory Corso. . . . A few months later, he came to me with the news that we were going to create the infrarrealista movement.[5]

When Roberto Bolaño came to say goodbye because he was going to live in Spain, we got into a discussion. He told me, "Now that I am going to live in

Spain, you need to stay here and lead the infrarrealistas because they are all dispersed and disorganized." I told him that, first, I didn't agree that the infras needed to be herded because my principles were libertarian and I wasn't going to impose anything. Second, I didn't take orders from him. And third, I was also going to travel, throughout Mexico. I concluded telling his that with his authoritarian attitudes he took himself to be the "Andre Breton of the infras." He responded with irony that "You take yourself to be the Antonin Artaud of the infras." That was our farewell.[6]

As happens with the other writers featured in this book, *infrarrealismo* is inseparable from the youthfulness of its members. In this literature, Mexico as a mythical place is tied to youth, adventure, ideals, poetry's ethical commitment to be critical of literary institutions, the canon, and the bourgeois culture of the consecrated, official writers like Octavio Paz. The poetry and youth of the beatniks resounds in the infrarrealista ideas, with Mexico as the scene and imaginary of "youth culture." In *Bolaño Infra*, Montserrat Madariaga Caro points out the importance of the magazine *El corno emplumado / The Plumed Horn*, edited by Sergio Mondragón and Margaret Randall in México. The magazine's bilingual content brought Beat poetry to young Mexican readers:[7]

All of the infrarrealistas interviewed in this project agree that the Beatniks were an inspiration and that *El corno emplumado* allowed them to read them. Medina recalls that they constantly read Allen Ginsberg, Jack Kerouac, and William Burroughs. Anaya translated *Howl and Other Poems* for UNAM in 83 and he has focused much of his published literary studies on the Beatniks. For his part, Bolaño confessed in a 1998 interview that he has always tried to follow Burroughs' advice: "For me, Burroughs is the paradigm of the writer. He is an absolutely self-sufficient writer, who can change scenes without having to change himself. When he returns to New York, he lives in a room that he calls The Bunker, a windowless hovel, somewhere in Manhattan."[8]

Burroughs was the oldest of the beatniks, but his adolescent, undisciplined, and rebellious attitude unites the group—an admirable quality in Bolaño's eyes. Youth and poetry converge in a mythical place: Mexico. As it was for Artaud and the beatniks, Mexico is for Bolaño the place to which Van Genn attributes to the rite of passage, the place of separation and liminality. Specifically, the journey to Mexico's northern border appears in Bolaño's work as a "place-myth." In *The Savage Detectives*, it is the place that attracts young writers with the centripetal force of an iconic poetic figure, Cesárea Tinajero. In *2666*, it is a dystopia driven by the femicides of Santa Teresa. In Bolaño's poetry, the northern frontier is a place of death, to where the poet's dreams travel with Mario Santiago.

Bolaño arrived in Mexico at the age of fifteen, in 1968, the same year as the Tlatelolco massacre, May in France, and the Prague Spring. The Mexican student movement in 1968 sprang from opposition to the PRI and manifested itself in the counterculture of rock, art, young poets, and radicalized groups of underground guerrilla resistance. These years, so important for Mexican youth, are narrated in Bolaño's novel *Amulet*, in the fictional voice of Auxilio Lacouture, who in real life was Alcira Sous Scaffo, an Uruguayan immigrant in Mexico. Lacouture tells how she survived several days locked in the women's bathroom at the UNAM during the Mexican army's seizure of the campus on September 18, 1968. The novel describes an experience that Bolaño did not live but heard about from the voice of an immigrant from the Southern Cone with whom the author identifies not only because of their common South American origins but also because of the experience of immigration to Mexico. Lacourture's mediation refracts Bolaño's political ideas regarding the leftist youth movements in the 1960s and 1970s. The final pages of *Amulet* discuss this idealist, committed, and somewhat naive youth that fought with the only tools they had—youth and courage. Auxilio says:

> And I heard them sing. I hear them singing still, faintly, even now that I am not in the valley, a barely audible murmur, the prettiest children of Latin America, the ill-fed and the well-fed children, those who had everything and those who had nothing, such a beautiful song it is, issuing from their lips, and how beautiful they were, such beauty, although they were marching deathward, shoulder to shoulder. . . . The young phantoms crossed the valley and fell into the abyss. A short trip. And their phantom song or the echo of their phantom song, which is to say, the echo of nothing, kept marching at the same pace, the pace of bravery and generosity, in my ears. A barely audible song, a song of war and love, because the children's certain march toward war recalled theatrical, arrogant attitudes. . . . And even though the song I heard spoke of war, of the heroic feats of a whole generation of Latin American youth sacrificed, I understood that above all it spoke of courage and mirrors, of desire and pleasure. And that song is our amulet.[9]

José Agustín notes that, "a very significant minority of society demanded true democracy and fought everywhere with enthusiasm to open spaces for expression. . . . The events of the political counterculture in 1968 generated silent effects that lasted for many years."[10] *The Savage Detectives* portrays how this countercultural movement also circulated in numerous literary workshops in Mexico in the 1970s. Some of these workshops gathered poets and intellectuals who were tired of the official culture represented by Carlos Monsiváis and, especially, Octavio Paz and his influential literary magazines, *Plural* (founded in 1971), *Vuelta* (founded in 1977), and the cultural supplement to *¡Siempre!*[11] Although the infrarrealistas were younger than the protest leaders of 1968, they arose in this context. Many came from working-class backgrounds and the ideology of their literature was deeply shaped by their social marginality, which drove their dissidence to elitist cultural circles.[12]

In the perception of these poets, the group was created informally without much systemization of principles. Raymond Williams has proposed the theoretical concept of *formations* for such groups, distinguishing them from literary and cultural *institutions*.[13] For Williams, the former ones are characterized by a loose structure in which the rules for belonging are not explicit or rigid, unlike institutions. A more practical sense of identity prevails in the group; the principles that confer identity are obvious, assumed, or tacitly understood. They may be articulated in programmatic speeches or manifestos, but they do not have a fundamentally strict quality. What is important is that the group perceives itself as different from other groups in the literary space and constitutes itself as a new reference of how to define literature. Williams highlights the specificity of the group as such and the possible coexistence of a diversity of formations within a cultural field. This position opposes traditional definitions of generations that considers social groups determined by age and era that assimilate all its members, leaving aside differentiated groups that coexist in the social (or literary) space.

It is impossible to conclude that all the members of a literary formation, such as the *infras*, perceive the group in identical ways. The principles that confer identity take the shape of a structure of feelings, in the sense that they are not intersubjectively identical. Once their connection in the literary space is presented, it can be said that the formation, and in the specific case of the *infrarrealistas*, is situated in the framework of the tradition of rupture proposed by Pierre Bourdieu to explain the rise of new groups. Bourdieu points out that the practice of rupture with previously consecrated groups is what explains the specificity of the field, its own functional logic. Once a group becomes consecrated, it is condemned to reproduce that which led to its consecration, which was precisely rupture. This reproduction prompts a "banalization" of production, an "automatization" of the perception of produced works. In the space of struggles and conflicts over the definition of symbolic capital, i.e. the literary field, the new groups strive to break with the consecrated groups to achieve institutional recognition in a field whose logic always requires something "new." For Bourdieu, "new" is not an "original invention"; rather, it is determined by previously existing objective and subjective conditions. [14]

It is in this light that we should understand the *infras'* habit of interrupting poetry readings by writers (including Octavio Paz) consecrated by official culture, who won state-sponsored grants. During presentations of other writers' books and literary prize ceremonies, the infras jumped on stage to read their own poems. This hatred toward the establishment and the "state" poets in a society that, like Mexico, valued respect for manners—where, as Juan Villoro puts it, poets and writers are expected to be "gentlemen"—generated rejection toward officialdom and the infrarrealistas were excluded from the circuits of consecration and recognition. They were not invited to participate in events or publications.

In *The Savage Detectives*, the characters Juan García Madero, Rafael Barrios, María and Angélica Font, Moctezuma, Piel Divina, Jacinto Requena, Xóchitl García, Ernesto San Epitafio, and especially Ulises Lima and Arturo Belano are dissident poets who protested the mandates of canon and where therefore marginalized from the Mexican literary establishment. They are parricides, irreverent, poor, vagabonds, intransigent. Testimony by Carlos Monsiváis, a character in the second part, describes them as two subjects, "both lost."[15] Another view from the Mexican literary field, Maples Arce, wrote that "All poets, even the most avant-garde, need a father. But these poets were orphans by vocation."[16] One of the occasions in which the novel represents the provocative and destabilizing attitude of the realvisceralistas is through the testimonies of Luis Sebastián Rosado and Alberto Moore, two young writers from wealthy families who belonged to groups led by Octavio Paz. Fear of the realvisceralistas is especially evident in Luis Sebastián, who also embarrassingly reveals his homosexuality by dancing with Piel Divina in the dive bar the realvisceralistas had dragged him to.

This occasion is also one of the rare moments in the novel that features a poem, recited by Ulises Lima. The poem "Le Coeur Volé" by Arthur Rimbaud is key to understanding the realvisceralistas' relationship with Rimbaud and the *poètes maudits*.[17] Ulises Lima is said to have recited it in perfect French, which surprised and even perturbed his friends. Ulises Lima tells the story of the poem, an autobiographical text that narrates the Rimbaud trip from Charleville to Paris to join the Commune, where a group of drunk soldiers mock and rape him. According to Lima, some of the same soldiers had participated in the French invasion of Mexico.

Like the realvisceralistas, Rimbaud scandalized the French literary field with his affairs with poets and his constant parricidal provocations of editors. Both the poetic voice in *A Season in Hell* and the realvisceralistas share the predominant feature of youth, of writing *being* young.[18] Citing Sartre and Luckács, Kristen Ross discusses the "calm" in the formation novel, which reconstructs the evolution of a young character's development of a trade or "métier."[19] It is precisely the gaining of this "métier" which defines his social insertion and the constitution of a bourgeois subject, with its moral of work and the objective rules of conformity and social ascent. This characteristic of the formation novel is absent in both *A Season in Hell* and *The Savage Detectives*. The calm is contradicted by the vertiginous rhythm of the succession of identities for both the poet in *A Season* (crazy, visionary, savage, civilization, pure, dammed, man, women, African, French) and the poets in *The Savage Detectives* revealed from a multiplicity of voices and perspectives. The profusion of voices and points of view underscores the impossibility of fixing them or knowing in their own voices—in a word, of shaping them according to a solid and stable image. Like the formation novel, *The Savage Detectives* narrates the experience of youth; yet, in contrast to the calm and the conformity of the bourgeois norms, its characters perennially live a season in hell. In this sense, they also seem to create a "queer" space of representation, in which disorder and excess undermine fixed categories.

Rimbaud fled from his country house in Charleville at sixteen to join Parisian life and the ideology of the proletariat. He wasn't alone. In 1889, six hundred thousand children (one-eleventh of the school-aged population) left school to wander the streets and move to Paris. In Europe at the time, the phenomenon of vagrancy was seen as the male equivalent of prostitution. The word, *vagaboundage* was a creation of the penal system, a term of repression, because although technically the vagabond did not violate any laws, he was virtually an insurrectional individual, especially during the agitation of the Commune.

In this sense, Bolaño's savage poets are Latin American vagabonds. They have no employment or profession, and indeed refuse to have one, but they are not idle, to the degree that idleness is defined in relation to work. Their poetic life is frenetic and combative. Their vagabondage is evidence of their rejection to be a body organized for work, where the hand carries out the orders of the brain. For both the poet of *A Season in Hell* and the savage poets, their labor is not for sale. This vertiginous poetic activity, together with the constant movement or vagabonding and idleness, has much in common with the Beat generation studied in the previous chapter and for whom Rimbaud was also a crucial reference.

This offers glimpses of a lingering distaste among the old aristocracy toward manual labor: any trade or "métier" is inferior to intellectual work. Yet, both Rimbaud and the savage poets are well aware of their social inferiority as upstarts in an intellectual field that marginalizes them. The Beats took this awareness to the extreme by calling themselves

"Beats"—as in beaten, pounded by society and the status quo. Resistance to work is a powerful, socially-inverting critique of the bourgeoisie because it implies being outside of the power relations established and controlled by capital. In *Mauvais Sang*, Rimbaud remarks on the body of workers: "business terrorizes me," "work is castration and I am intact."[20] Thus, the vagabond experience of the Beats, García Madero, Lima, and Belano resembles that of the young author of *A Season in Hell*.

The Damned Journey of Arthur Rimbaud and Arturo Belano

Although the objective of this chapter is to study travel to Mexico, it is necessary to open a parenthesis to examine Belano's identification with Rimbaud and his journeys, particularly his trip to Africa. The voyage to the northern frontier of Mexico will be addressed below. Now, in the second section of *The Savage Detectives*, Lima and Belano travel through Europe, Asia, and Africa after the death of Cesárea Tinajero, the poet mother of the avant-garde who preceded the realvisceralistas in the 1920s. Her death—or what is worse, her unveiling as the idealized mother figure of realvisceralismo—sets into motion the pilgrimage and expatriation of Ulises and Arturo beyond Mexico.[21] Like Rimbaud in Abyssinia, the poets travel through Europe, Asia, and Africa, and work to travel even more.[22] To travel to Israel, Ulises Lima works as a fisherman in a French port, but not a day more than needed to purchase his plane fare. In Tel-Aviv, we know that Ulises travels to meet with Claudia, the woman he loves, but she demands that he work. Ulises pretends to find a job to please her but instead takes on an obscure urban pilgrimage as a beggar and travel companion to a frontier character through prisons and neo-Nazi underworlds.

Belano visits other hells in Africa, prompted by a sword duel with Iñaki Echavarme in Barcelona, a critic who supposedly will write a negative review of his book. With no money and no connections to literary markets, Belano takes on the duel as a way to safeguard his honor and at the same time enter into this world without resources or contacts. After the duel, the critic and the poet end up as friends (Echavarme sends Belano medicine in Africa when he is sick).

In his study of duels in the eighteen century, Ute Frevert notes that duels served as a means of social ascent. If the duel carries the possibility of social ascent and entrance into the literary field through his friendship with the critic, why does Belano decide to go to Africa anyway? The answer is in the explanation Belano gives to why he felt offended by the critic, when previously he wouldn't have cared. "Now I care. I must be turning bourgeois."[23] Belano's confession as a vain writer wounded by criticism would subjugate him to the imperatives of the market. Although in a subtler manner, Belano was becoming one of the Mexican writers that the realvisceralistas mocked.

Belano's decision to go to Africa is motivated by the need to live poetry more radically, away from the promotional levers and market conditions. This living poetically, in the fashion of poètes maudits, is often how Rimbaud's trip to Africa is interpreted and it is, I argue, the model that Belano follows. In the essay "Literature + Illness = Illness," Bolaño reflects on the trip that he associates with Rimbaud and French poetry: "That great poetry . . . begins with Baudelaire, gains its maximum tension with Lautréamont and Rimbaud, and ends with Mallarmé."[24] Bolaño says that after boredom and resignation with life, all a poet can do is travel: "It's as if Mallarmé had said that it is necessary to sail, not to live."[25] For Bolaño, this is how Mallarmé responds to "Le voyage," the poem by Baudelaire that speaks of the traveler's motivations—flight, forgetting, conquest—but ultimately affirms that travel is for the condemned; it is to lose oneself in unknown territories, renounce everything and, at the same time, have nothing to lose. "It resembles the trip made by the sick man aboard a stretcher toward the operation table" (such was Rimbaud's trip from Africa to Marseille to have a leg amputated). The traveler thus finds himself in an "oasis of horror."[26] For Bolaño, it is a battle lost before it was fought, like most of the poets' battles: "Falling into the abyss, heaven, hell, what does it matter? / At the death of the unknown to find what is new."[27] What is new is the art that adds to the horror, as it was for Lautréamont and Rimbaud, poets submerged with identical fervor in the futility of books, sex, and journeys. Bolaño still calls on Mallarmé to carry out the trip anyway, despite the inevitable condemnation: "We have to keep moving through sex, books, and voyages, even knowing that they will take us to the abyss, which is, coincidentally, the only place where one can find the antidote."[28]

It is from this perspective that I understand Belano's trip to Africa. There is an exoticist interpretation of Rimbaud's trip, in which the western subject (ethnographer or poet) tests his conventions and himself amid otherness. There is a more utilitarian version of Rimbaud's trip that suggests he was a merchant and even a slave trader in Africa. Rimbaud wanted to be rich and orchestrated frustrated attempts to sell arms, taking advantage of local civil wars that favored the interests of France and Italy in the region. His reports to the French Geographical Society opened new commercial routes and safe roads for France in Africa and thus served European imperialism.[29] Nonetheless, when Bolaño speaks of Rimbaud's trip, he is thinking of a more poetic version because, having read Rimbaud's letters in this light, it is possible to find that "oasis of horror" of a obstinate and delirious voyage.

Jacobo Urenda is the character in *The Savage Detectives* who gives testimony of Belano's trip to Africa, when both were correspondents for the European press in Luanda, Angola, and Liberia. In the first encounter, in Luanda, Urenda thinks that Belano does not care about anything in life and only came to Africa looking for an unusual death or "some imbecility like that because my generation read Marx and Rimbaud till their guts turned."[30] But Belano was ill and was taking care of himself; he did not want to kill himself. In a crepuscular conversation, Belano suggested that he was there to get himself killed: "Do you think it's possible for someone to travel to such a remote place to get himself killed? I asked my wife, Urenda says. It's perfectly possible, she said. Even for a forty-year-old guy? If he has an adventurous spirit, it's perfectly possible, said my wife who has always had a bit of a romantic bent."[31] In Liberia, in the middle of a civil war, bullets fly over their heads, colleagues die or live huddled in a barn, surrounded by snipers. They initially conceive of an escape plan, but at the last minute Belano decides to go with the photographer López Lobo who joins a group of Mandingo soldiers: Belano himself recognized that it was an inviable and desperate move, but he was not going to let the photographer López Lobo go alone, for the night before he had told him that he come to Africa to get himself killed because he could not get over the death of his son. The next morning, Belano says goodbye to Urenda in a scene that recalls the end of *La Vorágine*: "Then Belano started running, as if at the last moment he thought the column would leave without him, he reached López Lobo, it seemed to me they were talking, it seem to me like were laughing, as if they were going on an expedition, and that's how they crossed the field and disappeared into the bush."[32]

The Belano who duels with a critic sees with horror the double face of the poet's slide into bourgeois norms and, like the idealized Rimbaud, decides right away to go to Africa. Bolaño the author, in contrast, did not lose himself in Africa. As a writer, he understood how to build himself critically within the publishing industry and to participate in the consecrated commercial circuits, as his multiple translations and literary prizes attest. Nonetheless, he was able to create a fictional character, Belano, *maudit* poetically, based on the "*illusio*" or the ideology of the literary.[33] To paraphrase Bourdieu, the legitimacy of a writer in the literary field, in this case a legitimacy acquired thanks to the figure of the "poèt maudit," contributes to the continual reproduction of belief in the game in the field, the *illusio* of the literary, of which it is also a product. The definition of poetry as life and death, as the inevitable destiny, defined as "legitimate" and "authentic" in the struggles over the symbolic power of the maudit artist vis-à-vis the market. This belief or "*illusio*" of the literary, which Bolaño fueled in his novels and essays through his alter-ego Belano, is the condition of the inner working of the game as well as its product.[34] In the following section, I will analyze other aspects in which Belano understood the *illusio* of the literary, especially in regard to exile and the value of the writer.

The Mexican Poems

Unknown University, the complete poems of Bolaño, begins with the poetic voice of a poor, undocumented, marginal immigrant in Spain. He intends to immigrate but has no work visa or legal residency in Spain. In the section titled, "My Life in the Tubes of Survival," we find poems about Bolaño's years in Mexico. Chronology is difficult to determine, but the general framework of the book evokes Mexico though Barcelona is the everyday experience. Mexico, or rather, the season in Mexico, is the space-time of lost youth, the place of memory. Chile, the country of his birth, is mentioned, but less.[35] The better part of the poems in this section speak of a South American's travels and nomadism.

The poems that refer to Mexico evoke autobiographical scenes and characters that are traceable in *The Savage Detectives*. The poem "Lupe," for example, recalls the character of the same name in the novel, a prostitute who travels in the Impala toward northern Mexico with the real-visceralista poets. The poem narrates the traumatic death of her son and her unfulfilled promise to the Virgin of Guadalupe to leave prostitution. Another poem, "Lisa" (Laura Jáuregui in the novel), addresses the topic of one true love, which repeatedly appears with regard to Lisa Johnson, Bolaño's girlfriend during his years in Mexico who left him and for whom the young author attempted suicide.

Beyond affection and characters, Mexico appears in these poems as a landscape, both urban and desertic. The poems evoke the "light of dawn in Mexico City," "Revolución Avenue," "Niño Perdido Street," and "The Altar of Sacrifices in Mexico City." The poet is "an adolescent lost in the streets of Mexico," where the light of the city is compared to a woman who "sucks her own vulva": "It tried to trap Mario Santiago. Ah, fucking light / As if it screwed itself."[36] In another poem, the characteristics that identify the Mexican symbol of the nopal now describe the adolescent poet: "The shining image of an adolescent alone / standing, arms outstretched, while in the endless horizon of Mexico / the storms appeared. / But he would survive. / Just like the nopales at the cliffs / his life would be suspended in dream / and monotony / at regular intervals and for a long time."[37] The young poet thus identifies with the nopal's resistance and endurance in the face of adversity. The poem furthermore begins with verses that refer to surrealism; as previous chapters have shown, André Breton internationalized the image of the nopal as a symbol of Mexico in his "Memories of Mexico." Bolaño writes: "He saw the nopal / but there, so far / must have been a dream. / From amidst the fog arose: shapes / round and soft, repeatedly, / in a long march from dream / to another dream."[38] The identification of Mexico with the definitions of the poetic is crucial to understanding how Bolaño used Mexico as a mythical place. Through Mexico, specifically the symbology of the nopal, Bolaño defines literature.

As in "Literature + Illness = Illness," Bolaño's poems speak of the "oasis of horror" to which the poet submits. Oasis of horror where, at the same time, the poet finds hope and bravery that serve as antidote and conjuring for *maldición*. Poetry is the antidote to desperation, illness, and death, as described in the poem "Devotion of Roberto Bolaño." Here, Mexico again is the prism through which to understand horror and its antidote:

> In late 1992 he was very ill / he had left his wife / this was the bitch truth: / he was alone and broke / and thought about the little time he had left. / But dreams, away from illness / came every night / with fidelity that amazed him. / Dreams carried him to a magical country / that he and no one else called Mexico City / and Lisa and the voice of Mario Santiago / reading a poem / and other good and dignified things / of the most electric praise / Sick and alone, he dreamed / and faced the days that marched on inexorably / and toward the end of another year / And from them he extracted a bit of strength and courage / Mexico, the phosphorescent steps in the night / the music playing on the corners / where the whores used to freeze / (in the icy heart of the Colonia Guerrero) / they gave him the nourishment he needed / to clench his teeth / and not cry out of fear.[39]

Mexico here appears as the cypher of the poet's courage ("And from them he extracted a bit of strength and courage"). Mexico is associated, inextricably, with the nostalgia for lost time and space, linked to lost youth, aesthetic and political ideals, that are the poet's *amulets* in the novel of the same name. At the same time, this loss and nostalgic feeling take on the humanistic benefits of writing, which Bolaño understands as the courage of poets. This courage is what survives beyond distance and time and it is what makes the poet a fundamentally nostalgic subject.

The recurrent dreams about Mexico in his poetry reinforce the idea of melancholy and libidinal energy of youth that survives in the poet: courage, adventure, passion for literature. In "Devotion of Roberto Bolaño," cited above, the phantasmagorical images of missing loved-ones, Lisa and Mario Santiago, return in dreams. Something similar happens in in the poem "The Burro (My Life in the Tubes of Survival)," where the poet repeatedly speaks of Mario Santiago in his dreams, on the black motorcycle that takes both to northern Mexico to chase the "unnamable unclassifiable dream/of our youth/that is, the most valiant dream of all out dreams." Mario Santiago, as a figure that returns from the dead to look for the poet on a black motorcycle, could be interpreted as the anticipated end of Bolaño himself, then seriously ill. The most interesting aspect is that the place that is visualized as the destination, perhaps in a Gothic fashion, is northern Mexico, the place where he will go to die and, at the same time, a mythical place for poets. "How could I refuse to jump on the swift black motorcycle / From the north and ride out over those road / that the saints of Mexico used to travel, / The mendicant poets of Mexico / the taciturn leeches of Tepito / Or the Colonial Guerrero, all on the same broad road / Where tenses mix and muddle: / Verbal and physical, yesterday and aphasia . . . / The only place possible for our poetry."[40]

In "The Burro," the poet takes up again the topic of courage and youth. It is a recurrent topic in his short stories, where Bolaño writes about the courage of poets and audacity of literature. "Sensini," in which the narrator refuses to send his poems to literary competitions, to throw his best work to the "hyenas," is a clear example.[41] The story "Enrique Martín" in a maudit tenor exclaims that "A poet can endure anything. Which is equivalent to saying that a man can endure anything. But it's not true: there are few things that a man can endure. Endure the truth. A poet, in contrast, can endure everything. We grew up with this conviction. The first sentence is true, but it leads to ruin, craziness, death."[42] (37).

The Mexican North, Femicides

The Savage Detectives foreshadows the Mexico in *2666*. In the third part of *Detectives*, the poet-mother of the avant-garde prophesizes the murders at the Mexican border in "The Part of the Crimes," in the posthumous novel. The poetic figure of Cesárea is contradictory in her evanescence and elephantine proportions. Materiality and spirituality live together in this maternal figure that brings life back to the realvisceralista poets Lima and Belano, thrusting them underground as fugitives of justice. By putting herself between them and the gangsters' bullet, she saves their lives and brings life back to them. Nonetheless, in the style of Borges, every one of his books contains the rest. The teacher friend of Cesárea whom Lima and Belano interview in their search for Cesárea reveals an important aspect of northern Mexico that *2666* later explores in greater detail: the maquiladoras and the femicides:

Then the teacher saw or thought she saw a map of the canning factory pinned to the wall. While she listened to the words that Cesárea had to tell, words that came out neither hesitantly nor rushed, words that the teacher would rather forget but she remembers perfectly and even understands, now she understands, her eyes scanned the map of the canning factory, a map that Cesárea had drawn, some spots in great detail and others blurred and vague, with notes in the margin that were sometimes barely legible and others in capital letters and even exclamation points, as if Cesárea with her handmade map were recognizing facets she had until then overlooked. And then the teacher had the fortitude to ask her why she had drawn a map of the facto-ry. And Cesárea said something about the approaching times, although the teacher wondered if Cesárea had entertained herself making that senseless map only because of the solitude she lived in. But Cesárea spoke to her of the times that were coming and teacher, changing the subject, asked her what times she meant and when. And Cesárea wrote down a date: some-where around the year 2600. Two thousand six-hundred something. And then, against the laughter that such a bizarre date provoked in the teacher, a suffocated laughter that was barely audible, Cesárea laughed again, al-though this time the racket of her laughter remained in the boundaries of own bedroom.[43]

The nostalgia for Mexico thus becomes dystopia in 2666. "The Part about the Crimes" provides an uninterrupted description of the series of women's raped and murdered bodies in the fictional city of Santa Teresa, Sonora, in northern Mexico. The aesthetic presages other scenes in his novels. For example, the protagonist of *Distant Star*, Tatiana von Beck Iraola ("a crazy, independent woman") enters the room where the repres-sive poet Carlos Wieder was exhibiting for the first time in Santiago, Chile his new avant-garde art or experimental poetry and photography. The exhibit featured photographs of dismembered women: "who looked like mannequins, in some cases, dismembered, destroyed mannequins, although, although in some thirty percent of the cases it is possible that they were alive at the moment of the photograph was taken. The pho-tos, in general, were of poor quality, but the impression they caused was vivid. The order in which they were displayed was not random: they fol-lowed a line, an argument, a history (chronological, spiritual), a plan."[44] The narrator says that "not a minute had passed when Tatiana von Beck turned around and left. She was pale and shaken . . . she looked at Wieder—it seemed like she was going to say something to him, but she couldn't find the words—and then tried to get to the bathroom. She couldn't. She vomited in the hallway and then, stumbling, she left the apartment."[45] In "The Part about the Crimes," Bolaño describes the femicides in northern Mexico between 1993 and 1997, also in chronological order. By juxtaposing multiple segments, each dedicated to a victim, he provokes in the reader a reaction similar to Tatiana von Beck's.

Like the photos in *Distant Star*, the forensic reports featured in *2666* provoke excess and vertigo. They note the age of each victim (generally fifteen to twenty-five), height, employment, clothing they were wearing, name, cause of death, and the official in charge of the case. The aesthetic is more descriptive and narrative; the fragmentation and the visual detail of each segment creates a photographic effect. Wieder's avant-garde art and the forensic reports, with their detailed descriptions of the corpses of the victims in Santa Teresa, tightly and inseparably join art and evil.

The character of Wieder in *Distant Star* and "The Part about the Crimes" has been read from the perspective of Georges Bataille, joining literature and absolute evil. Nonetheless, placing this union in the context of the Mexican frontier offers another reading. Mexico goes from the space-time of nostalgia in *The Savage Detectives* to the "oasis of horror in a desert of boredom," as an epigraph in *2666* from Charles Baudelaire reads, but in the context of a neoliberal economy in the space-time of the Mexican frontier. It should not be overlooked that violence is unleashed on the bodies of women who work in foreign factories. In this sense, the mythical space of northern Mexico becomes the "badland of Modernity."[46] How does the novel think about femicide by rooting it in the modern inequalities generated by global neoliberalism?

The violence against women is not exclusive to contemporary capitalist societies. In a complementary reading of Karl Marx, Silvia Federici, in *Caliban and the Witch: Women, the Body, and Primitive Accumulation*, examines how the passage from a feudal to a capital economy, through the primitive accumulation of capital, subordinated women's labor and bodies to a patriarchal system of production. Her thorough study shows that the witch hunts of the sixteenth and seventeenth centuries were as important for the development of capitalism as colonialization and expropriation of peasant lands. The new sexual division of labor that relegated women to reproductive, rather than productive, functions in the labor force and therefore excluded them from remunerated work, subordinated women in an androcentric system that persecuted and exterminated women's dissident practices, demonizing them as "witches." The outbreak of modernity redefined the relationships of gender domination now within the family. Federici argues that each phase of capitalism intensifies violence not only against peasants and (neo)colonialized subjects, but also against women:

Marx assumed that the violence that had presided over the earliest phases of capitalist expansion would recede with maturing of capitalist relations, when the exploitation and disciplining of labor would be accomplished mostly through the workings of economic laws (Marx 1909 Vol 1.). In this, he was deeply mistaken. A return of the most violent aspects of primitive accumulation has accompanied every phase of capitalist globalization, including the present one, demonstrating that the continuous expulsion of farmers from the land, war and plunder on a world scale, and the degradation of women are necessary conditions for the existence of capitalism in all times.[47]

Since the 1980s, in the phase of neoliberal capitalism that imposed flexibilization and state deregulation to establish the economy as the head of governmental administration, a model of a weak state was implemented and economic rationality was extended to non-economic areas like birth, family, health, delinquency, and penal policies. The state thus plays an ambivalent role. On the one hand, it deregulates local economies and promotes the global economy by eliminating economic borders; on the other, its immigration policies reinforce national boundaries and intensify surveillance systems. Furthermore, the state often becomes the defender of corporate interests. Sayak Valencia identifies the main factors of the neoliberal economy and the weak state: "the liberation of prices, the deregulation of markets, limited support in the country (agricultural and ranching), the de-structuralizing and inefficiency of state functions, lack of attention to minimal guarantees of human rights, spectralization of market, infomercial bombardment, constant frustration and precarization of labor that fosters the popularization of the criminal economy and the use of violence as an instrument of business."[48]

The recrudescence of the precariousness of life in the neoliberal economy undermines the social mandate of masculinity as provider and protector of the clan through employment instability and erosion of community and local ties.[49] Adding to this is the progressive socialization of consumption that defines individual and gender identities according to buying power in the material and symbolic market. The impossibility of access to the market or the constant desire and dissatisfaction generate, as Valencia notes, a type of gory violence—among, but not exclusively, genders—that rises from a gore capitalism and gore consumption. As Heather A. Brown argues in *Marx on Gender and the Family*, the situation becomes more problematic if the position of women in global capitalism is analyzed in light of United Nations reports indicating that women carry out 66 percent of work in the world and 50 percent of all food production, but earn 10 percent of income and own 1 percent of property.[50] Once again, it is clear that, in this phase of capitalism, gender is not separate from the global economic violence and its consequences in other orders.

Femicides and Neoliberalism

In *Huesos en el desierto*, journalist Sergio González highlights the hybrid spatial condition of Ciudad Juárez,[51] where different temporalities coexist and the mythical border with the United States symbolizes the loss of one identity and the risky search of another. At the threshold of the twenty-first century, the New Mexico Land Office considered it to be one of the borders of the greatest movement of people in the world: "Like so many Mexican cities, Juárez appears like an enormous backyard where masses, obsolete things at rest, sporadic vegetation, uneven asphalt and dirt roads mingle with the efficacy of machines, telecommunications, modern services, cutting-edge industry. A prosthesis of concrete, high technology, garbage in urban lots, decorated by plastic, potholes, rust, and strips of rags."[52]

As González points out, the map of Ciudad Juárez is difficult, for it overflows in conflictive, abrupt, and variegated ways. Crime, night life, bars, and the business of drug trafficking are rampant in the slums of precarious constructions. What Valencia says about Tijuana goes for many other cities—a gore market where the products offered are drugs, prostitution, human organs, intimidating violence, murders for hire, and so forth: "These demands have a specific geopolitical position that conceives of developing countries as the factories of gore merchandise produced for the consumption and satisfaction of international practical and playful demands."[53]

From the late nineteenth century to the early twenty-first, Ciudad Juárez was the "Passage to the North," a site of transit, smuggling, and violence that attracted American tourism during Prohibition in the southern states. The city was seen as a place of vacation without restrictions. During WWII, soldiers from Fort Bliss, Texas, went to Juárez for rest and relaxation. Migratory flows attracted commerce. Also during WWII, due to the shortage of labor in the United States, the Bracero Program allowed Mexican workers to enter the United States to meet labor demands. However, with the end of the war and the program, employment among rural workers grew along the US-Mexico border. The Mexican government instituted the Industrialization of the Border program (1965) that would later open avenues for the maquiladora industry: factories of foreign capital where different pieces of a product are manufactured or assembled by cheap labor for export. The program aimed to attract foreign (American) capital to Mexico and generate employment by keeping Mexican labor cheap and competitive. Here is where women occupy a place in the machinery of primitive accumulation of capital in the neoliberal age. The Mexican women who work in the maquiladoras earn far less than the minimum wage in the United States. Turnover is high, due to health problems and precarious working conditions in many factories. The crimes committed against women perpetuate the economic development of the zone and capital, disposing of the bodies that in their brief existence and death favor the gears of the productive system.

In "The Part about the Crimes," the head of the department of sexual crimes notes that the ratio of murders in all of Mexico was ten men for every woman; however, in Santa Teresa, the fictional version of Ciudad Juárez, it was four women for every ten men: "Do you know what city has the lowest rate of female unemployment in Mexico? Santa Teresa, said the head of the department of sexual crimes. Here, almost all women have jobs. Poorly paid and exploitative, with terrible shifts and no union guarantees, but jobs all the same. For many women from Oaxaca or Zacatecas, it's a blessing."[54] Martha Pérez, the (real) head of the Department of Sexual Crimes in Ciudad Juárez explained in an interview with Sergio González in *Huesos en el desierto* that the department received more than six reports of rape a day. Most of these rapes in factories were against minors who used fake documents to get jobs.[55]

The possibilities of employment and the type of economic independence that this situation creates for women becomes more problematic when combined with a masculine perception that sees them as mere sexual objects who fail to fulfill the role of the pure woman, wife and mother. A woman who works undermines the need for masculine protection: "By being free from a young age, from puberty even, women are identified as dirty—they like sex, earn money, and spend it on what they want, entertainment and clothing."[56] As Ana Bergareche notes in González's book, a fundamental problem is the identity of women who welcome the social change that comes from economic independence, but at the same time assimilate the socialization that being alone, without a family or a husband, makes them more vulnerable, and this vulnerability becomes more intense at the border. These studies of the episteme of gender violence show that although economic independence (albeit in precarious conditions) and the capacity of consumption could provide feminine empowerment, they cannot be separated from the systemic violence that undermines this empowerment.

Some of the traps of media and artistic representation of this phenomenon are the models known as sensationalist melodrama, humanitarian, conventional political narrations, noir novels and its subgenres. They fail to address the complex economic and geopolitical realities; far from creating an episteme of gender violence, they favor its normalization and make it, once again, an object of consumption (gore).

What Sergio González's research on the femicides makes clear is that, despite efforts by local authorities and the media to resort to the classic topic of the "serial killer" in Gothic and political literature, no single person is responsible for the deaths. The same thing happens in *2666*. In the novel, the supposed assassin of the first victims is Klaus Hass, a German-born American citizen residing in Mexico where he had computer businesses. Haas is taken to prison, from where he calls several press conferences. He declares that the assassin is Daniel Uribe, a member of a wealthy family. Nonetheless, the murders continue while Hass is in jail. The history of Hass, descendent of Germans, is inspired by the real case of the Egyptian citizen Omar Sharif Latif, declared guilty of three murders and sentenced to jail in 1996. Nonetheless, after his arrest, the murders continued. The authorities stated that Sharif from prison led members of the "Rebeldes" gang (the "Bison" in the novel) to continue the murders. The gang members were also charged and sentenced, but they declared that police had used torture to force them to confess to crimes they did not commit.

Throughout the investigation in the novel carried out by the fictional character and alter-ego of the journalist Sergio González, and thanks to a polyphony of voices and discursive genres such as forensics, politics, and journalism that converge to tell intersecting stories, suspicions, and counter-proofs, it is clear that there no single person responsible for the more than one-hundred narrated deaths. A collection of systemic factors constitute the framework of the story and go beyond the conventional models of representation of crime: government corruption, the ineffective legal system, the copycat effect, the lack of public lighting in poor neighborhoods, the networks of drug traffickers and parties with women as entertainment, the deeply sexist and misogynous society. In a frontier zone like Ciudad Juárez/Santa Teresa, the migratory flows, the cultural nomadism, and the mobile overpopulation exponentially increase violence in general and femicides, becoming the epitome of the consequences of global neoliberalism in women's bodies, and not only along the Mexican border.

This is the framework that creates the mass killing of women, in which they are literally waste. And I say literally waste because once killed, they are thrown into dumps, vacant lots, along the highway and in the desert, but mostly in clearings and dumps:

> Emilia Mena Mena died in June. Her body was found in the clandestine dump near Yucatecos Street, on the way to the Corinto brothers' brick facto-

ry. The forensic report indicates that she was raped, stabbed, and burned, but did not specify if death was caused by the stabbing or the burns or if Emilia Mena Mena was burned before or after death. Fires, most voluntary, some fortuitous, are regularly reported in the dump where she was found. The possibility therefore that the burns on her body were caused not by homicidal will but by a fire of these characteristics cannot be discarded. The dump has no official name, because it is clandestine, but it does have a popular name: it is called El Chile. During the daytime, not a soul can be seen in El Chile nor in the surrounding lots that the dump will swallow soon enough. At night those who have nothing or less than nothing ventured out. In Mexico City they're called "teporochos," but a teporocho is an opportunist, a contemplative cynic, and a humorist compared to the human beings who swarm around El Chile alone or in pairs. They are few, and their slang is difficult to understand. The police conducted a roundup the night after Emilia Mena Mena's body was found and all they brought in were three children who were looking through boxes of garbage. The nocturnal habitants of El Chile are scarce. Their life expectancy is brief. At most, they die after six months of moving through the dump. Their eating habits and sex life are a mystery. They may have forgotten how to eat and screw. Or perhaps food and sex are beyond their reach, indescribable, beyond action and expression. They are all, without exception, sick. To strip the clothing from a corpse in El Chile is to skin it. The population remains stable: never fewer than three, never more than twenty.[57]

The quote highlights the abject condition of the people who live in the dump. They are individuals who have lost their humanity, their ability to communicate and even their physiological functions. Their skin is rotting clothing, marking the absence of any separation between subject and object. Here is where the victims' bodies are thrown. The dump is comparable to the waste management industry, an allegory of the result of unequal economic globalization.

Mexico and Literature

Bolaño derived a literary theory from his vision of Mexico. In works such as *Amulet* and *The Savage Detectives*, literature is defined with the topic of the expelled, "exiled" writer. Mexico is the mythical place of youth and nostalgia for its loss. The admiration for the adolescent, poètes maudits led him to model Arturo Belano and Ulises Lima after Rimbaud and Lautremont, for whom travel, adventure, and vagrancy defined the poetic experience. In *Amulet*, Mexico extends into Latin America and the experience of a generation of militant youth. The amulet object is a lifesaver, as it was for Artaud. It expresses the luck of the poet—neither good nor bad, but inescapable—and is nothing more than his courage to face everything.

In Bolaño's poetry, Mexico is the scene of his phantasmagoric memories at the edge of death. The poet seizes onto these Mexican phantoms to recover his courage. But Mexico is not only the scene of a poetic life. In his poems, Mexico becomes poetry itself: it is the light—vagina dentata—that wanted to swallow Mario Santiago. It is the nopal that appears, in dreams; it is the figure of the poet himself. Once again, the nopal as a symbol of Mexico is associated with surrealism, in this case with Breton and the durability in the face of adversary and despite death.

Finally, Mexico is the oasis of horror in *2666*. In keeping with the doctrine of mauditism, Bolaño defines literature and Mexico in the words of Baudelaire as: "an oasis of horror in the middle of a desert of boredom." Drawing on the forensic reports on murdered women and the fragmented polyphony of "The Part about the Crimes," the novel aims to examine the deep social, economic, political history of the continent. There is a confidence in the writing/literature as a tool to know/experiment evil and its antidote. Literature, like Mexico, is an inescapable fate. The map of the factory in the room of the iconic poet Cesárea Tinajero in northern Mexico dated "2.600 something" points to the events in the maquiladoras in *2666*. Mexico is defined, inseparable from Bolaño's vision of literature, embedded in all of his work.

Conclusion

In the foregoing chapters, I have read travel experiences in Mexico in different discursive manifestations—essays, letters, poems, chronicles, diaries, and fictional narrative. Although I have considered the case of travelers, like Désiré Charnay, whose writings were addressed to and financed by metropolitan agencies in Europe and the United States, my reading has diverged from critiques of imperial travel. Following Edward Said, Stephen Greenblatt, David Spurr, Mary Louise Pratt, Ricardo Salvatore, and others, I examined the informal, economic, and cultural definitions of empire, as well as the symbolic machinery behind the representation of otherness. Nonetheless, my aim has also been to explore the experiences of non-imperial travelers such as Gabriela Mistral and Roberto Bolaño, as well as those travelers—like Alexander von Humboldt, Frances Calderón de la Barca, John Reed, Antonin Artaud, and the Beats—whose relationship with informal and formal empires was conflictive and critical. Drawing on what Van Den Abbeele proposes in this classic study *Travel as Metaphor* on the economy of travel and travel narratives in relation to the oikos—that is, the home or the point of departure against which the experience and the profit of the itinerary is evaluated—I have read these texts to study the extent to which they distanced themselves from, and dared to question, domestic economies in their representations of cultural encounters that are more protean and less determined by the travelers' origins.

My objective was to show that, for these travelers, travel is a judgment of domesticity, a vital narrative stand that expresses its impossibility. The impossible domesticity of these travelers redefines the economy of travel subjected to the oikos. Here oikos is not only criticized but also uninhabitable: these travelers do not feel comfortable with the securities of the habitual. These are the travel experiences and narratives that defy the *habitus* and its promise of conventional happiness, as Sara Ahmed posits. They propose an alternative history of happiness that derives from a radical cultural encounter, from the danger of succumbing and dying, and from failure. All these travelers fail and triumph literarily.

Mexico catapulted the professional and artistic fame of all these travelers. Mexico, and Latin America more broadly, made Humboldt the most prominent scientist of his age, given his involvement in independence struggles. Charnay became famous as the first photographer in the Maya area. Fanny Calderón was the first foreign woman to write about traveling in Mexico; her work as an intermediary helped strengthen Hispanism in the United States. Reed's chronicles for *Metropolitan Magazine* were a trampoline for war correspondents in Europe. Thanks to Mexico, Mistral became "America's teacher." Artaud's experience with the Tarahumaras legitimized his avant-garde theater, giving him the keys to develop his theory on theater and its double. For the Beats and Bolaño, the Mexico experience shored up their symbolic capital in the literary field wherein Mexico became a place of poetry: adventure and horror. For many, like Mistral and Bolaño, the trip to Mexico was their first time out of their countries. The trip and stay were decisive: these two travelers would never return to live in their country; they became migrant subjects for the rest of their lives.

Many books and movies address the travel experience in Mexico: *The Plumed Serpent* by D. H. Lawrence (1926), *Under the Volcano* by Malcolm Lowry (1957), or *¡Que viva México!* by Sergei Eisenstein (1931). *Impossible Domesticity* focuses not only on major works like Jack Kerouac's *On the Road* and Bolaño's *Savage Detectives* and *2666*, but also on a collection of secondary works, often overlooked by the general public. The aim was to shed light on a corpus that, although less well-known, influenced the overall work of these authors. At the same time, my intention was to use the marginal quality of these works to explore the possibilities of fragmenting and contesting the established, stereotypical images and discourses about Mexico.

The book thus posited theoretical problems of travel and travel writing in three sections. The first, encompassing chapters on Humboldt, Charnay, and Calderón, studied the agency of objects found on the way, as "quasi-subjects," in constant production and questioning of social relations and disciplines of knowledge, as Bill Brown, Bruno Latour, Martin F. Manalansan IV, and Jean Baudrillard have shown. In the case of the travelers in this first section, it is not so much them as the objects of their journey that resist discipline. The second section studied utopian aspects of Mexico during the revolutionary and postrevolutionary periods in contrast to other parts of Latin America, for Mistral, and the United

States and the Soviet Union, for Reed. Here the aim was to approach the political and pedagogical aspects of utopia and arcadia by drawing on concepts from Ernst Bloch, Fredric Jameson, and Roger Bartra. The third section, on Artaud, the Beatniks, and Roberto Bolaño, addressed the question of space in regard to art and literature. The aim was to explore spatial definitions of literature to see how Mexico was constituted as a poetic experience in spaces such as the desert and the border. Drawing on Rob Shields, Victor Turner, Pierre Bourdieu, and Kevin Hetherington, and reading travel and art as "queer" failure, as Jack Halberstam and Sara Ahmed, this third section analyzed the relationship between these texts and space.

Impossible Domesticity did not seek to read how these travelers influenced Mexican intellectuals and their definitions of the Mexican nation. It did not attempt to discover their "influence" on local discourses of identity or how Mexicans reacted or responded, in creative transcultural ways, to these foreigners. In a decolonizing reading, this book explored what Mexico gave to these travelers, their disciplines, professions, and life experiences. Drawing on Aníbal Quijano's work on the coloniality of power and the intrinsic relationship between modernity and coloniality, *Impossible Domesticity* shifted the angle of queries, situating Mexico in its undeniable and vigorously active position in the global production of knowledge, politics, and art.

Notes

Introduction

1. For definitions of this concept, see Shields, *Places on the Margin*. See also Rogers, *Jungle Fever*.

2. Bartra, *El salvaje en el espejo*; Mignolo, *Idea of Latin America*.

3. Clifford, *Predicament of Culture*.

4. Hetherington, *Badlands of Modernity*, 36.

5. Quijano, *Cuestiones y Horizontes*; Mignolo, *Darker Side of Western Modernity*.

6. Van Den Abbeele, *Travel as Metaphor*, xvii–xviii.

7. See Gómez, "Philosopher Traveler."

8. Brown, "Thing Theory."

9. Manalansan IV, "'Stuff' of Archives," 103.

10. Among postcolonial critics, see especially Spurr, *Rhetoric of Empire*; Greenblatt, *Marvelous Possessions*; Pratt, *Imperial Eyes*; Joseph, LeGrand, and Salvatore, eds., *Close Encounters of Empire*; and Said's classic *Orientalism*. My book *Iluminados y tránsfugas* follows along similar lines.

11. See, among others, Gómez, preface to *Travel Narratives*; Clark, ed., *Travel Writing and Empire*; Porter, *Haunted Journeys*; Stagl, *History of Curiosity*; Van Den Abbeele, *Travel as Metaphor*; and Ziff, *Return Passages*.

12. The rise of these disciplines has been studied as a part of a movement of global imperial expansion involving both formal practices of coercion (territorial annexation, military occupation, and colonial settlements) and more informal practices of economic and financial nature (Gallagher and Robinson, "Imperialism of Free Trade"). This formal and/or informal imperial expansion has rested on rhetorical machinery that situated the empire as the site of civilizing forces, reason, and the white masculine subject. As it determined categories of subalternity based on race and gender in colonialized territories, such discourse idealized, infantilized, eroticized, and demonized members of these categories on a symbolic plane (Spurr, *Rhetoric of Empire*). In a double movement of admi-

ration and usurpation, desire and rejection, the rhetorical and epistemological apparatus around Mexico provided justifications for exploitation, exploration, and extraction of goods and bodies while projecting Romantic/artistic/scientific/adventurous/utopic images of colonial otherness (Young, *Colonial Desire*; and Bhabha, *Location of Culture*).

13. Wallerstein, *Modern World-System*; Segato, *La crítica a la colonialidad*; Mignolo and Walsh, *On Decoloniality*.

14. Mignolo, *Darker Side of Western Modernity*, 2.

15. In my previous books, I studied how imperial travelers influenced the writing of local Latin American intellectuals and politicians. See Gómez, *Iluminados y tránsfugas*, and *Darwinism in Argentina*. *Impossible Domesticity* did not attempt to study how Mexicans reacted or responded to foreign travelers to produce discourses of national identity. Other critics have engaged in this task. See Pitman, *Mexican Travel Writing*.

16. Brown, "Thing Theory"; Latour, "Where Are the Missing Masses?"; Baudrillard, "Subjective Discourse"; Manalansan IV, "'Stuff' of Archives."

17. Humboldt and Trabulse, *Tablas Geográficas Políticas Del Reyno*, 217; translated by Robert Weis.

18. Latour, *Science in Action*.

19. Manalansan IV, "'Stuff' of Archives."

20. Manalansan IV, "'Stuff' of Archives," 97.

21. The title of this book, *Impossible Domesticity*, is inspired by Manalansan's original use of the phrase in his article "The 'Stuff' of Archives," in which the author studies the immigrants' experience in relation to household objects.

22. I take this term from M. L. Pratt, *Imperial Eyes*.

23. Desmond, *Yucatán through Her Eyes*; and Desmond and Messenger, *Dream of Maya*.

24. Charnay and DeBroise, *Claude Désiré Charnay*.

25. Ahmed, *Cultural Politics of Emotion*, 90–91.

26. Cabañas, *Cultural "Other."*

27. Bloch, *Principle of Hope*; Jameson, *Archaeologies of the Future*; Bartra, *El salvaje en el espejo*.

28. Bartra, *El salvaje en el espejo*, 1; translated by Robert Weis.

29. Homberger, *John Reed*.

30. Shields, *Places on the Margin*; Turner, *Ritual Process*; Bourdieu, *Rules of Art*.

31. Halberstam, *Queer Art of Failure*; and Ahmed, *Promise of Happiness*.

32. Halberstam, *Queer Art of Failure*, 2.

33. Halberstam, *Queer Art of Failure*, 2–3.

34. Halberstam, *Queer Art of Failure*, 3.

35. Ahmed, *Promise of Happiness*, 9.

36. Ahmed, *Promise of Happiness*, 17.

37. Price, *Primitive Art in Civilized Places*, 2001.

38. Anzaldúa, *Borderlands / La frontera*.

39. Valencia, *Capitalismo Gore*.

40. Nonetheless, in his novel *Amulet* (1999), Bolaño recognized the significance of Mexico as a destination and refuge for many Latin Americans, himself included, who were exiled by dictatorships. *Amulet* offers a key to the relationship of the travelers in *The Savage Detectives* with youth culture. In the novel, Auxilio Lacourtour locks herself in a bathroom in the National Autonomous University of Mexico for ten days in October 1968 while the army seizes the campus and massacres youth protesting in Tlatelolco Plaza. As he does in many of his novels, Bolaño speaks here of youth in Latin America. All the travelers I study in this book are young, and Mexico represents for them a voyage of initiation, of radically new experiences that are therefore risky, immeasurable, and transformative.

Chapter 1. Humboldt in Mexico

1. Humboldt, *Political Essay*, vol. 1, 10–11.

2. Latour, *La esperanza de Pandora*, chapter 2 (99–136).

3. Latour, *Science in Action*.

4. Leask, *Curiosity and the Aesthetics*. This chapter follows Leask's reading of Humboldt and his use of Latour's theory to explain the transfer of objects to the metropole. My objective is to extend this reading and, much like Latour, highlight the agency of nonhumans.

5. Humboldt, *Cartas americanas*, 54; translated by Robert Weis.

6. Humboldt, *Personal Narrative*, vii.

7. Humboldt, *Cartas americanas*, 24; translated by Robert Weis.

8. Humboldt, *Views of Nature*, 127.

9. Humboldt, *Views of Nature*, 128.

10. Humboldt, *Views of Nature*, 128.

11. Humboldt, *Views of Nature*, 129.

12. Clavijero, *Historia antigua de Mexico*, vol. 4, 228; translated by Robert Weis.

13. Ette, "'Not Just Brought about by Chance.'"

14. Humboldt, *Political Essay*, vol. 1, 125–26.

15. Humboldt, *Political Essay*, vol. 1, 124.

16. Humboldt, *Political Essay*, vol. 1, 211.

17. Humboldt, *Political Essay*, vol. 1, 212.

18. Humboldt, *Political Essay*, 223.

19. Ortega y Medina, *Humboldt desde México*, 22; translated by Robert Weis.

20. Bernal, *History of Mexican Archaeology*, 101.

21. Thomas Jefferson to Alexander von Humboldt, Monticello, April 14, 1811. Quoted in Rebok, *Humboldt and Jefferson*, 151–52.

22. Amid the wars for independence, it is interesting to note that Humboldt, a defender of democratic and liberal ideals and a fervent abolitionist, did not write widely about the Haitian Revolution, the first anti-slavery revolution in America. Although Humboldt never went to Haiti, the revolution was raging during the years of his voyage. His silence was perhaps political, for he would return to France, his residence for twenty-three years. In the context of the Napoleonic wars, the safety of his traveling companion, Bonpland, a French citizen, could also account for his silence. Nonetheless, slavery would be an important topic in his *Political Essay on the Island of Cuba* and a source of dissidence with Jefferson, though never explicitly.

23. In this work on different accelerated globalizations, Ette identifies the second one, during the eighteenth and nineteenth centuries, as "a more intensive system of trade and communication put into place, dictated by European interests and operated from London, Paris and Amsterdam, a system which implemented innovative forms of presenting and arranging knowledge, following the needs of European political power and science" ("'Not Just Brought about by Chance,'" 3). In this second phase, Cornelius DePauw played an outstanding role with his 1768 publication of *Recherches philosophiques sur les Américains*, in which the philosopher shows himself to be a thinker of globalization, characterized by an acutely asymmetrical structure in which America and Europe are compared in a dichotomy of inferiority–superiority, respectively. For Ette, it is plausible to think that DePauw, aware of the frustrated colonial designs of the Dutch and the Germans in Africa and America, had in mind a possible revitalization of the Brandenburgisch-Africanische-Americanische Compagnie ("'Not Just Brought about by Chance,'" 10–11). The sale and transport of slaves from Africa to the Caribbean appeared to be a way to rethink Europe's expansionist intentions.

24. Rebok, *Humboldt and Jefferson*.

25. On the *Naturgemälde*, Humboldt wrote the names of the plants in accordance with details on their altitude on the volcano's slope. In columns on both sides of the image, he recorded details about the humidity, temperature, and blue color of the sky, all according to the altitude of Chimborazo.

26. Rebok, *Humboldt and Jefferson*, 105.

27. Humboldt, *Views of Nature*, 1.

28. Humboldt, *Views of Nature*, 1.

29. Humboldt, *Views of Nature*, 32.

30. Humboldt, *Views of Nature*, 53.

31. Humboldt, *Views of Nature*, 216–17.

32. Humboldt, *Views of Nature*, 11.

33. Humboldt, *Views of Nature*, 11.

34. Humboldt, *Views of Nature*, 11.

35. Humboldt, *Views of Nature*, 14.

36. Humboldt, *Views of Nature*, 16; emphasis added.

37. Echenberg, *Humboldt's Mexico*.

38. Humboldt, *Political Essay*, vol. 1, 52–53.

39. Humboldt, *Political Essay*, vol. 1, 18.

40. Humboldt, *Political Essay*, vol. 1, 44–45.

41. Humboldt, *Political Essay*, vol. 1, 70.

42. Humboldt, *Political Essay*, vol. 1, 47.

43. Humboldt, *Political Essay*, vol. 1, 78.

44. Humboldt, *Political Essay*, vol. 1, 79.

45. Ortega y Medina, *Humboldt desde México*, 30–43.

46. Humboldt, *Political Essay*, vol. 3, 304–5.

47. Borges, "The Aleph," 128.

48. Wulf, *La invención de la naturaleza*, 121.

49. Humboldt, "On Account of Two Attempts," 13.

50. This rhetoric was not exclusive to Humboldt but was shared by other nineteenth century travelers. Shipwrecks, for example, almost always led to threats of cannibalism, famine, and the loss of sanity within a rhetoric of pilgrimage down a via crucis that took scientific progress as a transcendental good. Other examples include the voyage of James Cook and his death in a cannibalistic rite of the Pacific and the extermination of dozens of men in the expedition of La Condamine in Ecuador (Gómez, "The Philosopher Traveler").

51. Humboldt, *Cartas americanas*, 54; translated by Robert Weis.

Chapter 2. Désiré Charnay in Mexico

1. Charnay, *Le Mexique*.

2. Davis, *Désiré Charnay*, 129.

3. Baudrillard, "Subjective Discourse," 41.

4. "Il était réservé à la France de secouer le Mexique de son engourdissement" (Charnay, *Le Mexique*, 98; translated by Robert Weis).

5. "Mais il a fallu des circonstances extraordinaires: le cataclysme d'un grand peuple et le génie d'un grand prince, pour l'arracher à la pente fatale qui l'entraînait à l'Amérique. La scission des Etats-Unis rejette pour un long temps le Mexique sous l'influence européenne, et l'expédition actuelle assure à la France une prépondérance sans conteste sur cette contrée la plus riche du globe. A son origine, l'expédition alliée, dirigée dans le simple but d'une réclamation de créance, s'engageait dans une entreprise impraticable, et ne pouvait que se heurter contre l'impuissance d'un débiteur insolvable. Le Mexique, dans l'état où l'a réduit la guerre civile, privé de ressources et malgré la meilleure volonté du monde, n'aurait pu rembourser la moindre échéance, et la saisie de ses douanes ne pouvait que le précipiter dans de nouveaux désordres. Mais il semble que la Providence ouvre à ce pays une perspective nouvelle" (Charnay, *Le Mexique*, 98; translated by Robert Weis).

6. Davis, *Désiré Charnay*, 35.

7. Ette, "Iconografía, caligrafía, autografía."

8. Benjamin, *Work of Art*.

9. Barthes, "Rhetoric of the Image."

10. Lerebours, ed., *Excursions daguerriennes*.

11. Davis, *Désiré Charnay*, 5–9.

12. Davis, *Désiré Charnay*, 5–9.

13. Davis, *Désiré Charnay*, 108–30.

14. Evans, *Romancing the Maya*, 106.

15. Charnay, *Ancient Cities*.

16. Charnay and Le-Duc, *Cités et ruins américaines*.

17. Quoted in Evans, *Romancing the Maya*, 54.

18. Evans, *Romancing the Maya*, 103.

19. Allen T. Rice, "Introduction," in Charnay, *Ancient Cities*, xxiii.

20. Latour, *Science in Action*, 215–39.

21. Brown, "Thing Theory," 140.

22. Tovar de Teresa, "Prefacio."

23. Riegl, "Modem Cult of Monuments," 21–51.

24. Baudrillard, "Subjective Discourse," 42.

25. Davis, *Désiré Charnay*, 16.

26. Charnay, *Ancient Cities*, 55–56.

27. Sarmiento, *Facundo, or, Civilization and Barbarism*.

28. Gómez, "Local Knowledge and Science."

29. "Les ruines sont à douze kilomètres au moins du village; c'est une course assez longue. Le bruit des cognées frappant sur les troncs d'arbres m'avertit que nous approchions; cependant on n'apercevait pas la moindre trace des monuments, la forêt vierge nous enveloppait dans l'épaisseur de ses ombres, et nous n'avancions qu'avec difficulté. J'arrivai bientôt dans l'éclaircie que venait de pratiquer la hache des travailleurs, et je n'apercevais toujours point le palais. 'Ah çà! mais l'ami, dis-je au guide, où donc se cache le palais?' 'Le voilà, señor,' répondit-il, me désignant une masse noirâtre, couverte d'une végétation aussi vigoureuse que celle du sol, et dont la façade était à moitié cachée sous un fouillis de lianes. En vérité, l'on pouvait passer à dix mètres et ne point l'apercevoir. Je compris aussitôt les difficultés qui m'attendaient dans la reproduction de ces monuments; tout était noir, vermiculé, ruiné, perdu; je ne pouvais, du reste, me mettre à l'œuvre de sitôt, car le travail des Indiens n'allait point aussi vite que je l'avais pensé d'abord, il leur fallait deux jours encore pour me permettre de prendre une perspective de la façade. Il fallait, de plus, abattre au moins les arbres les plus gênants qui couvraient les toits de l'édifice et débarrasser la façade des plantes grimpantes qui en obstruaient la vue" (Charnay, *Le Mexique* , 416–17; translated by Robert Weis).

30. "Depuis deux jours, don Agustin avait envoyé à mon intention douze Indiens dans les ruines pour couper les bois et dégager les palais; l'ouvrage devait avancer, et je partis pour les rejoindre. J'étais accompagné de mon domestique et

d'un guide que l'État de Chiapas impose aujourd'hui à chaque voyageur, moyennant une solde de cinq francs par jour. Celui-ci devait me servir à deux fins: guider mes explorations dans les monuments et surveiller ma conduite à l'égard des palais, sa consigne étant de m'empêcher de commettre toute dégradation quelconque; quatre Indiens nous suivaient également, chargés de mes bagages, d'une table, de divers ustensiles de cuisine et de provisions de bouche" (Charnay, *Le Mexique*, 312; translated by Robert Weis).

31. The *volcanero* is the adroit local agent accustomed to the highlands due to his training in the extraction of sulfur from volcanoes and his familiarity with the inhospitable local conditions.

32. Charnay, *Les anciennes villes*, 166–67.

33. Baudrillard, "Subjective Discourse," 41.

34. Charnay, *Ancient Cities*, 222–23.

35. Jacob, *Sovereign Map*, xvi.

36. Shields, *Places on the Margin*.

37. "Je dormais seul dans le palais; les Indiens se refusèrent constamment à passer la nuit dans les ruines; l'idée seule leur inspirait une frayeur mortelle"(Charnay, *Le Mexique*, 367; translated by Robert Weis).

38. Kristeva, *Powers of Horrors*.

39. "La nuit vint, je me roulai sur mon hamac, où je ne tardai pas à m'endormir du sommeil du juste. Mais, hélas! juste, je ne l'étais point, car je m'éveillai soudain en proie à d'atroces douleurs. Un bruit d'ailes remplissait la chambre, et, portant les mains au hasard, je sentis une multitude d'insectes froids et plats de la taille d'un grand cafard. Horreur! une multitude d'entre eux passèrent sur ma figure; je me précipitai pour allumer une bougie, et mes yeux furent frappés du spectacle le plus désolant qui se pût voir. Dans mon hamac, plus de deux cents de ces affreuses bêtes restaient comme prises au filet; trente, au moins, de ces animaux, que je me hâtai de secouer, restaient encore sur moi; j'avais à la figure, aux mains, sur le corps, des enflures qui me causaient une douleur insupportable. Une grande quantité, parmi ceux du hamac, étaient gras, rebondis et gonflés du sang qu'ils m'avaient tiré; les murailles étaient couvertes de compagnons de même espèce, qui paraissaient attendre que leurs amis, rassasiés, leur cédassent la place. Comment me défaire de tant d'ennemis? Je m'armai d'une petite planche et je commençai le massacre. C'était une besogne atroce et dégoûtante à soulever le cœur; le combat dura deux heures, sans pitié, sans merci: j'écrasai tout. Quand je vis la place nettoyée, qu'il n'y eut plus que des cadavres, je fermai hermétiquement la porte et tâchai de me rendormir, deux heures après il fallait recommencer. . . . Pendant huit jours, j'endurai ce supplice, qui fut bien un des plus atroces de ma vie de voyage. Quinze jours après, je portais encore les marques des piqûres de mes adversaires" (Charnay, *Le Mexique*, 376–77; translated by Robert Weis).

40. Baudrillard, "Subjective Discourse," 42.

Chapter 3. Fanny Calderón in Mexico

1. Texidor, "Prólogo," ix–x; translated by Robert Weis.

2. Manuel Payno, *Revistas literarias de México*, La Iberia Editions, Mexico, 1868, 16. Quoted in Texidor, "Prólogo," x; translated by Robert Weis.

3. Fossey, *Le Mexique*, 542. Quoted in Texidor, "Prólogo," xi; translated by Robert Weis.

4. Elizabeth Eastlake, "Lady Travellers," *Quarterly Review* 76 (1845): 115. Quoted in Lindsay, "Postcolonial Anxieties," 171.

5. Franco, *Plotting Women*.

6. See Jagoe, "Visible Horizon Bounds Their Wishes"; Kaplan and Gerassi-Navarro, "Between Empires"; and Leask, "Ghost in Chapultepec."

7. Ahmed, *Cultural Politics of Emotion*, loc. 1941 of 6419, Kindle.

8. Latour, "Where Are the Missing Masses?," 235.

9. Calderón, *Life in Mexico*, 57–58.

10. Lindsay, "Postcolonial Anxieties," 181.

11. Letter from Prescott to Charles Dickens, Boston, December 1, 1842. Quoted in Texidor, "Prólogo," x.

12. Pi-Suñer Llorens, *La deuda española en México*, 31–76

13. Ahmed, *Cultural Politics of Emotion*, loc. 1937 of 6419, Kindle.

14. Calderón, *Life in Mexico*, 106.

15. See Alejandra Araya Espinosa, "De los límites de la modernidad a la subversión de la obscenidad: vagos, mendigos y populacho en México, 1821–1871," in Romana, *Culturas de pobreza*, 45–71.

16. Both Esther Aillón and Vanesa Teiltelbaum note that there were substantial changes in vagrancy laws after independence, not only in the creation of the tribunal but also in the expansion of the category of "vagos" to include beggars, false beggars, and child beggars who during the process of secularization lost the help of religious organizations. In 1845, the category of "vagos" included anyone who did not have a legally recognized trade—the acrobats in the plazas and other public spaces, people without permanent residence, and those who offended social superiors with obscene artistic expression. See Teiltelbaum, "La corrección de la vagancia," and Aillón Soria, "Moralizar por la fuerza."

17. Leask, "Ghost in Chapultepec," 193.

18. Leask, "Ghost in Chapultepec," 198.

19. Youngs, "Buttons and Souls," 119.

20. Pratt, *Imperial Eyes*, 77.

21. Calderón, *Life in Mexico*, 407.

22. Calderón, *Life in Mexico*, 79.

23. Ahmed, *Cultural Politics of Emotion*, loc. 1949 of 6419, Kindle.

24. Calderón, *Life in Mexico*, 203.

25. Calderón, *Life in Mexico*, 227.

26. Calderón, *Life in Mexico*, 220.

27. Calderón, *Life in Mexico*, 608.

28. Borges, "Historia del guerrero."

29. Kristeva, *Powers of Horrors*, 39.

30. Jaksić, "Lessons of Spain." For more biographical information, see Jaksić, *Hispanic World*.

31. Prescott, *Correspondence*, 315–16.

32. Eipper, "Canonizer De-Canonized," 422.

33. This was one of the main criticisms made by José Ramírez on *Historia de la Conquista de México* and Prescott's "limited" reading of Spanish sources. See Gómez, "El hispanismo en viaje."

34. Women traveler writers could not entirely identify with the traditionally masculine genre of travel narratives, especially with respect to the eroticized metaphors of "feminized" nature explored or described by male travelers. Most women, furthermore, wrote about their experiences as travelers in letters to relatives or in private diaries. See Bassnett, "Travel Writing and Gender," 229–30.

35. See Kaplan and Gerassi-Navarro, "Between Empires," and Leask, "Ghost in Chapultepec."

36. Prescott, *Correspondence*, 285.

37. Prescott, *Correspondence*, 263.

38. Prescott, *Correspondence*, 262.

39. Prescott, *Correspondence*, 285.

40. Cortés died on December 2, 1547, in Castilleja de la Cuesta, Spain, at the age of sixty-two. He was buried in the town monastery. In 1566, a will was discovered in which Cortés asked to be buried in the monastery in Coyoacán, Mexico. Since the building was still under construction, he was buried in a crypt in the church of San Francisco in Texcoco. Another will was discovered in 1794 that stipulated he be buried in the chapel of the Hospital de Jesús, which had been the site of Cortés's first encounter with the Aztec emperor Moctezuma. During the war of independence, as Alamán noted, the tomb ran the risk of profanation, which is why Alamán and the head chaplain of the hospital hid the remains in a loft inside the building and spread the rumor that they had been sent to Italy. The remains were later deposited in a "secret" niche built in the wall of the church next to the original funerary monument. They remained hidden there for 110 years. Although Alamán informed the Spanish embassy, most Mexicans only found out where the remains were hidden when a group of historians from the Colegio de México found Alamán's account in 1946. In 1947, the remains were placed in the same wall of the chapel of the Hospital de Jesús with a 1.26 by .85–meter plaque with the conquistador's coat of arms. See "Hernán Cortés encuentra reposo tras 400 años de muerto," *Informador*, December 1, 2014, https://www.informador.mx/Cultura/Hernan-Cortes-encuentra-reposo -tras-400-anos-de-muerto-20141201-0127.html.

41. Prescott, *Correspondence*, 112.

42. Baudrillard, "Subjective Discourse," 42.

43. Raphael Semmes, *Service Afloat and Ashore during the Mexican War*, 339. Quoted in Eipper, "Canonizer De-Canonized," 420.

44. Jaksić addresses the topic in chapter 7 of *Hispanic World*.

45. Eipper, "Canonizer De-Canonized," 421.

46. De la Torre Villar, "Dos historiadores de Durango," 406–7. See also Sáenz Carrete, "José Fernando Ramírez."

47. Ramírez, "Notas y esclarecimientos," 305; translated by Robert Weis.

48. Ramírez, "Notas y esclarecimientos," 313; emphasis in the original; translated by Robert Weis.

49. Leask, "Ghost in Chapultepec," 201.

50. "His figure was slender, at least until later life; but his chest was deep, his shoulders broad, his frame muscular and well proportioned. It presented the union of agility and vigor which qualified him to excel in fencing, horsemanship, and the other generous exercises of chivalry. In his diet he was temperate, careless of what he ate, and drinking little; while to toil and privation he seemed perfectly indifferent. His dress for he did not disdain the impression produced by such adventitious aids, was such as to set off his handsome person to advantage; neither gaudy nor striking, but rich. He wore few ornaments, and usually the same; but those were of great price. His manners, frank and soldier like, concealed a most cool and calculating spirit. With his gayest humor there mingled a settled air of resolution, which made those who approached him feel they must obey; and which infused something alike awe into the attachment of his most devoted followers. Such a combination, in which love was tempered by authority, was the one probably best calculated to inspire devotion in the rough and turbulent spirits among whom his lot was to be cast" (Prescott, *History of the Conquest*, 143).

51. Benjamin, "Unpacking My library," 258.

52. Prescott, *Correspondence*, 112–15; emphasis in the original. Leask analyzes other examples of Prescott's correspondence that follow this same Hispanist direction. See "Ghost in Chapultepec," 199–208.

53. Benjamin, "Unpacking My Library," 258.

54. Castro-Klarén, "Nation in Ruins."

55. Kagan, "Prescott's Paradigm."

56. Jaksić, "Lessons of Spain," 215.

57. Jaksić, "Lessons of Spain," 215.

Chapter 4. John Reed in Mexico

1. Jameson, *Archaeologies of the Future*, xi.

2. The fundamental dynamic of political utopia rests on a dialectic of identity and difference. The imagined reality is imagined from the known reality. "On the social level, it means that our imaginations are hostages to our own mode of productions. . . . It suggests that at best utopia can serve the negative purpose of

making us more aware of our mental and ideological imprisonment—and that therefore the best utopias are those that fail the most comprehensively" (Jameson, *Archaeologies of the Future*, xii–xiii).

3. As told in *Ten Days that Shook the World*, originally published in 1919.

4. Bloch, *Principle of Hope*, 763.

5. Michel de Certeau, "Figures du sauvage," in *La fable mystique: XVIe-XVIIe siécle*, 277–405. Quoted in Bartra, *Artificial Savage*, 36.

6. Bartra, *Artificial Savage*, 17.

7. Bakhtin, *Teoría y estética de la novela*, 449–86.

8. Bartra, *Artificial Savage*, 1–17.

9. Reed, "War in Paterson," *Masses*, June 1913. Quoted in O'Connor and Walker, *Lost Revolutionary*, 78. Paterson was also fundamental for the conjunction of art and worker mobilization both for Reed and the striking workers. Reed wrote the script for a pageant in New York in which the Paterson workers were to act. The objective was to raise money for the cause. Although the pageant was a huge success and attracted a large public, the play's expenses exceeded the ticket revenues. Still, it works on a level of symbolism and diffusion.

10. Reed, "Colorado War," 11.

11. I visited the Ludlow Massacre Monument in Ludlow, Colorado. An archaeological project organized by several institutions that aims to reconstruct the everyday life of the Ludlow strike corroborates Reed's research.

12. Reed, "Colorado War," 13.

13. Reed, "Colorado War," 12.

14. Reed, "Whose War?," *Masses*, April, 1917, https://www.marxists.org/archive/reed/1917/masses02.htm.

15. Reed, "Whose War?"

16. Reed, *Ten Days that Shook the World*, chap. 2.

17. Lamont, ed., *John Reed Centenary*, 4.

18. Lamont, ed., *John Reed Centenary*, 29.

19. Homberger, *John Reed*, 63.

20. Roosevelt, "Uncle Sam and the Rest," 11.

21. Homberger, *John Reed*, 73.

22. Reed, "If We Enter Mexico," 4.

23. *Metropolitan*, 4.

24. "Villa, Bandit and Brute," 3.

25. "Villa, Bandit and Brute," 3.

26. Reed, "With Villa in Mexico," 72.

27. Dabove, *Bandit Narratives in Latin America*, 26–27.

28. Reed, *Insurgent Mexico*, part 2, chap. 3, http://www.gutenberg.org/files/48108/48108-h/48108-h.html.

29. Reed, *Insurgent Mexico*, part 2, chap. 4, http://www.gutenberg.org/files/48108/48108-h/48108-h.html.

30. Reed, *Insurgent Mexico*, part 2, chap. 7, http://www.gutenberg.org/files/48108/48108-h/48108-h.html.

31. Reed, *Insurgent Mexico*, part 2, chap. 7, http://www.gutenberg.org/files/48108/48108-h/48108-h.html.

32. Reed, *Insurgent Mexico*, part 2, chap. 7, http://www.gutenberg.org/files/48108/48108-h/48108-h.html.

33. Reed, *Insurgent Mexico*, part 2, chap. 8, http://www.gutenberg.org/files/48108/48108-h/48108-h.html.

34. Reed, *Insurgent Mexico*, part 2, chap. 6, http://www.gutenberg.org/files/48108/48108-h/48108-h.html.

35. Bartra, *Artificial Savage*, 2–10.

36. Bartra, *Artificial Savage*, 10.

37. Bartra, *Artificial Savage*, 17.

38. Walter Lippman, *New Republic*, 1914. Quoted in Lamont, ed., *John Reed Centenary*, 16–17.

39. Reed, *Insurgent Mexico*, part 1, chap. 9, http://www.gutenberg.org/files/48108/48108-h/48108-h.html.

40. Keely, "My Experiences with War Correspondents," 18.

41. Keely, "My Experiences with War Correspondents," 18.

42. Reed, *Insurgent Mexico*, part 1, chap. 4, http://www.gutenberg.org/files/48108/48108-h/48108-h.html.

43. Reed, *Insurgent Mexico*, part 1, chap. 4, http://www.gutenberg.org/files/48108/48108-h/48108-h.html.

44. Reed, *Insurgent Mexico*, part 1, chap. 4, http://www.gutenberg.org/files/48108/48108-h/48108-h.html.

45. Azuela, *Los de abajo*.

46. Reed, *Insurgent Mexico*, part 4, chap. 13, http://www.gutenberg.org/files/48108/48108-h/48108-h.html.

47. Reed, *Insurgent Mexico*, part 4, chap. 13, http://www.gutenberg.org/files/48108/48108-h/48108-h.html.

48. Rosenstone, *Romantic Revolutionary*, 282.

49. Reed, *Ten Days that Shook the World*, 40.

50. Reed, *Ten Days that Shook the World*, 42.

51. Reed, *Ten Days that Shook the World*, 380.

52. Reed, *Ten Days that Shook the World*, 303.

53. Reed, *Ten Days that Shook the World*, 341.

Chapter 5. Gabriela Mistral in Mexico

1. Moraga Valle, "'Lo mejor de Chile,'" 1198.

2. Vasconcelos's relationship with the Ateneo is important to understand his relationship with the Mexican Revolution. In 1912, the Ateneo embraced Madero's ideas against Porfirio Díaz and thus ceased to be an exclusively cultural fo-

rum. With the triumph of the Constitutionalists, Carranza named Vasconcelos as director of the National Preparatory School. Later, the Conventionalist president Eulalio Gutiérrez named Vasconcelos as secretary of education. From 1916 to 1919, Vasconcelos lived in exile due to his partisan diatribes, but with Obregón and Huerta he consolidated his position within the field of education, becoming the president of the National University (Arreola Martínez, "José Vasconcelos," 6).

3. Moraga Valle, "'Lo mejor de chile,'" 1202; translated by Robert Weis.

4. Arreola Martínez, "José Vasconcelos," 8–9.

5. Arreola Martínez, "José Vasconcelos," 7. Translated by Robert Weis.

6. Raby and Donís, "Ideología y construcción del Estado," 21.

7. Raby, *Educación y revolución social*, 309.

8. Mistral, *Gabriela y México*, 62; translated by Robert Weis.

9. Mistral, *Gabriela y México*, 62; translated by Robert Weis.

10. Shields, *Places on the Margin*.

11. Bloch, *Principle of Hope*, 763. Quoted in Jameson, *Archaeologies of the Future*, xii–xiii.

12. Raby, *Educación y revolución social*, 314.

13. Castellanos, *Balún Canan*, 142–43; translated by Robert Weis.

14. "Before the Revolution, education in Mexico was available only and almost exclusively to the urban middle class and the wealthy. Despite the development of progressive ideas in some circles since the Reforma era (1855–1867), no serious effort had been made to educate peasants and ordinary people of the cities. Although Mexico produced and imported educators of the stature of Gabino Barreda, Joaquín Baranda, Enrique Rébsamen, and Justo Sierra, there were almost no schools in rural areas. Hence, although estimates vary, it is generally accepted that illiteracy in 1910 exceeded 80 percent. In addition, even the education offered by existing schools did not meet general norms. The government had established urban elementary schools, where middle-class children received a reasonably modern and liberal education, but in other ways the clerical monopoly on education remained intact. The rich sent their children to religious schools and seminaries. When the offspring of the lower classes received any education, it was always in parochial schools run by the clergy" (Raby, *Educación y revolución social*, 11; translated by Robert Weis).

15. Raby, *Educación y revolución social*, 14.

16. Mistral, "To the Mexican woman," in *Gabriela y México*, 66–67; translated by Robert Weis.

17. See González Jimenez, "Normal School for Women," 33–36.

18. López, "Women Teachers," 59.

19. Lopez, "Women Teachers," 59.

20. Mistral, *Lectura para mujeres*, 9; translated by Robert Weis.

21. Woolf, "Professions for Women," in *Death of the Moth*, http://gutenberg.net.au/ebooks12/1203811h.html#ch-28.

22. Fiol-Matta, *Queer Mother for the Nation*.

23. Moraga Valle, "'Lo mejor de Chile,'" 1185.

24. Rubilar, "Gabriela Mistral," 12; translated by Robert Weis.

25. Rubilar, "Gabriela Mistral," 12; translated by Robert Weis.

26. Mistral, *Gabriela y México*, 214; translated by Robert Weis.

27. Mistral, *Gabriela y México*, 215; translated by Robert Weis.

28. Mistral, *Gabriela y México*, 216; translated by Robert Weis.

29. Mistral, *Gabriela y México*, 217; translated by Robert Weis.

30. Guillory, "Canonical and Non-Canonical," 494.

31. Mistral, *Gabriela y México*, 250; translated by Robert Weis.

32. Vázquez de Knauth, *Nacionalismo y educación*, 162–63.

33. Vasconcelos, *El desastre*, 20

34. Mistral, *Gabriela y México*, 251; translated by Robert Weis.

35. Saavedra Molina, "Gabriela Mistral," cxxxiv; translated by Robert Weis.

36. Alegría, *Gabriela Mistral íntima*, 42; translated by Robert Weis.

37. Luis Ganderads, *Antología Mayor*, vol. III, 232. Quoted in Caballé, "Gabriela Mistral en Madrid," 235; translated by Robert Weis.

38. Caballé, "Gabriela Mistral en Madrid," 107; translated by Robert Weis.

39. Carrión, *Santa Gabriela Mistral*; translated by Robert Weis.

40. López, "Women teachers of postrevolutionary Mexico," 59.

Chapter 6. Antonin Artaud in Mexico

1. Hayman, *Artaud and After*, 103.

2. Borges, "Historia del guerrero y la cautiva."

3. Quoted in Luis Mario Schneider, "Artaud y México," in Artaud, *Viaje al País de los Tarahumaras*, 37; translated by Robert Weis.

4. Ahmed, *The Promise of Happiness*, 24.

5. Schneider, "Artaud y México," in Artaud, *Viaje al país de los Tarahumaras*, 24; translated by Robert Weis.

6. Artaud, "For the Theater and Its Double," 219–20.

7. Artaud, "For the Theater and Its Double," 256.

8. Artaud, "For the Theater and Its Double," 255.

9. Rousselet, "Revolucionar la idea del teatro," 44.

10. Schneider, "Artaud y México," in Artaud, *Viaje al país de los Tarahumaras*, 30; translated by Robert Weis.

11. Artaud, "Mensajes revolucionarios," 165. Quoted in Ortiz Bullé-Goyri, "Antonin Artaud y el ambiente teatral mexicano de los años treinta," 45; translated by Robert Weis.

12. Artaud, *Obras Completas*, t. VIII, 1971, p. 235. Quoted in Schneider, "Artaud y Mexico," 47; translated by Robert Weis.

13. Nicholson, "Surrealism's 'Found Object,'" 29. See also Schneider, *México y el surrealismo*.

14. Breton, "Souvenir du Mexique," 13; translated by Robert Weis.

15. But there is something still more important for Breton, who makes his trip to Mexico a pilgrimage to the mythical place: Leon Trotsky. For Breton and many other intellectuals in Europe and the Americas who opposed Stalin's regime, Trotsky was the emblematic and mythical figure of the Russian Revolution. In "Visita a León Trotsky," his speech delivered in the anniversary of the Revolution, organized by the P.O.I. in Paris in 1938, Breton recalls his emotional arrival at the Casa Azul, where Trotsky lived in Coyoacán in Mexico City where Diego Rivera and Frida Kahlo offered him refuge. "I introduced myself to that man who was the head of the 1905 revolution and one of the two heads of the 1917 revolution, not only the many who put his genius and all his vital strength to the service of the greatest cause I know, but also the only witness, the deepest historian whose works more than instruct, they provoke in man the desire to rise up" ("Visita a León Trotsky," 144, translated by Robert Weis). Although he signed it with Rivera, Breton wrote his essay "For a Revolutionary and Independent Art" in Mexico with Trotsky.

16. Valle R., "Diálogo con André Breton." Quoted in Nicholson, "Surrealism in Latin American Literature," 36.

17. Breton, "Recuerdo de México," 162; translated by Robert Weis.

18. Clifford, *Predicament of Culture*, 121–22.

19. Clifford, *Predicament of Culture*, 218.

20. Clifford, *The Predicament of Culture*, 132.

21. Lautréamont, *Les chants de Maldoror*, 1869.

22. The painting is part of the Collection of Daniel Filipacchi, in Paris, France. See https://historia-arte.com/obras/lo-que-el-agua-me-dio-de-frida-khalo.

23. Breton, "Frida Kahlo," 143.

24. Grimberg, *I Will Never Forget You*, 21.

25. The catalogue and some works of the exhibition can be seen at http://www.andrebreton.fr/work/56600100107091. Frida's opinion on the exhibit was highly negative. See Grimberg, *I Will Never Forget You*, 21–2.

26. Tibol, *Frida Kahlo, una vida abierta*, 95; translated by Robert Weis.

27. Monsiváis and Vázquez Bayod, *Frida Kahlo, una vida, una obra*, 163; translated by Robert Weis.

28. Grimberg, *I Will Never Forget You*, 21–22.

29. Nonetheless, in 1940, Frida Kahlo attended the grand surrealist party organized in Mexico by César Moro and André Breton. All the big names in painting, literature, and the arts were there: the photographer Manuel Álvarez Bravo, Alice and Wolfgang Paalen, the poet Xavier Villaurrutia, the painters Roberto Montenegro, and Antonio Ruiz, and Carlos Mérida. For some critics, though, the gathering was a wake for the movement, which had "become absurd due to the rise of fascisms in Europe and the break of the nation of socialism with revolutionary ideals" (Le Clézio, *Diego y Frida*, 150); translated by Robert Weis.

30. Artaud, "La pintura de María Izquierdo," 202–3. Translated by Robert Weis.

31. Artaud, "La pintura de María Izquierdo," 206–7; translated by Robert Weis.

32. Artaud, "La pintura de María Izquierdo," 208; translated by Robert Weis.

33. "Although she had Indian blood in her veins, she was hardly a 'pure' Indian in the cultural sense that Artaud seems to imply. She was raised in a very traditional, European way in the small town of San Juan de las Largos, Jalisco. Her family was middle class. She spent most of her childhood with her grandparents in Aguas Calientes, where her grandfather owned a jewelry store" (Tarver, *Issues of Otherness and Identity*, 8).

34. Geis, "The Voyaging Reality," 8.

35. Deffebach, *María Izquierdo and Frida Kahlo*, 111–30.

36. More than twenty of Artaud's articles on the Tarahumaras were translated into Spanish and published in Mexican newspapers, especially *El Nacional Revolucionario*, between April and November 1936. From the group known as the Contemporáneos, the poet Bernardo Ortiz de Montellano published "Artaud y el sentido de la cultura en México" in July 1936 in *El Nacional*. He examined Artaud's desire to renew European culture and identified it as surrealist. For Ortíz de Montellano, it was a spiritualism of a mystical order, a magical pantheist order of unity with nature, a genuine expression of the Indigenous cultures of America. See Nicholson, *Surrealism in Latin American Literature*.

37. Artaud, "La montaña de los signos," in Artaud, *Viaje al país*, 273; translated by Robert Weis.

38. Artaud, "La montaña de los signos," in Artaud, *Viaje al país*, 273; translated by Robert Weis.

39. Artaud, "La montaña de los signos," in Artaud, *Viaje al país*, 272; translated by Robert Weis.

40. Artaud, "El país de los reyes magos," in Artaud, *Viaje al país*, 276; translated by Robert Weis.

41. Artaud, "El país de los reyes magos," in Artaud, *Viaje al país*, 276; translated by Robert Weis.

42. Artaud, "El rito de los reyes de la Atlantida," in Artaud, *Viaje al país*, 278; translated by Robert Weis.

43. Artaud, "El rito de los reyes de la Atlantida," in Artaud, *Viaje al país*, 280; translated by Robert Weis.

44. Artaud, "The Peyote Dance," in Artaud, *Selected Writings*, 385.

45. Artaud, "Peyote Dance," in Artaud, *Selected Writings*, 387.

46. Artaud, "Peyote Dance," in Artaud, *Selected Writings*, 388.

47. Artaud, "Peyote Dance," in Artaud, *Selected Writings*, 391. Artaud was not the first nor the only traveler interest in the Tarahumara peyote ritual. This

plant, to which so many magical virtues are attributed, struck the interest of scientists and writers, among them Carlos Castañeda, who wrote a series of books about his learnings derived from peyote in Sonora, and Aldous Huxley in his *Doors of Perception* (1954) and *Heaven and Hell* (1955). Fernando Benítez, for his part, narrates the pilgrimage ceremony to Wirikuta in a sacred place for the Huicholes in *En la tierra mágica del peyote* (1968). Ramón Mata Torres describes the Huichol legend of the creation of peyote in *Los peyoteros* (1976). Carlos Castañeda and Aldous Huxley describe in their literature their lived experiences with this cactus. Huxley mentions that one of the major problems in describing a peyote experience is the difficulty in communicating it since the hallucinogen causes the disorientation of all the senses and the perception of time and space become vastly distorted. See Rojas Aréchiga, "El controvertido peyote."

48. Bonfiglioli, "Jíkuri Sepawa'ame," 158; translated by Robert Weis.

49. Bonfiglioli, "Jíkuri Sepawa'ame," 168; translated by Robert Weis. Like Artaud, Bonfliglioli speaks of *sipáwame* (shamans or priests) and coincides with Artaud in that the oneiric revelations remain secret during the first three years, to be developed then in isolated spots high in the mountains for helping other shamans. The sipáwame travel three times to a spot in the Chihuahua desert to find the sacred cactus and receive its teachings, and to take it with them to carry out the ceremony to help people. Thanks to intervention by the sipáwame, the divine influences come together in the ceremonial space and especially toward the allied peyote, to counteract the sorcerers and remove the illness. In other words, it is as if God offered up the "grand remedy" to the sipáwame and men, according to interpretation registered by Lumholtz in his *El México desconocido* (Bonfiglioli, "Jíkuri Sepawa'ame," 169).

50. Bonfiglioli, "Jíkuri Sepawa'ame," 180.

51. The ritual itself described by Artaud is very similar to that offered by later and contemporary anthropologies, with the exception of the interpretation attributed to the dancer, who, according to the anthropologist, makes circular movements that represent the circle of life. For Artaud, in contrast, the dancer's movements challenge the illnesses contained in the circle to move in and out.

52. Artaud, "El rito del Peyote," in Artaud, *Viaje al país*, 312; translated by Robert Weis.

53. Artaud, "El rito del Peyote," in Artaud, *Viaje al país*, 303; translated by Robert Weis.

54. Artaud, "El rito del Peyote," in Artaud, *Viaje al país*, 313; translated by Robert Weis.

55. Dawson, *Peyote Effect*, 3.

56. Dawson, *Peyote Effect*, 67.

57. Artaud, "Postscriptum," in Artaud, *Viaje al país*, 327; translated by Robert Weis.

58. Artaud, "A Henri Parisot," in Artaud, *Viaje al país*, 370; translated by Robert Weis.

Chapter 7. The Beats in Mexico

1. Ahmed, *Promise of Happiness*, 21–49.

2. Morgan, *The typewriter Is holy*, xviii. Regina Weinreich holds that "the very term 'Beat' was essential to the early Beat writers' self-definition. A term used in jazz circles after World War II, Beat meant 'down and out,' or 'poor and exhausted.' Another version goes that the con-man Herbert Huncke coined the term in 1944 when he exclaimed, 'man, that's Beat' in front of Burroughs when Burroughs was in Times Square looking for drugs. Burroughs passed the term on to Ginsberg who passed it on to Kerouac before the future author of *On the Road* left Columbia University to join the merchant marines. The term also kept its musical connotation, but also took on other resonances, such as beatific and social rejection. The category of 'Beat Generation' officially appeared in a November 1952 *New York Times* article and in some early novels by the Beat John Clellon Holmes. Nonetheless, the seminal figures of the Beat movement were Jack Kerouac, Allen Ginsberg, and William S. Burroughs. Other figures include Lawrence Ferlinghetti, Michael McClure, Gregory Corso, Gary Snyder, Carl Solomon, Neal Cassady, LeRoi Jones (Amiri Baraka). Women Beats, less studied than the men, include Joyce Johnson, Hettie Jones, Diane di Prima, etc." (Weinreich, "Beat Generation Is Now," 74–75).

3. Shields, *Places on the Margin*, 73–116.

4. Van Den Abbeele, *Travel as Metaphor*, xvii.

5. Morgan, *Typewriter Is Holy*, 183.

6. See also the two volumes by Charters, ed., *Beats: Literary Bohemian*.

7. Jonnes, *Cold War American Literature*, 5.

8. Jonnes, *Cold War American Literature*, 14–17.

9. United States, National Security Resources Board, *United States Civil Defense*, 7.

10. Gerstell, *How to Survive*, 119.

11. Jonnes, *Cold War American Literature*, 32.

12. Lardas, *Bop Apocalypse*, 21.

13. Ellwood, *Fifties Spiritual Marketplace*, 160–71.

14. Lardas, *Bop Apocalypse*, 5.

15. Hetherington, *Badlands of Modernity*, 20–38.

16. Bolaño, *Entre paréntesis*, 147–48; translated by Robert Weis.

17. Burroughs, *Naked Lunch*, x–xi.

18. Hetherington, *Badlands of Modernity*, 36.

19. Burroughs was not the only Beat who took scientific experimentation with drugs seriously. Allen Ginsberg, for example, volunteered for the earliest LSD tests on humans at Stanford in 1959. The scientific objective was never far

from his experimental or sacred poetic activities since drugs led him to a state of consciousness free from restrictions on creativity.

20. Latour, *La esperanza de Pandora*, 141.

21. Burroughs and Ginsberg, *Yage Letters*, 29.

22. Burroughs, *Everything Lost*, 165.

23. Burroughs and Ginsberg, *Yage Letters*, 12.

24. Manalansan IV, "The 'Stuff' of Archives."

25. Burroughs and Ginsberg, *Yage Letters*, 12–13.

26. Burroughs and Ginsberg, *Yage Letters*, 19–20.

27. Burroughs and Ginsberg, *Yage Letters*, 22.

28. Halberstam, *Queer Art of Failure*, 1–25.

29. Burroughs, *Everything Lost*, 175.

30. Burroughs, *Everything Lost*, 192–93.

31. Burroughs, *Everything Lost*, 155. "Sometimes I feel sorry for Allerton / he is such a child in a / selfish, and / callow sulky, and sweet. / But he doesn't realize / what he is involved in. Like / the pity I felt for my severed / finger, as if it was innocent victim of violent, unpredictable / forces. Sometimes he looks / hurt and puzzled, by the / warped intensity of my emotions. He wants / my fucking, not a relationship bordering on insanity. / A no more suited for this the / part I anger him than / I am suited to endure the fear / or pain and misery." Burroughs, *Everything Lost*, 129.

32. Burroughs, *Everything Lost*, 123.

33. Jonnes, *Cold War American Literature*, 124.

34. Jonnes, *Cold War American Literature*, 125.

35. Jonnes, *Cold War American Literature*, 129.

36. Kerouac, *On the Road*, 174.

37. Kerouac, *On the Road*, 175.

38. Sedgwick, *Between Men*, 696.

39. Weinreich, "Beat Generation Is Now," 76.

40. In fact, Galatea Dunkel also criticizes Dean because her husband Ed Dunkel left her to travel with a friend to Denver.

41. Kerouac, *On the Road*, 248.

42. In "Political outlaws: Beat cowboys," Kurt Hummer notes that "Late in his life, while working on the novel *The Place of Dead Roads* (1984), Burroughs began to identify himself with the American Western outlaw. In the popular imagination, the American Western outlaw is best represented by the legends surrounding Jesse James and Billy the Kid. Burroughs's own criminal life gave him a strong psychic connection to the outlaws of the Old West, yet he was relatively late in using a Western motif in his work. Other writers associated with the Beat Generation had used a Western motif effectively before, most notably Michael McClure in his play *The Beard* (1965), Brenda Frazer in her memoir published under the name Bonnie Bremser entitled *Troia: Mexican Memoirs*, and

Edward Dorn in his epic poem *Gunslinger* (1975)" (Hummer, "Political Outlaws: Beat Cowboys," 2).

43. Hummer, "Political Outlaws: Beat Cowboys," 2.

44. Quoted in Hummer, "Political Outlaws: Beat Cowboys," 4.

45. Hummer, "Political Outlaws: Beat Cowboys," 4. According to Gene Autry's classification, the cowboy hero: 1) Never takes unfair advantage; 2) Never goes back on his word; 3) Always tells the truth; 4) Is always gentle to old people, children, and animals; 5) Is never racially or religiously intolerant; 6) Always helps people in distress; 7) Never smokes and drinks; 8) Is always clean in thought, word, deed and personal grooming; 9) Respects women and the nation's laws; 10) Is a patriot (above all). Quoted in Hummer, "Political Outlaws: Beat Cowboys," 2.

46. Kerouac, *On the Road*, 248.

47. Kerouac, *On the Road*, 248.

48. Kerouac, *Lonesome Traveler*, 645–66.

49. Shields, *Places on the Margin*, 83–5.

50. Shields, *Places on the Margin*, 91.

51. Kerouac, *On the Road*, 74

52. Kerouac, *On the Road*, 87.

53. Kerouac, *On the Road*, 85.

54. Spurr, David, *Rhetoric of Empire*.

55. Kerouac, *On the Road*, 90–91.

56. Youngs, "Buttons and Souls," 119.

57. Kerouac, *On the Road*, 161.

58. Mexico likewise occupies the place of clandestinity and illegality for the fugitive. Following Burroughs, who flees to Mexico in order to evade jail in Louisiana, Jack Kerouac also plans his flight to Mexico to avoid paying alimony.

59. Kerouac, *Mexico City Blues*, no pagination.

60. Kerouac, *Mexico City Blues*, no pagination.

61. Lardas, *Bop Apocalypse*, 180.

62. Lardas, *Bop Apocalypse*, 181. Burroughs believed that Mexicans had been forever corrupted by their historical experience—not only by the "expansion of Western soul" but also by the totalitarian legacy of Mayan civilization and its ritual calendar (Lardas, 180–81).

63. Burroughs, *Naked Lunch*, x–xi.

64. Van Gennep, *Rites of Passage*.

65. Weinreich, "Beat Generation Is Now," 73.

Chapter 8. "An Oasis of Horror in a Desert of Boredom"

1. Bolaño, interview by Cristián Warnken. In the same interview, Bolaño compares Ulises Lima with Rimbaud and Lautreamont.

2. Morgan, *Typewriter Is Holy*, 226.

3. Pollack, "Latin America Translated (Again)."

4. Locascio, "My Bolaño Archive." https://lareviewofbooks.org/article/my-bolano-archive/.

5. Ramón Méndez, interview with Ricardo House for the documentary *Batalla futura I*. Quoted in Maristain, *El hijo de Mister Playa*, 81; translated by Robert Weis.

6. José Vicente Anaya, interview with Mónica Maristain. Quoted in Maristain, *El hijo de Mister Playa*, 101–2; translated by Robert Weis.

7. Madariaga Caro notes that the magazine had a cult following. Between 1962 and 1969, thirty-two issues were published. The ideology of the magazine was "pacifist revolution and liberation of the soul." It featured poems by the Beats and T. S. Elliot, as well as poetry from Argentina, Nicaragua, etc. (Madariaga Caro, *Bolaño Infra*, 43–44).

8. Roberto Bolaño, "De aquí a la eternidad," interview by Sergio Paz, December 13, 1998. Quoted in Madariaga Caro, *Bolaño Infra*, 44; translated by Robert Weis.

9. Bolaño, *Amulet*, 126–27. In his "Caracas Speech" upon accepting the Rómulo Gallegos prize, Bolaño returned to his generation of militant youth: "This comes to mind because much of what I have written is a love letter or a farewell to my own generation, those of us born in the 1950s who chose to engage in militias, or rather militancy. We offered up what little we had, our youth, to a cause that we believed to be the most generous of causes in the world and, in a certain way it was, but it really wasn't. Needless to say, we fought as hard as we could, but we had corrupt bosses, cowardly leaders, a propaganda machine that was worse than leprosy, we fought for parties that, if victorious, would have immediately sent us to work camps, we fought and gave all our generosity for an ideal that had been dead for fifty years, and some of us knew it, how could we not know it, we had read Trotsky or were Trotskyists, but we did it anyway, because we were stupid and generous, like young people are, they offer everything without asking anything in return, and now there is nothing left of those young people, those who didn't die in Bolivia, died in Argentina or Peru, those who survived went to Chile or Mexico where they died, and the ones who weren't killed there were later killed in Nicaragua, Colombia, in El Salvador. All of Latin America is sowed with the bones of forgotten youth" (Bolaño, *Entre paréntesis*, 37–38; translated by Robert Weis).

10. José Agustín, *Tragicomedia mexicana 2: La vida en México de 1970 u 1982*, 7. Quoted in Madariaga Caro, *Bolaño Infra*, 25; translated by Robert Weis.

11. Madariaga Caro, *Bolaño Infra*, 23–24.

12. The *infras* are the *realvisceralistas* in *The Savage Detectives*, that is Mario Santiago (Ulises Lima), Roberto Bolaño (Arturo Belano), José Vicente Anaya, Juan Esteban Harrington (Chilean), Jorge Hernández (Piel Divina), Rubén Medina (Rafael Barrios), Ramón and Cuauhtémoc Méndez (Pancho and Moctezu-

ma Rodríguez), Lisa Johnson (Laura Jáuregui), Mara and Vera Larrosa (María and Angélica Font), Gelles Lebrija (cousin of the Larrosas), Pedro Damián, Victor Monjarrás-Ruiz, Bruno Montané (Chilean, Felipe Müller), Guadalupe Ochoa (Xóchitl García), José Peguero (Jacinto Requena), Estela Ramírez, Lorena de la Rocha, and José Rosas Ribeyro (Peruvian) (Madariaga Caro, *Bolaño Infra*, 51).

13. Williams, *Marxism and Literature*, 115–20.

14. Bourdieu, *Las reglas del arte*, 227–31.

15. Bolaño, *Los detectives salvajes*, 160–61; translated by Robert Weis.

16. Bolaño, *Los detectives salvajes*, 177; translated by Robert Weis.

17. In the novel, Belano is constructed as a poét maudit, or a "damn poet" for editor Lisandro Morales, who published his anthology of poets before Belano left Mexico: "When Arturo Belano's book finally came out, he was a phantom author and I was about to become a phantom editor. I always knew it. There are editors of ash, jinxed, from whom you should flee, whether or not you believe in bad luck, whether you are a positive or a Marxist, avoid those people like the plague" (*Detectives salvajes*, 300; translated by Robert Weis). Parallels may be drawn with Poulet-Malassis, editor of *Les fleurs du mal*, who had to go into exile after publishing Baudelaire's book (Bourdieu, *Las reglas del arte*, 108).

18. *A Season in Hell* was published in 1873 in Brussels, in an edition financed by Rimbaud himself. Only a few dozen of the first edition circulated since Rimbaud never paid in full and the editor stopped the printing. *A Season in Hell* had eight sections in prose, the most famous of which is the first *Mauvais Sang*. Throughout the sections, the poetic voice describes the tribulations of a suffering soul, fighting against Western culture and the bourgeois values of Christianity, reason, science, morality, work, progress, monogamy, and so forth.

19. Ross, "Rimbaud and the Resistance to Work," 64.

20. Here I am paraphrasing verses from *Mauvais Sang*, quoted in French and translated to English by Kristin Ross ("Rimbaud and the Resistance to Work," 64).

21. According to Andrea Cobas Carral and Verónica Garibotto, the novel explores the modernizing project of the avant-guard of the 1920s in order to understand the roots of the revolutionary project of the 1970s. The first *realvisceralismo* shows how the revolution, on institutionalizing and coinciding with the state program, ceases to be effective, and how literature is one of the agents of this change, thus losing its subversive quality. During their adventure in the desert, the young writers of the second *realvisceralismo* walk upon the residues of the institutionalized revolution and the shambles of the state project: poverty, marginality, and violence (Cobas Carral and Garibotto, "Un epitafio en el desierto," 185–86).

22. His biographers note that Rimbaud's lifelong goal was to leave. From his teenage journey to Paris to join the Commune and his trips to Belgium, London, Stuttgart, Milan, and elsewhere around the world, nothing could stop

him. He traversed the Alps into Italy on foot. Some biographers hold that he joined a circus as an interpreter and traveled through Denmark and Sweden. In Africa, he lived in Aden, Harar, Abyssinia, and Kairo between 1880 and 1891. His letters reveal a restless traveler who wants to keep moving but is forced to settle, albeit temporarily, to pay for his freedom. What Bolaño observes in his essay "Literature + Illness = Illness" is evident in Rimbaud's letters: travel makes you ill. Rimbaud becomes weak in his journeys and contracts so many diseases that he ends up with an amputated leg. His wandering thus paradoxically makes him, literally and symbolically, a prisoner. Bolaño speaks of how he was made ill by his journeys from Chile to Mexico, from Mexico to Chile, on a bus at the end of Allende's government, during his imprisonment in Chile, and on his later trips. "I started to travel very young, since I was 7 or 8. First, on my father's bus, on solitary highways in Chile that seemed like post-nuclear highways, they gave me goosebumps. Then on trains and buses, until I was 15 and flew in a plane for the first time, I went to Mexico. From then on, I traveled constantly. The result: multiple illnesses" (*Entre paréntesis*, 147–48; translated by Robert Weis).

23. Bolaño, *Los detectives salvajes*, 474; translated by Robert Weis. I thank Kristie Soares for this observation.

24. Bolaño, "Literatura + enfermedad= enfermedad," in Bolaño, *El gaucho insufrible*, 143; translated by Robert Weis.

25. The reference is to Mallarmé's poem, "Brise Marine": "Both the flesh and the spirit weary me; I am no longer in love and I have read all my books. I long to get away, to flee from this world to where the birds are wild with joy to be flying across unknown seas and skies." https://www.poetica.fr/poeme-109/stephane-mallarme-brise-marine/ (translated by Robert Weis).

26. Bolaño, "Literatura + enfermedad= enfermedad," in Bolaño, *El gaucho insufrible*, 151; translated by Robert Weis.

27. Bolaño, "Literatura + enfermedad= enfermedad," in Bolaño, *El gaucho insufrible*, 154; translated by Robert Weis.

28. Bolaño, "Literatura + enfermedad= enfermedad," in Bolaño, *El gaucho insufrible*, 158; translated by Robert Weis. For more on the idea of travel and mauditism, see Spiller, "Roberto Bolaño."

29. The photographs Rimbaud took in Africa and sent to his relatives are famous. He acquired the camera, together with other instruments of measurement, in order to draft the maps he intended to send to the French Geographic Society. The "Relación sobre el Ogaden," a zone unknown to Europeans, was written by Rimbaud and sent with a report by a colleague to the society. The society published it in 1884 and used it to open commercial routes (Monteleone, "El nómade," 168–69).

30. Bolaño, *Los detectives salvajes*, 528; translated by Robert Weis.

31. Bolaño, *Los detectives salvajes*, 529; translated by Robert Weis.

32. Bolaño, *Los detectives salvajes*, 548; translated by Robert Weis.

33. Matei Chihaia notes that "Arturo Belano's name expresses an entire aesthetic program. Arturo recalls Arthur Rimbaud, not only the biography of the 'suicidal artist in Africa,' as the prologue to *Distant Star* says but also his writings on the interior experience of the poet, and in particular the key phrase in *Lettres de Voyant*, that states 'je est un autre.' I believe Bolaño refers to this experience when, in an interview, he describes Arturo Belano as an 'alter ego in the sense that things happen to him that have happened to me, but in other ways, no, of course not. Like with any alter ego'" ("Bolaño y yo," 143; translated by Robert Weis).

34. Bourdieu, *Las reglas del arte*, 337.

35. Bolaño arrives in the country of his birth, Chile, in 1973, after having lived in Mexico since 1968. His arrival coincides with the military coup against Salvador Allende. He was a political prisoner for a few days before voluntarily going into exile. He returned to Mexico and then settled definitively in Spain from 1980 till his death. The poems in *La universidad desconocida* can be read in dialogue with the essays in *Entre paréntesis*, especially the section titled "Exiles," which also discusses travel. Bolaño argues that every poet is an exile and every trip is one of exile. The essays thus express a poetics of travel: "Probably all of us, writers and readers alike, set out into exile, or at least into a certain kind of exile, when we leave childhood behind. This leads to the conclusion that the category of exile, especially in regard to literature, does not exist. The immigrant, the no-mad, the traveler, the sleepwalker all exist, but not the exile, since every writer becomes an exile simply by venturing into literature, and every reader becomes an exile simply by opening a book" (Bolaño, *Entre paréntesis*, 51; translated by Robert Weis). "All literature carries exile within it, no matter if the writer has had to leave for twenty years or if he has never moved from his house" (49); translated by Robert Weis.

36. Bolaño, "Luz," in *La universidad desconocida*, 36; translated by Robert Weis.

37. Bolaño, "Nopal," in *La universidad desconocida*, 367; translated by Robert Weis.

38. Bolaño, "Nopal," in *La universidad desconocida*, 367; translated by Robert Weis.

39. Bolaño, "Devoción de Roberto Bolaño," in *La universidad desconocida*, 397; translated by Robert Weis.

40. Bolaño, "El burro," in *La universidad desconocida*, 383; translated by Robert Weis.

41. Bolaño, "Sensini," in *Llamadas telefónicas*, 13.

42. Bolaño, "Enrique Martin," in *Llamadas telefónicas*, 37.

43. Bolaño, *Los detectives salvajes*, 596; translaud by Robert Weis.

44. Bolaño, *Estrella distante*, 97; translated by Robert Weis.

45. Bolaño, *Estrella distante*, 95; translated by Robert Weis.

46. As I mentioned in the introduction, I take this term from Kevin Hetherington's *Badlands of Modernity*.

47. Federici, *Caliban and the Witch*, 12–13.

48. Valencia, *Capitalismo Gore*, 36; translated by Robert Weis.

49. See Segato, "Una falla del pensamiento feminista."

50. Brown, *Marx on Gender and the Family*, 1–2. Nonetheless, the liberal discourse presents globalization as a reality based on equality due to the fact of "equal access to everything." This leads to an acceptance of the market as an equalizing field, instituting artificially naturalized needs that incite undifferentiated consumption (Valencia, *Capitalismo Gore*, 32).

51. Santa Teresa, in "The Part about the Crimes," is of course Ciudad Juárez. Bolaño followed events in Juárez thanks to his close friendship with the journalist Sergio González.

52. González, *Huesos en el desierto*, 27; translated by Robert Weis.

53. Valencia, *Capitalismo Gore*, 61; translated by Robert Weis.

54. Bolaño, *2666*, 710; translated by Robert Weis.

55. González, *Huesos en el desierto*, 25.

56. González, *Huesos en el desierto*, 35; translated by Robert Weis.

57. Bolaño, *2666*, 466–67; translated by Robert Weis.

<h1 style="text-align:center">Bibliography</h1>

Ahmed, Sara. *Cultural Politics of Emotion.* New York, NY: Routledge, 2004.

Ahmed, Sara. *The Promise of Happiness.* Durham, NC: Duke University Press, 2010.

Aillón Soria, Esther. "Moralizar por la fuerza: El decreto de reformulación del Tribunal De Vagos de la Ciudad de México." In *Trabajo, ocio y coacción: Trabajadores urbanos en México y Guatemala en el siglo xix*, edited by Clara E. Lida and Sonia Pérez Toledo, 67–113. Mexico City: Universidad Metropolitana, 2001.

Alegría, Ciro. *Gabriela Mistral íntima.* Santiago de Chile: Antártica SA, 1989.

Altamirano, Carlos, and Beatriz Sarlo. *Literatura, sociedad.* Buenos Aires: Hachette, 1983.

Anzaldúa, Gloria. *Borderlands / La Frontera: The New Mestiza.* 2nd ed. San Francisco: Aunt Lute Books, 1999.

Arreola Martínez, Betzabé. "José Vasconcelos: El caudillo cultural de la nación." *Tiempo Laberinto* 25, no. 4 (2009): 3–10.

Artaud, Antonin. "For the Theater and Its Double, 1931–1936." In *Selected Writings*, edited by Susan Sontag, translated by Helen Weaver, 215–76. Berkeley, CA: University of California Press, 1976.

Artaud, Antonin. "La pintura de María Izquierdo." In *Viaje al país de los tarahumaras*, edited by Luis Mario Schneider, 202–6. Mexico City: FCE, 1984.

Artaud, Antonin. *Nouvelles révélations de l'Être.* Paris: Denoël, 1937.

Artaud, Antonin. "The Peyote Dance." In *Selected Writings*, edited by Susan Sontag, 383–91. Berkeley, CA: University of California Press, 1976.

Artaud, Antonin. *Viaje al país de los Tarahumaras.* Edited by Luis Mario Schneider. Mexico City: FCE, 1984.

Azuela, Mariano. *Los de abajo.* Paris: ALLCA XX, Colección Archivos, 1988.

Bakhtin, Mikhail. *Teoría y estética de la novela.* Madrid: Taurus, 1975.

Barthes, Roland. "Rhetoric of the Image." In *Classic Essays on Photography*, edited by Alan Trachtenberg, translated by Stephen Heath, 269–85. New Haven, CT: Leete's Island Books, 1980.

Bartra, Roger. *The Artificial Savage: Modern Myths of the Wild Man*. Ann Arbor, MI: University of Michigan Press, 1997.

Bartra, Roger. *El salvaje en el espejo*. Mexico City: Coordinación de Difusión Cultural, Universidad Nacional Autónoma de México, 1992.

Bassnett, Susan. "Travel Writing and Gender." In *The Cambridge Companion to Travel Writing*, edited by Peter Hulme and Tim Youngs, 225–41. Cambridge, MA: Cambridge University Press, 2002.

Bataille, Georges. *La literatura y el mal*. Madrid: Taurus, 1971.

Baudelaire, Charles. "Le Voyage." "Charles Baudelaire's Fleurs du mal / Flowers of Evil" webpage. FleursDuMal.org. https://fleursdumal.org/poem/231.

Baudrillard, Jean. "Subjective Discourse or the Non-Functional System of Objects." In *The Object Reader*, edited by Fiona Candlin and Raiford Guins, translated by James Benedict, 41–63. London: Routledge, 2009.

Benjamin, Walter. "Unpacking My Library." In *The Object Reader*, edited by Fiona Candlin and Raiford Guins, translated by Harry Zohn, 257–62. London: Routledge, 2009.

Benjamin, Walter. *The Work of Art in the Age of Mechanical Reproduction*. Translated by Harry Zohn. New York: CreateSpace Independent Publishing Platform, 2010.

Bernal, Ignacio. *History of Mexican Archeology*. London: Thames and Hudson, 1980.

Bhabha, Homi. *Location of Culture*. London: Routledge, 1994.

Bloch, Ernst. *The Principle of Hope*. Cambridge, MA: MIT Press, 1986.

Bolaño, Roberto. *Amuleto*. Nueva York, NY: Vintage Español, 2017. First published 1999 by Anagrama.

Bolaño, Roberto. *Entre paréntesis*. Barcelona: Editorial Anagrama, 2004.

Bolaño, Roberto. *Estrella distante*. Barcelona: Editorial Anagrama, 2006.

Bolaño, Roberto. Interview by Cristián Warnken. *La belleza de pensar*, Canal 13 UC, 1999. Available at https://www.youtube.com/watch?v=4opmK0SO-J8&t=904s.

Bolaño, Roberto. Interview by Sergio Paz. "De aquí a la eternidad." Revista El Domingo, *El Mercurio*, December 13, 1998, 4–6.

Bolaño, Roberto. *La universidad desconocida*. Barcelona: Editorial Anagrama, 2007.

Bolaño, Roberto. "Literatura + enfermedad= enfermedad." In *El gaucho insufrible*. Barcelona: Anagrama, 2003, 135–58.

Bolaño, Roberto. *Llamadas telefónicas*. Barcelona: Editorial Anagrama, 2006.

Bolaño, Roberto. *Los detectives salvajes*. Barcelona: Editorial Anagrama, 1998.

Bolaño, Roberto. *2666*. Barcelona: Editorial Anagrama, 2004.

Bonfiglioli, Carlo. "Jíkuri Sepawa'ame (La raspa del peyote): una danza de curación en la sierra Tarahumara." *Anales de Antropología* 39, no. 2 (2005): 151–88.

Borges, Jorge Luis. "The Aleph." In *The Aleph and Other Stories, 1933–1969*, translated by Norman Thomas di Giovanni, 22–30. New York: Dutton, 1970.

Borges, Jorge Luis. "Historia del guerrero y la cautiva." In *El Aleph*, 47–50. Buenos Aires: Emecé, 1949.

Bourdieu, Pierre. *Las reglas del arte: Génesis y estructura del campo literario*. Barcelona: Anagrama, 1992.

Breton, André. "Frida Kahlo." In *Antología (1913–1966)*, edited by Margarite Bonnet, translated by Tomás Segovia, 140–43. Mexico City: Siglo Veintiuno Editores, 1983.

Breton, André. "Por un arte revolucionario independiente." In *Antología (1913–1966)*, edited by Maragarite Bonnet, translated by Tomás Segovia, 154–61. Mexico City: Siglo Veintiuno Editores, 1983.

Breton, André. "Recuerdo de México." In *Antología (1913–1966)*, edited by Margarite Bonnet, translated by Tomás Segovia 162–64. Mexico City: Siglo Veintiuno Editores, 1983.

Breton, André. "Souvenir du Mexique." *Minotaure*, no. 12–13 (1939): 29–52.

Breton, André. "Visita a León Trotski." In *Antología (1913–1966)*, edited by Margarite Bonnet, translated by Tomás Segovia 144–53. Mexico City: Siglo Veintiuno Editores, 1983.

Brown, Bill. "Thing Theory." In *The Object Reader*, edited by Fiona Candlin and Raiford Guins, 139–52. London: Routledge, 2009.

Brown, Heather. *Marx on Gender and the Family*. Chicago, IL: Haymarket Books, 2013.

Burroughs, William. *Everything Lost: The Latin American Notebook of William S. Burroughs*. Edited by Oliver Harris. Columbus: Ohio State University Press, 2008.

Burroughs, William. *Naked Lunch*. New York: Grove Press, 2009.

Burroughs, William, and Allen Ginsberg. *The Yage Letters*. Edited and with an introduction by Oliver Harris. San Francisco, CA: City Lights Books, 2006.

Caballé, Ana. "Gabriela Mistral en Madrid." *Anales de literatura hispanoamericana*, no. 22: 231–45. Madrid: Editorial Complutense, 1993.

Cabañas, Miguel A. *The Cultural "Other" in Nineteenth-Century Travel Narratives: How the United States and Latin America Described Each Other*. Lewiston, NY: Edwin Mellen Press, 2008.

Calderón de la Barca, Frances. *Life in Mexico, during a Residence of Two Years in that Country*. London: Chapman and Hall, 1843.

Carrión, Benjamín. *Santa Gabriela Mistral*. Editorial Casa de la Cultura Ecuatoriana, 1956.

Castellanos, Rosario. *Balún Canan*. Mexico: Fondo de Cultura Economica, 1957.

Castro-Klarén, Sara. "The Nation in Ruins: Archaeology and the Rise of the Nation." In *Beyond Imagined Communities. Reading and Writing the Nation in the Nineteenth-Century Latin America*, edited by Sara Castro-Karen and John Charles Chasteen, 161–94. Baltimore, MD: Johns Hopkins University Press, 2003.

Charnay, Désiré. *The Ancient Cities of the New World: Being Voyages and Explorations in Mexico and Central America from 1857–1882*, translated by J. Gonino and Hellen Conant. London: Chapman & Hall, 1887.

Charnay, Désiré. *Le Mexique: Souvenirs et impressions de voyage*. Paris: E. Dentu, 1863.

Charnay, Désiré, and Olivier DeBroise. *Claude Désiré Charnay: 150 años de la fotografía*. Mexico City: Consejo Nacional para la Cultura y las Artes; Oaxaca: El Centro Cultural Santo Domingo, 1989.

Charnay, Désiré, and Eugène Viollet-Le-Duc. *Cités et ruins americaines*. Paris: Gide Editeur, 1863.

Charters, Ann, ed. *The Beats: Literary Bohemian in Postwar America*. Detroit, MI: Gale Research, 1983.

Chihaia, Matei. "Bolaño y yo." In *La obsesión del yo. La auto(r)ficción en la literatura española y latinoamericana*, edited by Sabine Slickers Toro Vera and Ana Luego, 141–54. Madrid: Iberoamericana Vervuert, 2010.

Clark, Steve, ed. *Travel Writing and Empire*. London: Zed Books. 1999.

Clavijero, Francisco Javier. *Historia antigua de Mexico. Disertaciones*. 4 vols. Mexico City: Porrúa, 1945.

Clifford, James. *The Predicament of Culture*. Cambridge, MA: Harvard University Press, 1988.

Cobas Carral, Andrea, and Verónica Garibotto. "Un epitafio en el desierto: Poesía y Revolución en *Los detectives salvajes*." In *Bolaño salvaje*, edited by Edmundo Paz Soldán and Gustavo Faverón Patriau, 163–89. Barcelona: Candaya, 2008.

Dabove, Juan Pablo. *Bandit Narratives in Latin America: From Villa to Chávez*. Pittsburgh: University of Pittsburgh Press, 2017.

Davis, Keith F. *Désiré Charnay, Expeditionary Photographer*. Albuquerque: University of New Mexico Press, 1981.

Dawson, Alexander. *The Peyote Effect. From the Inquisition to the War on Drugs*. Berkeley, CA: University of California Press, 2018.

Deffebach, Nancy. *María Izquierdo and Frida Kahlo*. Austin: University of Texas Press, 2015.

De la Torre Villar, Ernesto. "Dos historiadores de Durango: José Fernando Ramírez y José Ignacio Gallegos." *Historia Mexicana*, vol. 24, no. 3 (1975): 403–441.

Den Abbeele, Georges Van. *Travel as Metaphor: From Montaigne to Rousseau.* Minneapolis: University of Minnesota Press. 1991.

Derrida, Jacques. "El teatro de la crueldad y la clausura de la representación." In *La escritura y la diferencia*, 318–43. Barcelona: Editorial Anthropos, 1989.

Desmond, Lawrence G. *Yucatán through Her Eyes: Alice Dixon Le Plongeon, Writer and Expeditionary Photographer.* Albuquerque: University of New Mexico Press, 2009.

Desmond, Lawrence G., and Phyllis M. Messenger. *A Dream of Maya: August and Alice Le Plongeon in Nineteenth-Century Yucatan.* Albuquerque: University of New Mexico Press, 1988.

Echenberg, Myron. *Humboldt's Mexico: In the Footsteps of the Illustrious German Scientific Traveler.* Montreal: McGill-Queen's University Press, 2017.

Eipper, John. "The Canonizer De-Canonized: The Case of William H. Prescott." *Hispania* 83, no. 3 (2000): 416–27.

Ellwood, Robert. *The Fifties Spiritual Marketplace.* New Brunswick, NJ: Rutgers University Press, 1997.

Ette, Ottmar. "*Iconografía, caligrafía, autografía*: On the Art of Visualization in the Journals of Humboldt's American Trip." *HiN—Humboldt im Netz. Internationale Zeitschrift für Humboldt-Studien* 16, no. 30 (2015): 29–53. http://www.unipotsdam.de/romanistik/hin/hin30/ette.htm

Ette, Otmar. "'Not Just Brought about by Chance': Reflections on Globalisation in Cornelius de Pauw and Alexander von Humboldt." *Studies in Travel Writing* 15, no. 1 (2011): 3–25.

Evans, R. Tripp *Romancing the Maya: Mexican Antiquity in the American Imagination, 1820–1915.* Austin: University of Texas Press, 2004.

Falcón, Romana, coord. *Culturas de pobreza y resistencia: Estudios de marginados, proscritos y descontentos. México, 1804–1910.* Mexico: Universidad de Querétaro, 2005.

Federici, Silvia, *Caliban and the Witch: Women, the Body and Primitive Accumulation.* New York: Autonomedia, 2014.

Fiol-Matta, Licia. *A Queer Mother for the Nation: The State and Gabriela Mistral.* Minneapolis: University of Minnesota Press, 2002.

Fossey, Mathieu de. *Le Mexique.* Paris: Henri Plon, 1857.

Franco, Jean. *Plotting Women: Gender and Representation in Mexico.* New York: Columbia University Press, 1989.

Frevert, Ute. *Men of Honour: A Social and Cultural History of the Duel.* Cambridge, MA: Blackwell, 1995.

Gallagher, John, and Ronald Robinson. "The Imperialism of Free Trade." *Economic History Review* 6, no. 1 (1953): 1–15.

Geis, Terri. "The Voyaging Reality: María Izquierdo and Antonin Artaud, Mexico and Paris." *Papers of Surrealism*, no. 4 (2005): 1–12.

Gennep, Arnold van. *The Rites of Passage*. Chicago: University of Chicago Press, 1960.

Gerstell, Richard. *How to Survive an Atomic Bomb*. New York: Bantam Books, 1950.

Gómez, Leila. *Darwinism in Argentina: Major Texts, 1845–1909*. Translated by Nicholas Callaway. Lanham, MD: Bucknell University Press, 2011.

Gómez, Leila. "El hispanismo en viaje: Prescott y México." *Revista de Crítica Literaria Latinoamericana* XLI, no. 82: 117–34.

Gómez, Leila. *Iluminados y tránsfugas: Relatos de viajeros y ficciones nacionales*. Madrid: Iberoamericana Vervuert, 2009.

Gómez, Leila. "Local Knowledge and Science: The Role of Pathfinders in Travel Narratives." In *Travel, Agency, and the Circulation of Knowledge*, edited by Gesa Mackenthun, 121–37. Münster: Waxmann, 2017.

Gómez, Leila. "The Philosopher Traveler: The Philosopher Traveler, Secularization in Learning in Spanish America and Brazil." In *A Companion to Latin American Studies Culture and Literature*, edited by Sara Castro-Klarén, 247–61. Malden, MA: Blackwell, 2008.

Gómez, Leila. "Presentación." Special issue, *Colorado Review of Hispanic Studies: Travel Narratives from Columbus to the New Age*, no. 3 (2005): 1–13.

González Jimenez, Rosa María. "The Normal School for Women and Liberal Feminism in Mexico City, Late Nineteenth Century and Early Twentieth Century." *Resources for Feminist Research*, no. 34 (2012): 33–55.

González Rodríguez, Sergio. *Huesos en el desierto*. Barcelona: Anagrama, 2002.

Greenblatt, Stephen. *Marvelous Possessions*. Chicago: University of Chicago Press, 1991.

Grimberg, Salomon. *I Will Never Forget You; Frida Kahlo to Nickolas Muray*. San Francisco: Chronicle Books, 2006.

Guillory, John. "Canonical and Non-Canonical: A Critique of the Current Debate." *E.L.H.* 54, no. 3 (1987): 483–521.

Halberstam, Jack. *The Queer Art of Failure*. Durham, NC: Duke University Press, 2011.

Hayman, Ronald. *Artaud and After*. Oxford: Oxford University Press, 1977.

Heliodoro Valle, R. "Diálogo con André Breton." *Universidad: Mensual de Cultura Popular* 29 (June 1938): 5–8.

Hemmer, Kurt. "Political Outlaws: Beat Cowboys." *American Studies Journal*, no. 50 (2007).

Hetherington, Kevin. *The Badlands of Modernity: Heterotopia and Social Ordering*. New York: Routledge, 1997.

"Hernán Cortés encuentra reposo tras 400 años de muerto." *Informador*. December 1, 2014. https://www.informador.mx/Cultura/Hernan-Cortes-encuentra-reposo-tras-400-anos-de-muerto-20141201-0127.html.

Homberger, Eric. *John Reed*. Manchester: Manchester University Press: 1990.

Humboldt, Alexander von. "On Account of Two Attempts to Ascend Chimborazo." *Athenaeum*, no. 524 (1837): 832–34.

Humboldt, Alexander von. *Cartas americanas*. Translated to Spanish by Lisandro Alvarado, José Nucete Sardi, and Eduardo Rohl. Caracas: Editorial Ayacucho, 1980.

Humboldt, Alexander von. *Personal Narrative*. Abridged and translated with an introduction by Jason Wilson, and a historical introduction by Malcolm Nicolson. New York: Penguin, 1995.

Humboldt, Alexander von. *Political Essay on the Kingdom of New Spain*. Translated by John Black. London: Longman, Hurst, Rees-Orme, and Brown, 1822.

Humboldt, Alexander von. *Views of Nature*. Edited by Stephen T. Jackson and Laura Dassow Walls, translated by Mark W. Person. Chicago: University of Chicago Press, 2016.

Humboldt, Alexander von. *Views of the Cordilleras and Monuments of the Indigenous Peoples of the Americas*. Edited by Vera M. Kutzinski and Ottmar Ette, translated by Ryan Poynter. Chicago: University of Chicago Press, 2012.

Humboldt, Alexander von, and Elías Trabulse. *Tablas geográficas políticas del reyno de Nueva España: Acompañadas de: Correspondencia Mexicana, 1803–1854; Diario de viaje (de Acapulco a Veracruz); Introducción a La Pasigrafía Geológica*. México: Secretaría de Gobernación, Archivo General de la Nación, 2003.

Jacob, Christian. *The Sovereign Map: Theoretical Approaches in Cartography throughout History*. Chicago: University of Chicago Press, 2006.

Jagoe, Eva-Lynn. "The Visible Horizon Bounds Their Wishes: Seclusion and Society in Fanny Calderón de la Barca's Postcolonial Mexico." *Imperial Objects: Essays on Victorian Women's Emigration and the Unauthorized Imperial Experience*, edited by Rita S. Kranidis, 170–89. New York: Twayne, 1998.

Jaksić, Iván. *The Hispanic World and American Intellectual Life, 1820–1880*. New York: Palgrave Macmillan, 2007.

Jaksić, Iván. "The Lessons of Spain: New England Intellectuals and the History of the Hispanic World, 1820–1880." *Massachusetts Historical Review* 18 (2016): 213–32.

Jameson, Fredric. *Archaeologies of the Future: The Desire Called Utopia and Other Science Fictions*. London: Verso, 2005.

Jonnes, Denis. *Cold War American Literature and the Rise of Youth Culture*. London: Routledge, 2015.

Joseph, Gilbert M., Catherine C. LeGrand, and Ricardo D. Salvatore, eds. *Close Encounters of Empire*. Dunham, NC: Duke University Press, 1998.

Kagan, Richard. "Prescott's Paradigm: American Historical Scholarship and the Decline of Spain." *American Historical Review* 101, no. 2 (1996): 423–46.

Kaplan, Amy, and Nina Gerassi-Navarro. "Between Empires: Frances Calderón de la Barca's *Life in Mexico*." *Symbiosis* 9, no. 1 (2005): 3–25.

Keely, James. "My Experiences with War Correspondents." *Metropolitan Magazine*, November 1914, 18, 63–65.

Kerouac, Jack. *Lonesome Traveler.* New York: Library of America, 2007.

Kerouac, Jack. *Mexico City Blues.* New York: Grove Weidenfeld, 1990.

Kerouac, Jack. *On the road.* New York: Library of America, 2007.

Kerouac, Jack. *Tristessa.* New York: Library of America, 2007.

Kristeva, Julia. *Desire in Language: A Semiotic Approach to Literature and Art.* New York: Columbia University Press, 1980.

Kristeva, Julia. *Powers of Horrors: An Essay of Abjection.* New York: Columbia University Press, 1982.

Lamont, Corlis, ed. *The John Reed Centenary.* New York: John Reed Centenary Committee, 1988.

Lardas, John. *The Bop Apocalypse: The Religious Visions of Kerouac, Ginsberg, and Burroughs.* Urbana: University of Illinois Press, 2001.

Latour, Bruno. *La esperanza de Pandora: Ensayos sobre la realidad de los estudios de la ciencia.* Translated by Tomás Fernández Aúz. Barcelona: Gedisa, 2011.

Latour, Bruno. *Science in Action: How to Follow Scientists and Engineers through Society.* Cambridge, MA: Harvard University Press, 1987.

Latour, Bruno. "Where Are the Missing Masses? The Sociology of a Few Mundane Artifacts." In *The Object Reader*, edited by Fiona Candlin and Raiford Guins, 229–53. London: Routledge, 2009.

Lautréamont, Comte de. *Les chants de Maldoror.* Paris: Gustave Balitout, Questroy et Cie, 1874.

Leask, Nigel. *Curiosity and the Aesthetics of Travel-Writing, 1770–1840.* London: Oxford University Press, 2004.

Leask, Nigel. "The Ghost in Chapultepec: Fanny Calderón de La Barca, William Prescott and Nineteenth-Century Mexican Travel Accounts." In *Voyages and Visions: Toward a Cultural History of Travel*, edited by Jás Elsner and Joan-Pao Rubiés, 184–209. London: Reaktion, 1999.

Le Clézio, J. M. G. *Diego y Frida.* Mexico: Editorial Diana, 1995.

Lerebours, Nöel, ed. *Excursions daguerriennes, représentant les vues et les monuments les plus remarquables du globe.* París: Noël-Marie Paymal Lerebours, 1840–1844.

Lindsay, Claire. "Postcolonial Anxieties: Fetishizing Frances Calderón de la Barca." *Women: A Cultural Review* 17, no. 2 (2006): 171–87.

Locascio, Lisa. "My Bolaño Archive." *Los Angeles Review of Books.* June 23, 2013. https://lareviewofbooks.org/article/my-bolano-archive/#!

López, Oresta. "Women Teachers of Post-Revolutionary Mexico: Feminisation and Everyday Resistance." *Paedagogica Historica International Journal of the History of Education* 49, no. 1 (2013): 56–69.

Löwerstern, Isidore. *Le Mexique, souvenirs d'un voyager par Isidore Löwerstern, auteur de les Etats Unis et la Havane.* Paris: Leipsick, 1843.

Lumholtz, Carl. *El México desconocido*. Clásicos de la antropología 11, Instituto Nacional Indigenista, 1981.

Madariaga Caro, Montserrat. *Bolaño Infra*. Santiago de Chile: RIL, 2010.

Manalansan IV, Martin F. "The 'Stuff' of Archives: Mess, Migration, and Queer Lives." *Radical History Review*, no. 120 (2014): 94–107.

Maristain, Mónica. *El hijo de Mister Playa*. Santiago de Chile: Alquimia Ediciones, 2017.

Mayer, Robert. "One Step Forward, Two Steps Back: On Lars Lih's Lenin." *Historical Materialism: Research in Critical Marxist Theory* 18, no. 3 (2010): 47–63.

Mignolo, Walter. *The Darker Side of Western Modernity*. Durham, NC: Duke University Press, 2011.

Mignolo, Walter. *The Idea of Latin America*. Malden, MA: Blackwell, 2005.

Mignolo, Walter, and Catherine E. Walsh. *On Decoloniality*. Durham, NC: Duke University Press, 2018.

Mistral, Gabriela. *Gabriela y México*. Edited by Pedro Pablo Zegers B. Santiago de Chile: Ril Editores, 2007.

Mistral, Gabriela. *Lectura para mujeres*. Mexico City: Porrúa, 1967.

Monsiváis, Carlos, and Rafael Vázquez Bayod. *Frida Kahlo, una vida, una obra*. Mexico City: Consejo Nacional para la Cultura y las Artes, 1992.

Monteleone, Jorge. "El nómade: Cartas de Jean-Arthur Rimbaud en Abisinia." *Abyssinia: Revista de Poesía y Poética*, 1, 157–78.

Moraga Valle, Fabio. "'Lo mejor de Chile está ahora en México': Ideas políticas y labor pedagógica de Gabriela Mistral en México (1922–1924)." *Historia Mexicana* 63, no. 3 (2014): 1181–247.

Morgan, Bill. *The Typewriter Is Holy: The Complete, Uncensored History of the Beat Generation*. New York: Free Press, 2010.

Nicholson, Melanie. *Surrealism in Latin American Literature: Searching for Breton's Ghost*. New York: Palgrave Macmillan, 2013.

Nicholson, Melanie. "Surrealism's 'Found Object': The Enigmatic Mexico of Artaud and Breton." *Journal of European Studies* 43, no. 1 (2013): 27–43.

O'Connor, Richard, and Dale Walker. *The Lost Revolutionary: A Biography of John Reed*. New York: Harcourt Brace & World, 1967.

Ortega y Medina, Juan. *Humboldt desde México*. Mexico City: Universidad Autónoma de México, 1960.

Ortiz Bullé-Goyri, Alejandro. "Antonin Artaud y el ambiente teatral mexicano de los años treinta." *Fuentes Humanísticas* 13, no. 24 (2002): 41–48.

Pi-Suñer Llorens, Antonia. *La deuda española en México*. Mexico City: El Colegio de México, 2006.

Pitman, Thea. *Mexican Travel Writing*. New York: Peter Lang, 2008.

Pollack, Sarah. "Latin America Translated (Again): Roberto Bolaño's *The Savage Detectives* in the United States." *Comparative Literature* 61, no. 3 (2009): 346–65.

Porter, Dennis. *Haunted Journeys: Desire and Transgression in European Travel Writing*. Princeton, NJ: Princeton University Press, 1991.

Pratt, Mary Louise. *Imperial Eyes*. London: Routledge, 1992.

Prescott, William. *The Correspondence of W. H. Prescott 1833–1847*. Translated and edited by Roger Wolcott. Boston, MA: Houghton Mifflin, 1925.

Prescott, William. *History of the Conquest of Mexico and History of the Conquest of Peru*. New York: Cooper Square Press, 2000.

Price, Sally. *Primitive Art in Civilized Places*. Chicago: University of Chicago Press, 2001.

Quijano, Aníbal. *Cuestiones y horizontes: De la dependencia histórico-estructural a la colonialidad/descolonialidad del poder*. Buenos Aires: CLACSO, 2014.

Raby, David. *Educación y revolución social en México, 1921–1940*. Mexico City: Secretaria de Educación Pública, 1974.

Raby, David L., and Martha Donís. "Ideología y construcción del Estado: la función política de la educación rural en México: 1921–1935." *Revista Mexicana de Sociología* 51, no. 2 (1989): 305–20.

Ramírez, José F. "Notas y esclarecimientos a la Historia de la Conquista de México, del Señor W. Prescott." In *Obras del Licenciado José Ramírez*, vol. 1, 291–537. Mexico City: Imprenta Victoriano de Agüeros, 1898.

Rebok, Sandra. *Humboldt and Jefferson: A Transatlantic Friendship of Enlightenment*. Charlottesville: University of Virginia Press, 2014.

Reed, John. "The Colorado War." *Metropolitan Magazine*, July 1914, 11–16.

Reed, John. *Diez días que estremecieron al mundo*. Mexico City: Porrúa, 2001.

Reed, John. "If We Enter Mexico." Editorial. *Metropolitan Magazine*, June 1914.

Reed, John. *Insurgent Mexico*. New York: D. Appleton and Company, 1914. http://www.gutenberg.org/ebooks/48108.

Reed, John. *Ten Days that Shook the World*. New York: Random House, 1960.

Reed, John. *War in Eastern Europe*. New York: Charles Scribner's, 1919.

Reed, John. "With Villa in Mexico." *Metropolitan Magazine*, February 1914, 72.

Riegl, Alois. "The Modem Cult of Monuments: Its Character and Its Origins" *Oppositions* 25 (1982): 39–75.

Rogers, Charlotte. *Jungle Fever: Exploring Madness and Medicine in Twentieth-Century Tropical Narratives*. Nashville, TN: Vanderbilt University Press, 2012.

Rojas Aréchiga, Mariana. "El controvertido peyote." *Revista Ciencias*, no. 91 (July–September) (2008): 44–49.

Roosevelt, Theodore. "Uncle Sam and the Rest of the World: The Sound of Laughter and Children Playing Has Been Still in Mexico." *Metropolitan Magazine*, March 1915, 11–13.

Rosenstonen, Robert. *Romantic Revolutionary: A Biography of John Reed*. New York: Vintage Books, 1981.

Ross, Kristin. "Rimbaud and the Resistance to Work." *Representations*, no. 19: 62–86.

Rousselet, Laurine. "Revolucionar la idea del teatro." *Archipiélago* 20, no. 79 (2013): 44–8.

Rubilar S., Luis. "Gabriela Mistral y el imaginario pedagógico chileno." *Memoria Chilena: Artículos para el Bicentenario*, December 2010: 1–20. http://www.memoriachilena.gob.cl/602/w3-article-123217.html.

Saavedra Molina, Julio. "Gabriela Mistral, vida y obra." *Revista Hispánica Moderna* 3, no. 2 (1937): 110–35.

Sáenz Carrete, Erasmo. "José Fernando Ramírez: Su último exilio europeo y la suerte de su última biblioteca." *es*, no. 25 (2011): 100–35.

Said, Edward. *Orientalism*. New York: Pantheon, 1978.

Sarmiento, Domingo Faustino. *Facundo, or, Civilization and Barbarism*. New York: Penguin, 1998.

Schneider, Luis Mario. *México y el surrealismo (1925–1950)*. Mexico City: Arte y Libros, 1975.

Sedgwick, Eve. *Between Men: English Literature and Male Homosocial Desire*. New York: Columbia University Press, 1985.

Segato, Rita. *La crítica a la colonialidad en ocho ensayos*. Buenos Aires: Prometeo, 2015.

Segato, Rita. "Una falla del pensamiento feminista es creer que la violencia de género es un problema de hombres y mujeres." Interview by Florencia Vizzi and Alejandra Ojeda Garnero. *La Tinta*, September 22, 2017. https://latinta.com.ar/2017/09/rita-segato-falla-pensamiento-feminista-violencia-genero-problema-hombres-mujeres/.

Shields, Rob. *Places on the Margin: Alternative Geographies of Modernity*. London: Routledge. 1991.

Smith, Geoffrey D., John M. Bennett, and Oliver Harris, eds. *Everything Lost: Latin American Notebook of William S. Burroughs*. Columbus: Ohio State University Press, 2017.

Spiller, Roland. "Roberto Bolaño: Fracasar con éxito o navigare necessum est." In *Poéticas del fracaso*, edited by Yvette Sanchez and Roland Spiller, 143–73. Tübingen: Gunter Narr, 2009.

Spurr, David. *The Rhetoric of Empire*. Durham, NC: Duke University Press, 1991.

Stagl, Justin. *A History of Curiosity: The Theory of Travel Writing, 1550–1800*. Chur, Switzerland: Harwood Academic Publishers, 1995.

Stephens, John L. *Incidents of Travel in Central America, Chiapas, and Yucatan*. New York: Harper & Brothers, 1841.

Tarver, Gina McDaniel. *Issues of Otherness and Identity in the Works of Izquierdo, Kahlo, Artaud, and Breton*. Albuquerque: University of New Mexico Press, 1996.

Teitelbaum, Vanesa. "La corrección de la vagancia: Trabajo, honor y solidaridades en la Ciudad de México, 1845–1853." In *Trabajo, ocio y coacción: Trabajadores urbanos en México y Guatemala en el siglo xix*, edited by Clara E. Lida and Sonia Pérez Toledo, 115–56. Mexico City: Universidad Metropolitana, 2001.

Texidor, Felipe. "Prólogo" to *La vida en México*, by Francis Calderón de la Barca, vi–lxvii. México: Porrúa, 2010.

Tibol, Raquel. *Frida Kahlo, una vida abierta*. Mexico City: Editorial Oasis, 1983.

Tovar de Teresa, Guillermo. "Prefacio" to *Ciudades de luz*, 5–8. Mexico City: Espejo de Obsidiana, 1993.

Turner, Victor. *The Ritual Process: Structure and Anti-Structure* London: Routledge & Kegan Paul, 1969.

United States. National Security Resources Board. *United States Civil Defense*. Washington, DC: Government Printing Office, 1950.

Valencia, Sayak. *Capitalismo Gore*. Barcelona: Melusina, 2010.

Van Den Abbeele, Georges. *Travel as Metaphor: From Montaigne to Rousseau*. Minneapolis: University of Minnesota Press, 1991.

Vasconcelos, José. *El desastre*. Mexico City: Ediciones Botas, 1951.

Vasconcelos, José. *Ulises criollo*. Mexico City: Universidad Nacional Autónoma de México, 2007.

Vázquez de Knauth, Josefina. *Nacionalismo y educación en México*. Mexico City: El colegio de México, 1970.

"Villa, Bandit and Brute, May Be Mexican President." *New York Times*, December 14, 1913, 3.

Wallerstein, Immanuel. *The Modern World-System*. New York: Academic Press, 1974.

Weinreich, Regina. "The Beat Generation Is Now about Everything." In *A Concise Companion to Postwar American Literature and Culture*, edited by Josephine G. Hendin, 72–94. Malden, MA: Blackwell, 2004.

Williams, Raymond. *Marxism and Literature*. London: Oxford University Press, 1977.

Woolf, Virginia. "Professions for Women." In *The Death of the Moth and Other Essays*. Available at Project Gutenberg Australia. http://gutenberg.net.au/ebooks12/1203811h.html#ch-28.

Wulf, Andrea. *La invención de la naturaleza: El Nuevo Mundo de Alexander von Humboldt*. Bogotá: Taurus, 2017.

Young, Robert. *Colonial Desire*. London: Routledge, 1995.

Youngs, Tim. "Buttons and Souls: Some Thoughts on Commodities and Identity in Women's Travel Writing." *Studies in Travel Writing* 1, no. 1 (1997): 117–40.

Ziff, Larzer. *Return Passages: Great American Travel Writing, 1780–1910*. New Haven, CT: Yale University Press, 2000.

Index